A BIRDER'S GUIDE

TO

SOUTHERN CALIFORNIA

A BIRDER'S GUIDE

TO

SOUTHERN CALIFORNIA

by
Harold R. Holt
1990

American Birding Association, Inc.

Library of Congress Catalog Card Number: 90-84063

ISBN Number: 1-878788-00-0

Third Edition

     1   2   3   4   5   6   7   8   9

Printed in the United States of America

Publisher

    ABA / William J. Graber, III, Chairman, Publications Committee

Editor

    Paul J. Baicich

Associate Editors

    Bob Berman
    Cindy Lippincott

Copy Editor

    Hugh Willoughby

Cover Design and Typography, and Interior Design

    Dianne Borneman / Shadow Canyon Graphics, Evergreen, Colorado

Maps

    Cindy Lippincott

Front Cover Photograph

    California Quail by James Gallagher

Back Cover Photograph

    Elegant Tern by Larry Sansone

Distributed by

    American Birding Association Sales
    PO Box 6599
    Colorado Springs, Colorado
    80934-6599 USA

    (800) 634-7736 (U.S. & Canada)
    (719) 634-7736

American Birding Association, Inc.

Since 1969, the American Birding Association has served the North American birding community by helping birders hone their field identification skills and telling them where to find birds. This membership organization exists to promote the recreational observation and study of wild birds, to educate the public in the appreciation of birds and their contributions to the environment, to assist in the study of birds in their natural habitat, and to contribute to the development of improved bird population studies. The organization also keeps North American birders informed about valuable resources, new publications, and top-notch birding equipment.

All ABA members receive _Birding_, the official bimonthly magazine of the organization, and _Winging It_, the monthly newsletter. Both publications are chock-full of birdfinding advice, identification details, and up-to-date birding news. Members also receive discounts from ABA Sales on bird books, tapes, optical equipment, and accessories. The ABA publishes the _ABA Birdfinding Guides_, a popular series to which this volume belongs. ABA also publishes an invaluable Membership Directory, conducts sell-out biennial conventions, and sponsors bird-related tours of various durations to domestic and foreign birding hot-spots.

All persons interested in these aspects of bird study are invited to join. If you bird beyond your backyard, ABA membership will help you discover a whole new world of birding adventure and expertise. A membership form is included in this book.

American Birding Association
PO Box 6599
Colorado Springs, Colorado 80934-6599

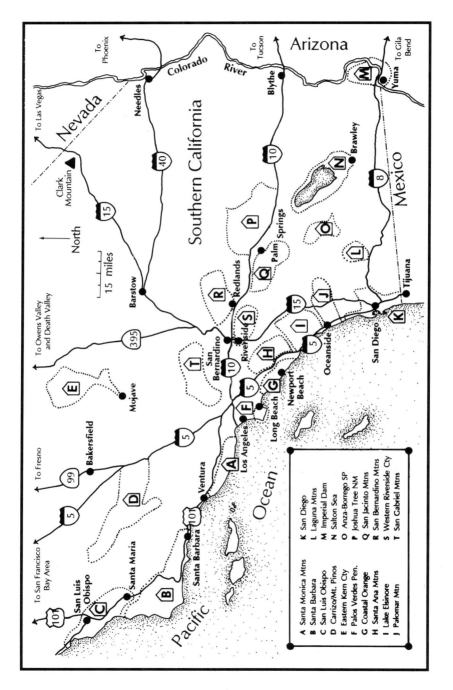

A Santa Monica Mtns
B Santa Barbara
C San Luis Obispo
D Carrizo/Mt. Pinos
E Eastern Kern Cty
F Palos Verdes Pen.
G Coastal Orange
H Santa Ana Mtns
I Lake Elsinore
J Palomar Mtn
K San Diego
L Laguna Mtns
M Imperial Dam
N Salton Sea
O Anza-Borrego SP
P Joshua Tree NM
Q San Jacinto Mtns
R San Bernardino Mtns
S Western Riverside Cty
T San Gabriel Mtns

TABLE OF CONTENTS

FOREWORD

by Roger Tory Peterson

When I heard that the American Birding Association had taken over publication of the Lane Guides, I was pleased for several reasons.

Throughout the twenty-two years that ABA has been growing as a vital, progressive resource for birders in North America, one of the hallmarks of the organization has been birders helping each other to improve field identification and birdfinding skills. It is appropriate—and not unexpectedly, it was Jim Lane's wish—that the American Birding Association ultimately take over stewardship of the Lane Guides. And recently, Jim Lane's long-time friend and collaborator Harold Holt decided the time had come to pass on that responsibility.

ABA members, both experts and knowledgeable amateurs, share their knowledge both in print and in the field and have produced, over the years, an impressive array of articles in *Birding* magazine on bird identification. ABA's journal, however, originally focused on helping members learn about locations where the birding was good, where rarities occurred regularly, how to get there, and how to bird the area productively. ABA's publication of the Lane Guides is a logical extension of this tradition.

To both update the current guides in the Lane series, and to produce new *ABA Birdfinding Guides*, ABA will call upon the field expertise and current local knowledge of its membership throughout North America. By utilizing this "institutional" knowledge rather that the resources of one individual author, ABA's guides will be the next generation in the progression from the pioneering efforts of Olin Sewall Pettingill and Jim Lane to the future of birding.

In this complete revision to *A Birder's Guide to Southern California*, Harold Holt and his collaborators have added new birding areas to this book, completely revised the 23 existing maps, added 33 new maps, and have included a number of valuable features that should be appreciated by birders everywhere. Furthermore, the ABA has done what they have done so well over the years—called on the experience, expertise, and goodwill of their members to examine and validate every bit of the text.

This book is indispensable for birdfinding in Southern California for residents and travelers alike. Don't leave home without it!

Old Lyme, Connecticut / September, 1990

PREFACE

Dr. James A. Lane (1926-87) was born in Orange County, California. His doctorate, earned from the University of California at Los Angeles, was in Ichthyology. After teaching a short time, he realized specialzing in fish was not what he really wanted to do since his real interest was in birds. He moved to Carr Canyon, Arizona, where, under the influence of his many friends, he decided to write a book about where to find birds. *A Birdwatcher's Guide to Southeastern Arizona* was written in 1965. In 1968 he published his second book, *A Birdwatcher's Guide to Southern California*. Dr. Lane had now found his real purpose in life—to help others find and enjoy the birds of all of North America. In the ensuing years he published another five titles—his *Birder's Guide to–* series. For these great works he was honored by the American Birding Association in 1986 with the prestigious Ludlow Griscom Award, presented for his outstanding contributions to the birding world.

I met Jim in 1972, and together we wrote the first of the Colorado titles. Shortly after, Jim joined the Massachusetts Audubon Society as a bird-tour leader. This, in combination with his continued authorship and updating of the guides, kept him very busy. About this time, I took over distribution of the books for Jim, and in 1982 I began to relieve him by doing revisions of all of his books. Jim's health gradually failed, and the birding community lost a great friend in March 1987.

No one could hope to replace Jim Lane, but I am trying to continue the work he started. I wish to thank everyone who has suggested and submitted changes for this new edition. I particularly wish to thank the following people: Keith Axelson, Ebbe Banstorp, Chuck Bernstein, Jenny Kate Collins, Brian Daniels, Dorothy Dimsdale, Jon Dunn, Tom Edell, Claude Edwards, Kimball Garrett, Sylvia Ranney Gallagher, Bill Grossi, Marjorie and Don Hastings, Fred Heath, Matt Heindel, Ken Hollinga, Ginger Johnson, Betsy Knaak, Mark Kincheloe, Paul Lehman, Jerry and Laurette Maisel, Guy McCaskie, Bob McKernan, Chet McGaugh, Art Morley, Mike Patten, Don Roberson, Larry Sansone, Cory Schlesinger, Brad Schram, Arnold Small, Betty Jo and Jim Stephenson, Monte Taylor, Gerald Tolman, Richard Webster, Douglas Willick, and Sandy Wohlgemuth. Artwork by Charles H. Gambill, Shawneen Finnegan, and Jonathan Alderfer is much appreciated, as are the cover photographs by James Gallagher and Larry Sansone. The ABA staff also deserves special praise for their help.

Harold R. Holt / Denver, Colorado / October, 1990

EDITOR'S NOTE

The American Birding Association was fortunate to have acquired the Lane Guide series this year. The original eight birder's guides in that series (Southeast Arizona, Colorado, Florida, Southern California, the Texas Coast, the Rio Grande Valley, and two by authors other than Jim Lane and Harold Holt, North Dakota and Churchill, Manitoba) have helped thousands of birders find and enjoy birds across the continent. These books have shown us where to go and what to look for. ABA hopes to continue that tradition started by Jim Lane years ago. Not only have we set for ourselves the goal of revising and reprinting those core Lane Guides, but we also aim to add new titles to the *ABA Birdfinding Guides*. *A Birder's Guide to Southern California* is the first of these guides published under ABA auspices.

The tasks entailed here were considerable; the results, quite satisfying. Harold Holt has been a cooperative and thoughtful author. Many other birders—mentioned in Harold's preface—helped with suggestions and changes. The final outcome, however, would have been impossible without the staff assembled for this book. Bill Graber was gracious in his guidance and advice. Bob Berman was always ready with his technical computer skills, organizational abilities, and business acumen. Cindy Lippincott served a vital dual role. She was the master mapmaker and doubled in essential editing tasks. Finally, Hugh Willoughby checked over the entire text for those nasty little errors that escaped everyone else. It exemplified fine teamwork indeed.

We hope that this book will launch an ongoing series of *ABA Birdfinding Guides* which will be beneficial to the organization and will be embraced by thousands of birders throughout the continent. You deserve the best!

Since this book will be revised in the future, I hope that you will advise us if you find errors or omissions.

Paul J. Baicich / Editor, *ABA Birdfinding Guides* / October, 1990

INTRODUCTION

Ask any native or politician what comprises the area known as Southern California and the answer will be that it is anything south of the Tehachapi Mountains (Tay-HATCH-ah-pea). Then ask where the Tehachapis are, and he or she will probably be unable to tell you. Out-of-staters and people from San Francisco often say erroneously that Southern California is everything south of Monterey, since that is where the fold in the map occurs. Then there are the purists who insist it is only the coastal plain that stretches from Santa Barbara to San Diego, or roughly the area affected by the Los Angeles smog. For the purpose of this guide, Southern California is defined as that part of the state south of a line from the Morro Bay area to the California-Nevada border east of Clark Mountain (at Interstate 15).

The physical character of Southern California is largely determined by the ocean, the mountains, and the deserts. This diverse region contains many different habitats, each with its own flora and fauna. By going from the ocean to the snow-capped mountains and then down to the deserts, you can find all of the traditional life zones, and you can do so in a one-day drive.

THE OCEAN

The character of the Pacific Ocean, which bathes the shores of Southern California, is largely determined by the California Current. After the North Pacific Current loops past Alaska, one branch of the current follows closely down the coast, bringing cool, foggy weather to the California coast. This branch is the California Current. At Point Conception, the coastline veers sharply to the east, but the California Current continues southward, passing several hundred miles west of San Diego. This allows the warmer water from the south (called the Southern California Countercurrent) to eddy northward along the southern coast, where the water temperature averages from 60 to 70 degrees in late summer and fall.

The prevailing winds from the west and northwest cross these warm waters and give the coastal plains an ideal climate, neither too hot nor too

1

cold. The plains are attractive to birds and people alike. Formerly, great numbers of birds wintered here, but they are being replaced by people. Although comprising only 15% of the land mass of California, the coastal plains contain 85% of the population.

THE MOUNTAINS

The biggest surprise for the first-time visitor to California is usually the mountains. Somehow, the travel folders fail to mention the towering peaks that dominate the landscape. The visitor is unprepared for the vast number of mountains, their ruggedness, and their beauty.

There are two major series of mountains in Southern California. One east-west series stretches eastward, roughly paralleling the San Andreas fault line, from Point Conception to north of the Salton Sea. These are known as the Transverse Ranges and consist of the Santa Ynez, Santa Monica, San Gabriel, and San Bernardino mountains. They act as an effective barrier to influences from the northwest, political as well as climatic. Another series of mountains follows a north-south trend. This group, known as the Peninsular Ranges, extends southward from San Gorgonio Pass at Beaumont into Baja California and consists of the Santa Ana, San Jacinto, Palomar, and Laguna mountains. Most of these mountains were formed by the block faulting that caused the great rift valley now occupied by the Salton Sea and the Gulf of California.

THE DESERTS

Winter storms do get past the towering peaks of the mountains, but the precipitation doesn't, so to the east we find the dry deserts. These are divided into two parts. The low desert around the Salton Sea and southward into Mexico is known as the Colorado Desert. Most of this area is less than 1,000 feet in elevation. In fact, much of it is below sea level. To the north and east is a higher area known as the Mojave Desert (Mo-HAH-vay), which ranges from 1,000 to 4,000 feet in elevation.

BIRDS

In the varied regions of Southern California, over 400 species of birds have been found, but only about 300 occur regularly. Of these, about 165 are permanent residents or year-round visitors; 40, summer residents; 65, winter visitors; and 30 appear only as migrants.

RARE BIRD ALERT TELEPHONE NUMBERS

The following rare bird alerts will provide the birder with up-to-date (usually revised weekly) bird information on the more unusual species for their areas:

Los Angeles	(213) 874-1318
Morro Bay	(805) 528-7182
San Bernardino	(714) 793-5599
San Diego	(619) 435-6761
daily updates	(619) 479-3400
Santa Barbara	(805) 964-8240

THE WEATHER

Because of the wide range in topography, it is possible to find almost any kind of weather at any time of year. The high mountain peaks are perennially cold. The low deserts are usually hot. In between these extremes, most of Southern California has an almost year-round spring-like climate. Precipitation is rather irregular. There is usually little or no rain along the coast between mid-May and mid-October. At other times rainstorms usually last one day, but a series of storms over a several-week period, or conversely, long periods in winter with no rain at all, are possible.

At irregular times during the year, high-pressure areas develop over the high deserts of Nevada and spill over the mountain passes to the coast. As this hot, dry air flows toward sea level, it is compressed by pressure and superheated by as much as an additional 27 degrees F. The results are strong, hot, dry winds known locally as "Santa Anas". During the 2 or 3 days when they blow, the coastal areas are completely cleared of fog and smog. In midwinter, they are responsible for periods of balmy 80-degree weather, but in fall they cause scorching heat-waves and contribute to the severity of disastrous fires.

HOW TO USE THIS BOOK

The main purpose of this guide is to help the birder find the various birds of Southern California and become acquainted with many of the better birding areas. Its usefulness is second only to that of a field guide and binoculars for birders making their first Southern California visits. At the same time, much of the material may be useful to resident Californians as they expand their birding horizons or seek up-to-date bird and route information for less-frequently-visited locales. While the main subject covered is birds, much information is provided about the general habitat requirements of various species with the aim of helping birders locate birds by knowing their preferred food or nesting plants, shrubs, or trees.

A quick inspection of the book will show that it is divided into *loop trips* (or sometimes linear routes) through the better birding areas. Most of the intersections and points of interest mentioned are followed by numbers, thusly (1.5). These numbers indicate the mileage *from the last point so marked*. Outstanding birding spots are shown in **bold-faced type**. If your time is limited, stops at these places will let you sample the loop's specialties at the most-promising locations. Some of the bold-faced areas are well-known migrant traps where you might find almost anything in the proper season.

Each chapter's trip can easily connect into the next chapter, although there are often alternative route choices. (Two short chapters—on the Laguna Mountains and Anza-Borrego—serve as "bridges" to the chapters preceding and following them.) Some birders using this book have simply sampled one or another loop without regard to the order of the chapters, and that's fine too.

WHEN TO COME

In Southern California, the weather and birding are good at any time of year. A full day afield in any good area at any season should yield 75 to 100 species to an experienced birder. The best birding is during April and early May when winter and spring birds overlap and spring migrants appear in full color. Four birders, on a big-day run from the Salton Sea through the Laguna Mountains to San Diego, once had 217 species in early May. The fall season, from late August to November, is best for rare and accidental birds. Christmas Counts in this area produce lists of 150 to 200 species. While still rewarding, mid- and late summer is the dullest time. It is also the fire season, and some of the mountain areas are closed.

WHAT TO WEAR

The mode of dress in the West is decidedly informal. Levis and slacks are fine for birding. Sport clothes are acceptable at most restaurants and motels. People wear almost anything on the streets and almost nothing on the beaches.

California weather is highly variable, particularly in the winter and at various elevations. Most summer days are mild, except on the deserts. However, the nights can be cool enough for a jacket. Winter days range from cool to balmy, but the nights are usually cool to cold. Be sure to take warm clothing on trips to the mountains in winter and on boat trips at any season. The wind off the water can be quite cold.

WHERE TO STAY

Finding a motel in Southern California is easy. The hard part is finding a spot where there isn't one. None of the motels caters particularly to birders. Reservations are usually not needed except around major tourist attractions.

Campgrounds are numerous, too. A few are listed at the end of each chapter. For a list of the state park campgrounds, write to the Division of Beaches and Parks, Box 2390, Sacramento, CA 95811. There is a charge in all state parks, and some of them are on a reservation system. Most entrance fees to the National Forest and Parks are covered by the Golden Eagle Passport ($25.00) and Golden Age Passport (free to citizens over 62 years of age); however, there is often an extra charge for camping. Some of the forestry campgrounds are also on the reservation system, particularly in summer.

Individual maps of the 17 National Forests in California are available at $3.00 each from the U.S. Forest Service, 630 Sansome Street, San Francisco, CA 94111. The four National Forests in this area are Angeles, Cleveland, Los Padres, and San Bernardino.

Camping is very pleasant here with few insects and little rain, but lots of people. Most campgrounds are filled to overflowing on weekends. Plan to camp during the week or get there early.

SUGGESTIONS FOR VIEWING WILDLIFE

Stop at any patch of chaparral and you will see a few birds flit away. Now purse your lips and give a series of short, interrupted hisses and squeaks. A surprising number of birds may pop into view. The birder who does not learn to hiss, squeak, or pish is missing a lot of birds.

Birds also respond to taped recordings of their songs, particularly in the breeding season. The songs can be pre-taped from bird-song records. All bird recordings should be used sparingly and responsibly in the field. Such recordings are about the only way to lure nocturnal birds into view. Owls, however, will react to the sound of an injured mouse. These sounds can be obtained by pinching the toes of a pet. Try not to record the sounds of your own injury if the pet bites you.

Many mammals and reptiles are nocturnal. Most are seen by chance, but driving little-used back roads after dark will improve your odds. The best roads are those with narrow shoulders, without embankments or ditches. Not all animals become active at the same time, so vary the hours of your trips.

To catch lizards for closer study, make a noose from a short piece of fishing line and attach it to a slender stick. A fly-fishing rod works very well. Most reptiles show little fear of such a contraption. It is easy to slip the noose over their head, and with a quick jerk you have them hooked. It is far harder to convince a policeman what you are doing running around the desert with a fishing pole.

CURRENT NAMES

The American Ornithologists Union nomenclature committee has published a 37th supplement (*Auk*, Vol. 106, No. 3, pp. 532-7, July 1989) to its *A.O.U. Check-list of North American Birds*. Several species have recently been "split" while some others have been "lumped". This list was compiled in an attempt to standardize the common names. Naturally, not everyone agrees. Many of the changes are simple ones made by adding "Common", "American", or "Northern" to separate American species from those of other lands. Others were made to bring our names into compliance with those used in other countries.

The birds names used herein follow the American Birding Association's *ABA Checklist, Fourth Edition*, 1990 (in preparation). Listed below are some names which differ from those used in our older, standard field guides. Old names are in parentheses.

Pacific Loon (split from Arctic)

Black-vented Shearwater (split from Manx)

Mottled (Scaled) Petrel

Wedge-rumped (Galapagos) Storm-Petrel

Green-backed (Green) Heron

Tricolored (Louisiana) Heron

Tundra (Whistling) Swan

Whistling-Duck (Tree Duck)

Northern (Common) Pintail

Black (Common) Scoter

Black-shouldered (White-tailed) Kite

Common Moorhen (Gallinule)

Red-necked (Northern) Phalarope

Yellow-footed Gull (split from Western)

Common Black-headed (Black-headed) Gull

Common (Thin-billed) Murre

Barn Owl (Common Barn-Owl)

Western Screech-Owl (split from Common)

Flammulated Owl (Flammulated Screech-Owl)

Northern Saw-whet Owl (Saw-whet Owl)

Common Poorwill (Poor-will)

Red-breasted Sapsucker (split from Yellow-bellied)

Western Wood-Pewee (Pewee)

Cordilleran Flycatcher (split from Western)

Pacific-slope Flycatcher (split from Western)

Dusky-capped (Olivaceous) Flycatcher

Brown-crested (Wied's Crested) Flycatcher

Greater Pewee (Coues' Flycatcher)

Northern Rough-winged (Rough-winged) Swallow

Common (Northern) Raven

American Dipper (North American)

California Gnatcatcher (split from Black-tailed)

Rufous-backed Robin (Thrush)

American (Water) Pipit

Northern Parula (Parula Warbler)

California Towhee (split from Brown)

Streak-backed (Scarlet-headed) Oriole

Rosy Finch (lumping of Gray-crowned, Black, and Brown-capped)

Dark-eyed Junco (Northern) (lumping of Oregon, White-winged, Slate-colored, and Gray-headed)

Occasionally, reference to a particular subspecies will occur in the text (e.g., when dealing with Clapper Rail, Least Tern, or Savannah Sparrow). The only regularly-used subspecies name in the book is "Pacific Golden-Plover", in expectation on an impending "split".

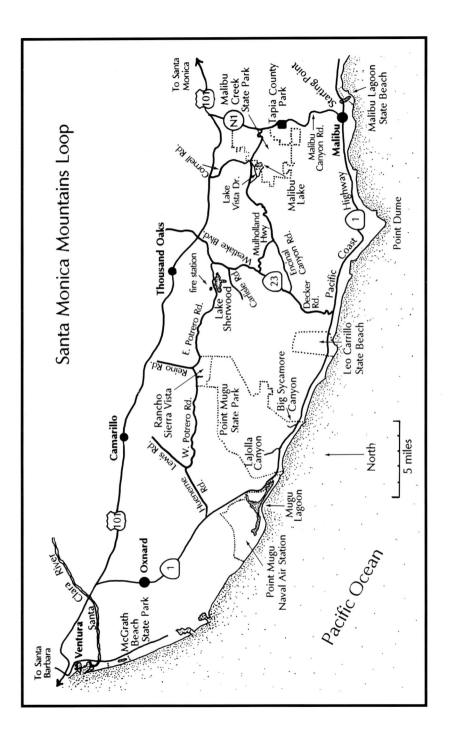

Santa Monica Mountains Loop

SANTA MONICA
MOUNTAINS LOOP

Compared with other California mountains, the Santa Monicas should probably be called hills. Their highest point is Sandstone Peak with an elevation of only 3,111 feet. However, what they lack in height is offset by their rugged canyons and inspiring views. The only forests are occasional stands of live oaks and sycamores along the streams. Most of the vegetation is lush chaparral. This loop will take you through these habitats as well as to some interesting coastal sites.

This is not one of the best birding areas in Southern California, but it *is* close to Los Angeles. The best time to visit is during April and May when the birds are singing and the flowers are in bloom, although the birding can be fairly good at any season. Most of the birds of Southern California's chaparral and oak-woodland habitats can be found on this loop.

The starting point is the intersection of the Pacific Coast Highway (Highway 1) and Webb Way in Malibu, about 13 miles west of Santa Monica. Before starting up Malibu Canyon, drive east on Highway 1 for one-quarter mile to **Malibu Lagoon**. On the right (south), just before the bridge over Malibu Creek, you will see the entrance to Malibu Creek State Beach (fee). The parking-lot fee is steep, but there is on-the-street parking on the south side of the Pacific Coast Highway or near the shopping mall across the highway.

The lagoon and beach can be very rewarding at any time of the year, with a varying assortment of gulls, terns, small shorebirds, large waders, ducks, and marshbirds. In late summer and fall check for Elegant Terns. A sudden mass flight of birds may mean only a playful dog in the water, but it could also mean a raptor overhead. Walk under the bridge and upstream to look for a variety of streamside songbirds.

A walk across the bridge over the creek (take a moment to scan the lagoon from here) takes you to Adamson House and Museum. Here, a fine growth of exotic trees and shrubs surrounds an attractive Spanish-style mansion. On your left, as you enter the grounds, is a brick wall covered with luxuriant Cape Honeysuckle, an excellent spot for Allen's and

9

occasionally Rufous Hummingbirds in spring. The property also offers access to the east side of the lagoon, which may not be accessible from the west side when the intermittent sandbar serving as a path is not there. A viewing platform on the bank above the lagoon is often productive of such secretive species as Sora and Virginia Rail.

Return to Webb Way and turn right. Go one block and turn left onto Civic Center Way, then turn right onto Malibu Canyon Road (0.7).

Turn left into Tapia County Park (4.5), where Malibu Creek, lined with dense willows, can offer good birding. Nearby are areas of large cottonwoods, sycamores, and Coast Live Oaks. Common, resident chaparral birds which you can expect are Acorn, Nuttall's, and Downy Woodpeckers, Scrub Jay, Plain Titmouse, Rufous-sided and California Towhees, and Lesser Goldfinch. California Quail, Bewick's Wren, Wrentit, and California Thrasher can be heard calling from the chaparral on the surrounding hills. Along the stream, Green-backed Heron, Belted Kingfisher, and Common Yellowthroat are found, and Red-shouldered Hawks often perch in the sycamores. Among the oaks, you may find Band-tailed Pigeon and Hutton's Vireo. Spring brings Lazuli Buntings and an assortment of flycatchers, vireos, and warblers. In winter, Golden-crowned Kinglet and Golden-crowned Sparrow may be seen. In fall, eastern vagrants show up regularly. At any time of year, an early-morning birder may luck upon a Bobcat.

Continue up Malibu Canyon Road and turn left into **Malibu Creek State Park** (1.3) (fee). This vast oasis of natural beauty is rapidly becoming encircled by development. Set in rugged, chaparral-covered mountains, the park contains creeks, grassy flats, thick groves of oaks, and a man-made lake. (The *M.A.S.H.* television series was filmed here—you may recognize the terrain from the title sequence and the outdoor scenes; remnants of the sets may still be found.) Birding here is good for the same species listed for Tapia Park. Phainopepla is fairly common, especially in spring and summer, and Lazuli Bunting can be seen in spring. Canyon Wrens are found regularly where the creek flows close to the steep cliffs. An occasional Black-shouldered Kite may be encountered, hovering like an American Kestrel. Be on the lookout for Golden Eagle and other raptors.

Turn left as you leave the park, then left again at the signal light onto Mulholland Drive (0.2). For the next 30 miles or so, you will be in a good area for Golden Eagle, but most of the large soaring birds will be Red-tailed Hawks and Turkey Vultures.

At the stop sign at Cornell Road (3.2) turn left onto Lake Vista Drive, which skirts Malibu Lake. The lake and the land on both sides of the road are private, but you might try to get permission at the office of the Malibu

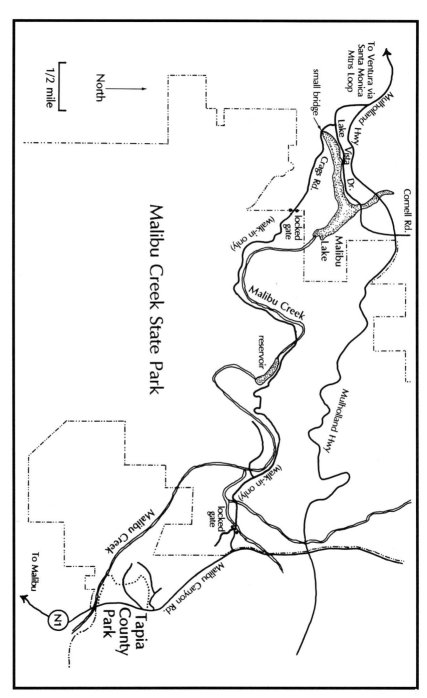

Lake Mountain Club (0.4) to bird the road on the east side of the lake and the property around the office and up the hill behind. The lake abounds with ducks and other water birds, particularly in winter. Crags Road (1.1) branches to the left for 0.7 miles and ends at the western entrance (walk-in only) to Malibu Creek State Park. Shortly after turning onto Crags Road, you will reach a small bridge. This is a good vantage point for scoping the lake on the left, and a reedy area to the right which can sometimes be productive. Turn left onto Lake Vista Drive as you leave Crags Road and almost immediately rejoin Mulholland Drive, where you will turn left. During the next 20 miles you will pass many side roads which may be explored, but the habitat is all about the same.

Stay on Mulholland Drive, bearing right at the fork (5.5) (do not go left down Encinal Canyon Road). The road, which in places winds sharply and climbs steeply, does not offer much in the way of birds, but it does provide some delightful mountain vistas. Turn right onto Westlake Boulevard (Highway 23) (2.4). For the next 2 miles, the road is narrow and winding, so drive slowly.

Turn left onto Carlisle Road (2.2). This dead-end road is only about two miles long, but it can be alive with birds, particularly after the first mile. Return to Westlake Boulevard, continue to Potrero Road (1.5), and turn left. At 0.6 miles, East Potrero Road leaves the new main road and turns left to reach Sherwood Lake. Those who have known this area in the past will be shocked at the changes. The road around the lake no longer exists, nor do the tules which held Red-winged and Tricolored Blackbirds. Most of the houses, trees, and other vegetation which formerly ringed the lake have been removed—all to make way for a development of about 600 million-dollar homes. But the ducks and other water birds don't seem to mind, and a flock of White Pelicans has been present here in recent winters. Stop near the fire station to scan the lake (1.5). At the stop sign (0.1) turn left onto East Potrero Road. Continue west through Hidden Valley, an area of beautiful farms and huge Valley Oaks (California White Oaks). The fields hold Western Meadowlark, Horned Lark, Lark Sparrow, and, in winter, American Pipit. Check the oaks for Plain Titmouse and Acorn Woodpecker. The utility poles in this area are often riddled with holes that these colorful woodpeckers drill to store acorns.

Turn left at Reino Road (5.5) onto West Potrero Road. At Pinehill Avenue (0.5) turn left into the Santa Monica Mountains National Recreation Area/Rancho Sierra Vista. The nature center is about a one-half mile walk from the parking lot (0.4). The area has several short trails which may be productive, and an 8-mile trail through Point Mugu State Park which ends at the ocean at Big Sycamore Canyon. The grasslands here have Western

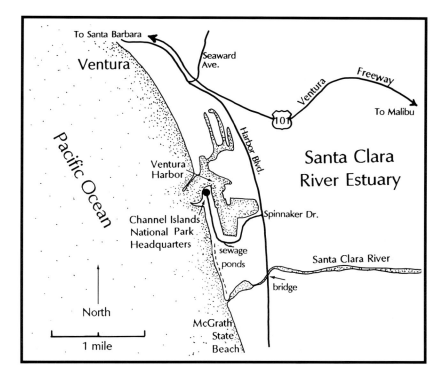

Kingbird in summer and Say's Phoebe in winter. On the hillsides you will see unusual, stalked plants, Giant Coreopsis or Sea Dahlia, which grows only on the Channel Islands and the adjacent mainland. Here they are small, but on the islands they may grow to 10 feet tall. Return to West Potrero Road and continue west.

Beyond the Camarillo State Hospital (5.5) the road is bordered by rocky hills with a heavy growth of cactus. Look for Cactus Wren and Rufous-crowned Sparrow. (This is the westernmost limit of the wren's range.) In winter you might find a Prairie Falcon here. Bear left across the bridge at Lewis Road (1.2) onto Hueneme Road (y-KNEE-me). The newly-plowed fields in this vicinity are good in winter for Horned Lark, Mountain Bluebird, and American Pipit. At Pacific Coast Highway (Highway 1) (2.3) turn left.

Mugu Lagoon (3.8) is located within the boundaries of the Point Mugu Naval Air Station and is, therefore, off-limits unless you can make special arrangements and receive written permission to enter the area. It usually abounds with birds, but unfortunately it can be birded only with difficulty through the chain-link fence along the Pacific Coast Highway. Since the birds are usually at a considerable distance, a good scope is necessary. Still, it is worth a try. With luck you may be able to identify one of the larger waders, such as Long-billed Curlew.

If you are particularly frustrated here and wish to visit a good, accessible coastal site on this loop, you may detour to the **Santa Clara River Estuary**. Otherwise you can complete the loop directly, skip the following instructions, and go straight to the directions for birding Point Mugu State Park.

For the detour, go west and north on Highway 1 to Highway 101 (9.9). Take Highway 101 west to the Seaward Avenue exit in Ventura (5.3). Go one-half block south, and turn left onto Harbor Boulevard, which parallels the highway. Turn right onto Spinnaker Drive (1.6), which borders the south edge of the Ventura Marina. At the end of Spinnaker Drive is the headquarters for Channel Islands National Park (see *Pelagic Birding Trips* section). In winter you will find loons, grebes, and scoters in the harbor and, on the beach, gulls, terns, Sanderlings, and Whimbrels.

To reach the estuary, go back to the chain-link fence at the south end of the harbor and park in the lot on the opposite side of Spinnaker Drive. Walk south along the beach to the Santa Clara River's mouth. You will pass a protected breeding-colony of the endangered California subspecies of the Least Tern. The river-mouth area is very good for waterfowl, gulls, and terns. Elegant Terns are numerous in summer and fall. A few Thayer's Gulls are present each winter in the large gull flock. Shorebirding is generally excellent here, but it's all highly dependent on the season and the water level (a low water level is best). The sewage ponds inside the fence are excellent for ducks, in both summer and winter. The entrance to the facility is a little farther along Spinnaker Drive. Birders are welcome to walk or drive around the ponds, but first must sign in at the office.

For alternative approaches to this estuary, return to Harbor Boulevard and turn right. Park just before reaching the bridge to check for swallows and terns. The estuary can be approached from here if you climb down the bank at the corner of the bridge. (You may have difficulty making your way through the dense vegetation, but a path can usually be found.) Birds can be found along the river all the way to the ocean. The south side of the estuary can also be checked from McGrath State Beach (camping; fee) (0.5). The brushy areas of the park are excellent for warblers and small landbirds during migration. Black-shouldered Kites can usually be seen hovering over the fields along Harbor Boulevard beyond the park.

You can continue the Santa Monica Mountains Loop by returning to Mugu Lagoon. *Alternately, you can get a jump on the Santa Barbara County chapter by heading north on Highway 101.*

From Mugu Lagoon, continue on Pacific Coast Highway to La Jolla Canyon in **Point Mugu State Park** (3.4). A dripping water-fountain near the restroom (unless some busybody fixes it!) attracts a variety of birds, most notably the easy-to-hear but difficult-to-see Wrentit. In recent years Big Sycamore Canyon has not been as productive as it used to be (since the creek has been dry), but it is always worth checking. You can park outside the entrance to avoid the fee.

As you continue east, stop occasionally to scan the beach for Snowy Plover, Whimbrel, Sanderling, Willet, Marbled Godwit, and other shorebirds. Check the trees on the ocean-side of the highway for migrants. The wooded area at Leo Carrillo State Beach (9.4) can be very good for warblers in migration. Continue on Highway 101 back to the starting point in Malibu.

Campgrounds are located at Point Mugu State Park (Sycamore Canyon), Leo Carrillo State Park, McGrath State Beach, and Malibu Creek State Park. Motels are clustered along Highway 1.

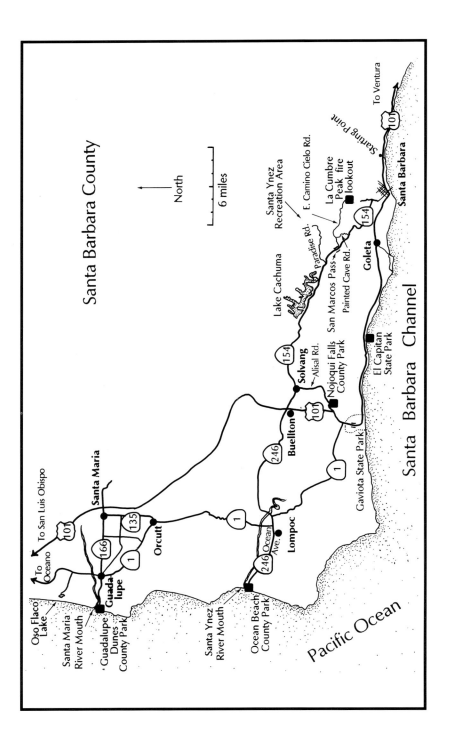

SANTA BARBARA COUNTY

When the Spaniards were picking sites for missions, they surely must have selected Santa Barbara for its ideal climate and beautiful setting. And what a setting! The mission nestles among majestic live oaks on rolling hills. To the north are the towering Santa Ynez Mountains and to the south, the blue waters of the Pacific. Even today's bustling city blends well with the natural surroundings. Over 400 species of birds have been recorded here. It is doubtful that you will find that many, unless you decide to retire and stay. After seeing this attractive town, you will probably think that this is not a bad idea.

Before beginning this route, visitors to the Santa Barbara area ought to be aware that the coast runs east-west, not north-south. So, the ocean is to the south (not west) and the mountains are to the north (not east).

The starting point is the intersection of Highway 101 and Cabrillo Boulevard toward the east end of Santa Barbara. Leave the freeway on Cabrillo Boulevard and go left (south) one block. Turn right on Los Patos Way to the parking area for the **Andree Clark Bird Refuge** (0.1). There are always ducks of some type on this freshwater pond. In winter there may be a fairly good selection. Check the *Myoporum* bushes on the islands for roosting Double-crested Cormorant, Great Blue and Green-backed Herons, and Black-crowned Night-Heron. All three phalaropes have occurred here in migration.

This is an excellent area to study gulls. They are accustomed to being fed and are very tame. Western, California, and Ring-billed Gulls are present all year. Glaucous-winged, Herring, Thayer's, Heermann's, Mew, and Bonaparte's come during the winter.

Continue on Cabrillo Boulevard to Stearn's Wharf on State Street (2.1). A walk on the wharf can be worthwhile, but it is probably better to spend your time on the breakwater which protects the harbor. To reach it, continue past the traffic light to Castillo Street (0.5), turn left at the next left, and park in the lot. Follow the sidewalk past the U.S. Naval Reserve Training Center and the seafood restaurants to the breakwater. At the end of the breakwater you will see a sandspit where Snowy Plover, Sanderling, Whimbrel, and other shorebirds rest between early fall and early spring. Gulls and terns are usually common. In late summer and fall, this is a good

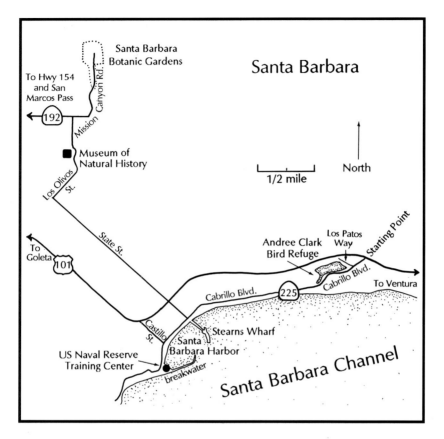

spot to pick out Heermann's Gull and Elegant Tern. Mew Gulls and Royal Terns come in late fall and winter.

Return to State Street and turn left, then left again onto Highway 101. As you cross Chapala Street (1 block), you will see the largest Moreton Fig tree in the United States. Continue on Highway 101 to Ward Memorial Boulevard (Highway 217) (5.4) and turn left to **Goleta Beach County Park** (2.0). From the inland side of the main parking lot check the channel to the mouth of the slough for herons, egrets, ducks, shorebirds, gulls, and terns. Elegant Terns occur from July to October, and Royal Terns are present from October to March. Walk out on the fishing pier to look for loons, grebes, and scoters. In winter and spring a handful of Tricolored Blackbirds is usually present in the parking area near the base of the pier.

Go back out of the park, turn left, go under the highway (0.2), and turn right onto Ward Memorial Boulevard to the gate of the University of

California at Santa Barbara (fee for parking, Monday-Friday) (ask for a campus map). Go left on Lagoon Road and bird the Campus Lagoon, fairly good from fall through spring for loons, grebes, cormorants, waterfowl, and terns.

Goleta Point (also called Campus Point), located near the Marine Sciences Building, can be good fall through spring for Ruddy and Black Turnstones at low tide, and for scanning the ocean. A scope is very helpful. This is the favored spot for observing the spring coastal seabird migration from mid-March through late May (with April being best). Many thousands of loons (mostly Pacific), Brant, scoters (mostly Surf), gulls, and terns may be seen moving up-coast (west). All sorts of surprises are possible. Afternoon is by far the best time of day to see a large number of birds here.

To reach the west side of the campus, return to the gate area and go left on University Road, left on Campus Road, and around to El Colegio

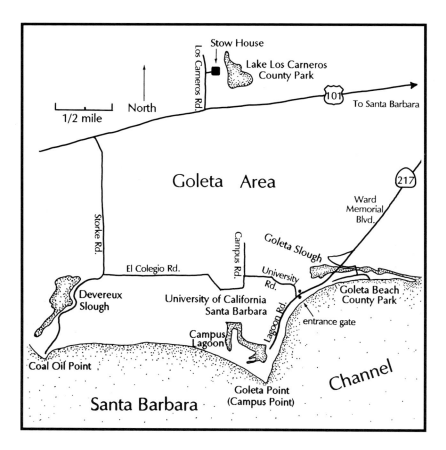

Road, and left at Storke Road to Devereux Slough. When it has water (usually dry by late summer) from late fall to mid-summer, the slough has good numbers of ducks, gulls, and terns. If water levels are low (late summer and early fall), it is very good for shorebirds. Over the years such rarities as Sharp-tailed Sandpiper, Ruff, Little Gull, and Eurasian Wigeon have been found. The vegetation bordering the slough can be good for migrating and wintering landbirds. One or two pairs of Cassin's Kingbirds are resident in the area. Allen's Hummingbirds breed in the area from March to July. One or two Tropical Kingbirds are found each fall or winter.

At Coal Oil Point at the end of the road, a low tide exposes rocks. Look for Ruddy and Black Turnstones during fall and winter. Also, large numbers of Brandt's Cormorants are found offshore. The point is fairly good for scanning the ocean at any season. A sizable wintering flock of Snowy Plovers frequents the beach several hundred yards up-coast, present late August to April.

To continue the loop, return to State Street in Santa Barbara (7.7) and turn left. Follow this street through the downtown area. Two blocks past Mission Street (2.0), turn right onto Los Olivos Street. Go past the mission (0.5), bear left onto Mission Canyon Road, and follow the signs for the free **Santa Barbara Museum of Natural History** (0.5). In addition to the excellent exhibits of native birds and mammals, it has a fine bookstore and friendly staff to answer your questions. In the Coast Live Oaks around the parking area, look for Hutton's Vireo, Plain Titmouse, Bushtit, Scrub Jay, Acorn Woodpecker, and Rufous-sided and California Towhees. This area can also be good for migrants in spring. Townsend's Warblers are fairly common from September to May.

Go back to Mission Canyon Road (0.1) and turn left. At Foothill Road (Highway 192) (0.3), jog right 2 blocks and continue on Mission Canyon Road to the **Santa Barbara Botanic Gardens** (fee) (1.0). If you can tear yourself away from the fine display of plants, you will find many chaparral and oak-woodland birds.

The trail that runs along the creek at the bottom of the canyon is particularly productive for woodland species. Permanent residents include California Quail, Anna's Hummingbird, Nuttall's Woodpecker, Wrentit, California Thrasher, Hutton's Vireo, and California Towhee. In addition, in summer look for Pacific-slope Flycatcher, Black-headed Grosbeak, and Hooded Oriole. In winter look for Winter Wren, Townsend's Warbler, and Golden-crowned Sparrow. Other things to look for here are Merriam's Chipmunk, California Ground-Squirrel, and Western Fence Lizard.

Return to Foothill Road (Highway 192) and turn right. At San Marcos Pass Road (Highway 154) (3.0), turn right onto the freeway for the climb up the pass. The hills here are covered with fine stands of chaparral (although impacted in part by the major wildfire of 1990). Stop anywhere and look for California Quail, California Thrasher, and Wrentit. The marble-dropping song of the Wrentit is heard more often than the bird is seen, but if you squeak, it may come out to investigate. In spring, it responds well to taped recordings of its song.

At the crest of the highway (San Marcos Pass) (8.4) turn right to drive out **East Camino Cielo Road**. At the fork with Painted Cave Road (2.0) keep left and bird your way out East Camino Cielo Road seven miles to the La Cumbre Peak fire lookout. All along this road in spring and early summer look for California and Mountain Quail, Costa's and Anna's Hummingbirds, California Thrasher, Canyon Wren, Lazuli Bunting, and Rufous-crowned and Black-chinned Sparrows. Townsend's Solitaires sometimes winter in the pines in the La Cumbre Peak area, and Golden-crowned and Fox Sparrows are common in winter.

Return to San Marcos Pass and continue north on Highway 154 to Paradise Road (3.2), where you turn right to the **Santa Ynez Recreation Area** (a county park and two campgrounds) (2.4). Birds that are typical of the chaparral and the oak woodlands are abundant here. By playing owl calls at night, you should be able to find Great Horned Owl and Western Screech-Owl.

Continue past the boys' camp (3.4) and, if the water is not too deep (a potential problem in winter), ford the stream. Beyond are more campgrounds which are sometimes worth a look.

Return to Highway 154 and turn right toward **Lake Cachuma** (2.5), which is best in winter when the ducks, grebes, Bald Eagles, and Ospreys are about. It is difficult to find a place from which to view the lake. The best three spots are the intake stands located where the lake first comes into view from Highway 154, the Cachuma County Park (fee) (4.3), and the vista point at the dam (2.4). From the County Park there are naturalist-led cruises on the lake twice a week in winter. The oak woodlands shelter such birds as Acorn Woodpecker, Plain Titmouse, and Western Bluebird. In winter look for Lewis's Woodpecker (rare). At the dam, look for Wrentit, California Towhee, and California Thrasher. Rock Wrens might be found on the dam itself.

At Highway 246 (5.0) turn left toward Solvang (5.0). This replica of a Danish village is famous for its pastry and artwork. It is a pleasant little tourist trap.

Near the Santa Ynez Mission at the east edge of town, turn left on Alisal Road for a drive down beautiful Alisal Canyon. Look over the golf course for Western Bluebird and Yellow-billed Magpie, the only California bird never verified outside the state. After you reach Alisal Creek, stop anywhere to check the lush vegetation. In summer you may see Hooded and Northern Orioles, Black-headed Grosbeak, Hutton's and Warbling Vireos, Lazuli Bunting, and Chipping Sparrow. Look for Hermit and Varied Thrushes, and numerous sparrows in winter. Stop at **Nojoqui Falls County Park** (nah-ho-WEY) (6.7) for the noisy flock of Yellow-billed Magpies (usually at the entrance or at the ranger's house). Approximately 15 pairs of Purple Martins (a rare and local bird in the West) breed in the sycamore trees around the ranger's house (April-August).

The short hike up to the falls takes you through typical woodland canyon habitat. Here you may find such resident birds as Band-tailed Pigeon, Anna's Hummingbird, Acorn, Nuttall's, Downy, and Hairy Woodpeckers, Northern Flicker, Scrub Jay, Plain Titmouse, Bushtit, Bewick's and House Wrens, California Thrasher, Hutton's Vireo, California Towhee, and Lesser Goldfinch. Summer brings Black-chinned and Allen's Hummingbirds, Pacific-slope and Ash-throated Flycatchers, Violet-green Swallow, Warbling Vireo, Yellow Warbler, and Black-headed Grosbeak. In winter look for Winter Wren, Ruby-crowned Kinglet, numerous Hermit Thrushes, Townsend's Warbler, and many Yellow-rumped Warblers. Resident Spotted Owls (rare) may be heard at night in the upper end of the park. It is best to bird this area early before the crowds arrive. Continue on Highway 154 to Highway 101 (1.9) and turn left.

When you reach Highway 1 (2.3), you have a choice. If you wish to turn north toward Lompoc, Santa Maria, San Luis Obispo, and Morro Bay, skip ahead to those areas (instructions for San Luis Obispo and Morro Bay are in the following chapter). If you want to go east to the beaches to camp, or head back to Santa Barbara, read on.

Continue south on Highway 101, and after going through Gaviota Pass, you will reach the ocean(2.5). There are several state parks along the route back to Santa Barbara. They are worth checking in migration and in winter, but are far too crowded in summer. Gaviota State Park (part of which you have just passed through) is best during spring and fall migrations. El Capitan State Park (12.5) has many of the same oak and riparian-woodland birds as above except for Yellow-billed Magpie and Purple Martin.

Continue on Highway 101 and exit at Los Carneros Road (9.8) (see Goleta Area map). Stow House, built in 1876, is on your right (0.4). Park in the lot behind the fire station and walk to the house. Walk the driveway to **Lake Los Carneros County Park**, a good spot for ducks and many other birds. Most of the 1,043-acre park, including the lake, is in a wild state. The trees around the house itself may be particularly good in migration and winter.

Yellow-billed Magpie
Shawneen Finnegan

To return to the loop's starting point, turn left onto Highway 101 and drive to Cabrillo Boulevard (12.3).

To continue the tour farther west and north, drive west on Highway 101 from Los Carneros Road to the junction of Highways 101 and 1 (26.1) and turn left toward Lompoc (19.2). Rather than turning north to follow Highway 1 in downtown Lompoc, continue west on Ocean Avenue (Highway 246) until you reach the mouth of the Santa Ynez River at **Ocean Beach County Park** (11.3).

The amount of water in the Santa Ynez River varies greatly, depending on the amount of rainfall in its drainage system. During high water levels, the mouth of the river is good for ducks, herons, gulls, and terns. On the other hand, shorebirds are numerous during periods of low water. Least Terns are very local breeders. The willow-riparian vegetation in the area is the most southern range for Chestnut-backed Chickadee. From May through August you should be able to use the parking lot at the beach as a vantage point for scanning the ocean for large numbers of Sooty

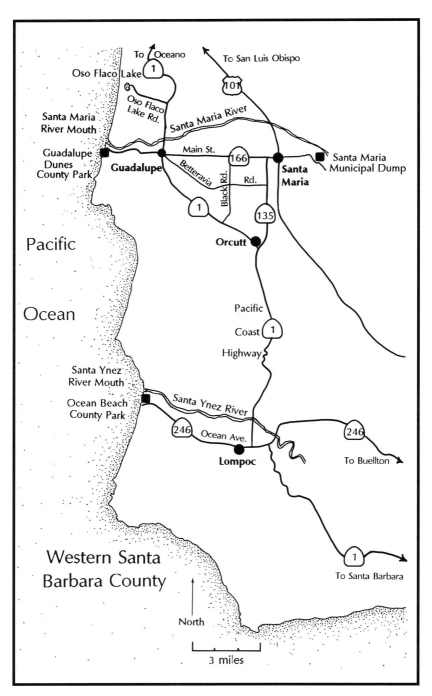

To Oceano

To San Luis Obispo

Oso Flaco Lake

1

101

Oso Flaco Lake Rd.

Santa Maria River

Santa Maria River Mouth

Guadalupe Dunes County Park

Guadalupe

Main St.

166

Santa Maria Municipal Dump

Betteravia

Black Rd.

Rd.

Santa Maria

1

135

Pacific

Orcutt

Ocean

Pacific

Coast

1

Highway

Santa Ynez River Mouth

Ocean Beach County Park

Santa Ynez River

246

Ocean Ave.

246

To Buellton

Lompoc

Western Santa Barbara County

North

1

To Santa Barbara

3 miles

Shearwaters, and in fall (mid-October to late November or December) you have a chance of seeing Black-vented Shearwater. In winter, the ocean off the river's mouth supports large numbers of Surf and White-winged Scoters and lesser numbers of Red-throated, Pacific, and Common Loons. Rarities may occur. In summer, from July to October, good numbers of Elegant Terns appear along with smaller numbers of Royal Terns (the Royals remain through the winter).

Return to Lompoc and continue north on Highway 1. At Orcutt (19.5) follow Highway 135 to the right and continue north on it to Betteravia Road (5.1), then turn left (west) to Black Road (3.1). Formerly, this area's lush pastures offered very good birding, but it is unfortunately becoming more and more developed. This is all *private property*, so please bird from the road.

In winter (October to mid-April) you may still find the Pacific Golden-Plover (which may soon be split from the Lesser Golden-Plover) in the lush pasture just to the south along Black Road. Also look in the pasture east of Black Road and south of Betteravia Road. Other shorebird species which you may see here include Black-bellied Plover, Long-billed Curlew, and Common Snipe. In 1984, when these fields were flooded, a Little Curlew was found here among the large numbers of birds using the fields. (Four years later there was another sighting of Little Curlew in a different pasture, some 7 miles farther west.) Other rarities here over the years have included Sharp-tailed Sandpiper and Ruff.

Just to the northeast of this intersection are short-grass fields and gently rolling hills (partially grazed by cattle and sheep) which somewhat regularly support small numbers of Mountain Plover from early November through mid-February. These birds prefer shorter, over-grazed grass and are not present every winter. Also, you may find one or two wintering Ferruginous Hawks.

Return to Highway 135 and continue east one mile to Highway 101. Drive north to Main Street in Santa Maria (2.0) and turn right (east) to the Santa Maria Municipal Dump (approximately 2.5 miles), located on the north side of Main Street. This is one of the best localities in Southern California for finding Thayer's Gull. From mid-November through late March as many as twenty Thayer's per day may be found. Almost all are in first-winter plumage. This number represents about five to ten percent of the Herring-type gulls there. Other gulls present are California, Ring-billed, Mew, and Glaucous-winged, but *no* Western Gulls. First-winter Thayer's are told from first-winter Herring Gulls by their more-gently-rounded head, black bill, checkered plumage, and light tan-brown wingtips with little white crescents on the tips of each primary.

Herring is paler-headed, has darker wingtips, and the underwing is dark (paler in Thayer's). At the entrance to the dump ask permission to enter; simply tell them that you would like to look over the gulls. Or you can park beyond the entrance, adjacent to where the active dumping is taking place, and bird from the road.

Drive west on Main Street (Highway 166) past Highway 1 and all the way to the ocean and **Guadalupe Dunes County Park** (about 12 miles). About a mile short of the ocean and the **Santa Maria River Mouth** is a guard station and parking lot. The park is open from 8 to 6 (or dusk depending on the season) seven days a week. Although the road is paved to the beach, *no four-wheel-drive vehicles are allowed*. Between the guard station and the dunes at the beach is a riparian area of thick willows, good to bird for the resident Chestnut-backed Chickadee (fairly common). Also found during the breeding season are Swainson's Thrush and Yellow and Wilson's Warblers. Migrants are attracted to this area in spring and fall. At the river's mouth, during low-water periods, you will find many shorebirds. A number of rarities have been recorded over the years, including several records of Ruff and Sharp-tailed Sandpiper. The area can also be fairly good for waterfowl in winter and fall. Snowy Plovers breed commonly, as do a few Least Terns.

In summer and fall you may find lots of Elegant Terns, Brown Pelicans, and Heermann's Gulls. And in winter it is a fine place to study gulls in the afternoon. (For this it may help if you're willing to get a little wet or muddy. Or bring your boots—but it's not a requirement.)

The dunes are an excellent platform from which to scan the ocean for large numbers of Sooty Shearwaters in summer and Black-vented Shearwaters in fall. In winter large numbers of Surf and White-winged Scoters are seen, as well as many loons of three species—Red-throated, Pacific, and Common. Occasionally a surprise turns up, such as a pelagic species.

Return to Highway 1 and go north to Oso Flaco Lake Road (4.8). Turn left to its dead-end, 3.2 miles, where thick willows and sand-dunes surround natural Oso Flaco Lake. In fall, migrant songbirds may be found here (best in September and October). Resident willow birds include Anna's Hummingbird, Nuttall's and Downy Woodpeckers, Chestnut-backed Chickadee, Hutton's Vireo, Black Phoebe, Marsh Wren, California Thrasher, and Wrentit. California Quail and California Towhee may also be found. The lake is better for ducks in winter. Common Moorhen (uncommon) is sometimes seen here, and Caspian, Forster's, and Least Terns are commonly seen in spring and summer. The spectacular dunes behind the lake and along the coast here are being preserved by The

Nature Conservancy, and if your schedule permits, take a walk through them in order to appreciate their sheer beauty.

You are not far from Oceano and Lopez Lake, the beginning of our trip through the San Luis Obispo and Morro Bay areas.

There are campgrounds in Santa Ynez Valley and at the state parks west of Santa Barbara. Motels are plentiful in Santa Barbara, Lompoc, and Santa Maria.

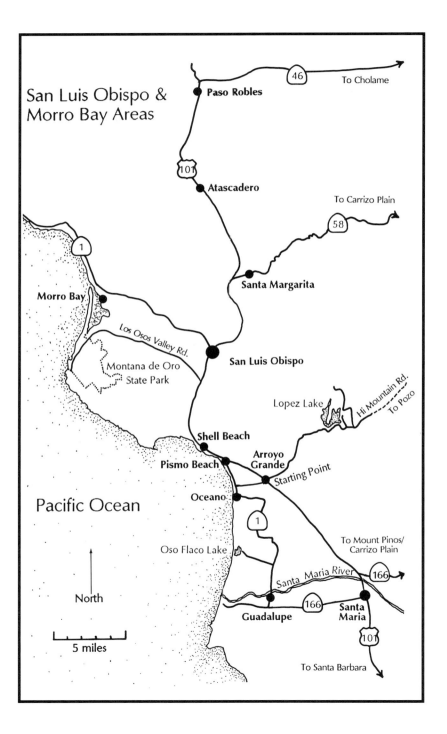

San Luis Obispo &
Morro Bay Areas

46
To Cholame

Paso Robles

101

Atascadero

To Carrizo Plain

58

1

Santa Margarita

Morro Bay

Los Osos Valley Rd.

Montana de Oro
State Park

San Luis Obispo

Lopez Lake

Hi Mountain Rd.
To Pozo

Shell Beach

Arroyo
Grande

Pismo Beach

Starting Point

Oceano

Pacific Ocean

1

To Mount Pinos/
Carrizo Plain

Oso Flaco Lake

Santa Maria River

166

North

166

Santa
Maria

Guadalupe

101

5 miles

To Santa Barbara

SAN LUIS OBISPO — MORRO BAY AREAS

by Brad Schram

This route will take the birder through the hillside and coastal habitats in the San Luis Obispo and Morro Bay areas. Two main north-south highways, the famous California Highway 1 on the coast and U.S. Highway 101 through the interior, provide parallel tracks from which all birding trips mentioned below depart. Visitors from the East may find many western and California specialties here with ease, given the right season and habitat. Conversely, westerners may be treated during migration (especially fall) to eastern vagrants in many of these locations.

Highway 101's Grand Avenue off-ramp in Arroyo Grande is the starting point for both the Lopez Lake and Oceano trips. It is located 12.3 miles north of the Santa Maria River, which marks the boundary between Santa Barbara and San Luis Obispo counties.

Lopez Lake is a large reservoir amid oak-covered rocky hillsides and cattle-grazing land. In winter its waters (especially at the east end) are good for diving ducks, Osprey, and the occasional Bald Eagle. The oak-covered slopes are year-round host to numerous species, including Red-shouldered Hawk, Band-tailed Pigeon, Western Screech-Owl, Acorn and Nuttall's Woodpeckers, Plain Titmouse, and Western Bluebird, while White-throated Swifts may be seen coursing overhead. Yellow-billed Magpies are resident in the hillside oak savannah, but are not plentiful. Chestnut-backed Chickadee is a permanent resident in the willow-riparian area along nearby Hi Mountain Road. The latter area is best visited in spring and early summer when breeding Western Wood-Pewee, Pacific-slope Flycatcher, Warbling Vireo, MacGillivray's Warbler, Yellow-breasted Chat, Black-headed Grosbeak, Lazuli Bunting, and Bullock's Northern Oriole may be seen. As with all stream-side habitat in San Luis Obispo County

29

(SLOCo to the locals), Black Phoebes are year-round residents, while California Thrasher and California Towhee populate the edges.

To reach Lopez Lake, turn east off Highway 101 at the Grand Avenue exit. Drive through the old village of Arroyo Grande, following the highway signs pointing east toward the lake. Be sure to bear right (following the sign) at the junction with Highway 227 (0.8). As you drive through the decreasingly populated countryside, stay alert for roadside birds (the first 1.3 miles off Highway 101 are good for Hooded Oriole between April and August). In spring and summer you may see Western Kingbird perched on the fences in open country, while Say's Phoebe takes over this territory in winter. Raptors might include Black-shouldered Kite (uncommon). After reaching the west end of Lopez Lake (no access), continue driving until you find a small, gated, dirt track off to the right behind a "no parking" sign (9.9). Park on the dirt drive and check the inlet waters, which extend under the highway and up a small oak-lined canyon. Birds often seen here

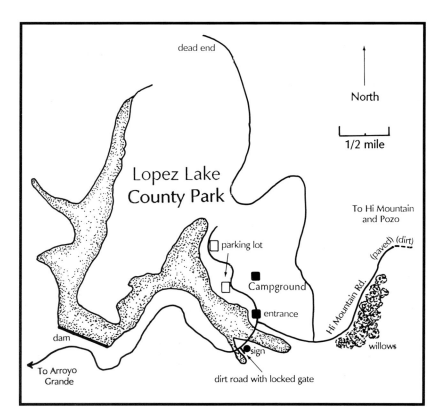

(November-March) include Gadwall, Hooded Merganser (rare), and Common Merganser.

After crossing a bridge, you will see paved Hi Mountain Road leading off to the right (0.1). Before investigating it, winter visitors will first want to continue straight on the main road into the **Lopez Lake County Park** (fee); the entrance is straight ahead (0.3). The park's oak-covered hillsides contain the birds typical of this habitat noted earlier, while the lakeshore has its own specialties. From the entrance kiosk proceed straight uphill on Lopez Drive to a large parking lot on the left (0.7). Between November and March there is usually a large, mixed flock of Ring-necked Ducks, Lesser Scaups, and Buffleheads on the lake at this location. Both Western and Clark's Grebes are regular here in winter. Tufted Duck (rare) has been seen here also. Drive to the end of the road (0.8), park, and walk a few hundred yards farther to a vantage point on the narrow Wittenberg Arm of the lake. During high water-levels this arm can be filled with diving ducks, possibly including all of those noted above. The enclosing oaks may be productive also. From mid-April through summer the lake will be unproductive, but the riparian and oak habitats will then be at their best.

Return to the junction of Hi Mountain Road and follow it 1.2 miles to an area of thick willows on a curve where roadside parking is easy. All land on both sides of the road is private here, so bird the edges of the oaks and willows from the lightly-traveled road. If you continue farther up 13-mile long Hi Mountain Road, it becomes a four-wheel-drive dirt track transecting some wonderful oak, grassland, sycamore-riparian, and chaparral habitat—but this is only for the hardy, and local advice should be sought before attempting this drive.

The **Oceano Campground** (or "Oceano" as locals abbreviate it) is also easily reached from the Highway 101/Grand Avenue junction. Drive west (toward the ocean) on Grand Avenue through Arroyo Grande and Grover City to the intersection with Highway 1 (2.7). Turn left onto Highway 1 and continue to the first street on the right, Coolidge Drive (0.9). Turn right onto Coolidge Drive and park at its end, one block away at its intersection with Norswing Drive. (One could also enter the park from its entrance on Pier Street, 0.2 beyond Coolidge Drive; in this case, turn right on Pier Street and park in front of the Oceano Campground entrance.) From Coolidge Drive and Norswing Drive you will see a path, entering the willows, behind wooden barrier posts. Turn right and follow this approximately one-mile-long path as it circles the pond. Bird the willows around the pond, the pines behind the tile-roofed homes across from the north end of the pond, the willows and cattails along the channel extending north from the pond's end, and the pines in the campground and along the

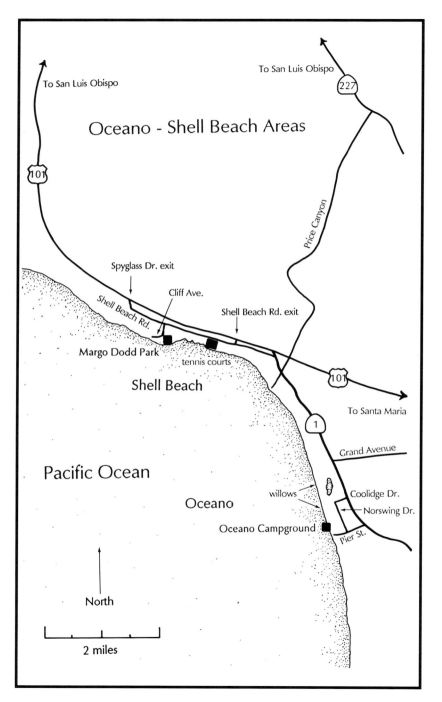

To San Luis Obispo

To San Luis Obispo

227

Oceano - Shell Beach Areas

101

Price Canyon

Spyglass Dr. exit

Shell Beach Rd.

Cliff Ave.

Shell Beach Rd. exit

Margo Dodd Park

tennis courts

101

Shell Beach

To Santa Maria

1

Grand Avenue

Pacific Ocean

Oceano

willows

Coolidge Dr.

Norswing Dr.

Oceano Campground

Pier St.

North

2 miles

dunes. These areas are good for western migrants. In fall, vagrant warblers, the primary target, have been found here in impressive numbers, but many other vagrant passerines have been found here, too. After a good migration flight-night this search should take no less than two hours, often more.

Oceano should be birded before 10:00 a.m. to avoid the regular afternoon winds. It is a classic coastal California "vagrant trap" during fall migration, centering on a small pond surrounded by willows with nearby pines, just a few hundred yards of sand-dunes inland from the ocean. The best time is in September and October, especially the latter month, although eastern vagrants have been found here through December. There are only a few records from spring. Winter finds an occasional vagrant enjoying the mild climate, but more predictable wintering birds include common puddle ducks and Wood Duck (uncommon). The resident willow birds include Anna's Hummingbird, Nuttall's and Downy Woodpeckers, Chestnut-backed Chickadee, and Hutton's Vireo. In winter you will also find a full complement of visiting warblers and sparrows such as you might see anywhere on the California coast. Black Phoebe is a permanent resident, as is Marsh Wren in the cattails and tules, while patches of dry scrub provide cover for California Thrasher and Wrentit, both common. California Quail may be found in many locations. California Towhees outnumber their Rufous-sided cousins.

An extension of the park, south of Pier Street from the entrance, has a pond surrounded on three sides by grass. This area holds the predictable assortment of domestic waterfowl and panhandling gulls, but an occasional wintering Snow or Ross's Goose (rare) may be found, and wintering Thayer's Gulls (uncommon) are sometimes seen after mid-October. Look among the Western Grebes on the pond for Clark's Grebe, occasionally seen here.

The cliffs at **Shell Beach**, just up-coast from Arroyo Grande, are a fine place for birding at any time of year. Wintering birds easily seen just offshore include three species of loons, both Western (abundant), and Clark's (uncommon) Grebes, and rafts of scoters (Surf is abundant, White-winged common, and Black rare). Resident Brandt's and Pelagic Cormorants are common on rocks just offshore, as is Black Oystercatcher. Winter shorebirds include Willet, Wandering Tattler (uncommon), Whimbrel, Marbled Godwit, Ruddy (uncommon) and Black (common) Turnstones, Surfbird (uncommon), and Sanderling, while the resident Western Gulls' numbers are augmented by the influx of wintering gulls from the north. From October to mid-March, small flocks of Black-vented Shearwaters (uncommon) may be seen offshore with the aid of a spotting scope.

Birding from the cliffs can be especially rewarding during spring through summer when migration is underway, cliff-nesting birds are breeding, and the summer influx of Brown Pelicans, cormorants, and gulls (especially Heermann's) make very impressive numbers here. Pigeon Guillemots arrive on the cliffs during April, and by May scores may be seen from numerous vantage points. From June to August scores of thousands of Sooty Shearwaters are commonly seen from this vantage point. From August through the fall, Royal Tern is often seen here, and Elegant Tern is common from mid-July through early October, when its numbers decrease until this species disappears locally by mid-November.

From northbound Highway 101, take the Shell Beach Road exit, 4.7 miles north of Grand Avenue. Turn left under the freeway to Shell Beach Road, which parallels the cliffs. Turn right onto it and drive to the tennis courts on the left side of the road (0.3); park in the lot. Peregrine Falcon is sometimes seen here in spring and summer, as is Osprey during migration. During spring and early summer of 1988 and 1989, a small number of Rhinoceros Auklets was seen regularly from this vantage point; although nesting was suspected, it was never proven.

Drive north from the tennis courts, turn left onto Cliff Avenue (0.6), and stop at very small, bluff-top Margo Dodd Park (0.3). The birds seen here are similar to those at the tennis courts, and close-range views of Pigeon Guillemots at the entrances to their nest burrows are available from mid-April to July. Several active Black Oystercatcher breeding territories are visible from this point. From here you have a panorama of the entire coast from Point Sal in Santa Barbara County to the Port San Luis Lighthouse up-coast to the right—this is an exquisite spot! Look closely at the low, flat rock just offshore for shorebirds and the numerous Harbor Seals normally hauled out there. Sea Otters are often seen from this point, as are Gray Whales during migration and Common Dolphins in the late spring and summer.

Montaña de Oro State Park, located just south of Morro Bay, is another productive birding area. The park's western border is a lovely series of cliffs, small beaches, and the finest tide-pools in the county. The cliffs and coastal waters, at the appropriate time of year, harbor the same species noted for Shell Beach. Winter scoping from the cliffs often produces sightings of Northern Fulmar (irregular), Parasitic and Pomarine Jaegers, Common Murre, Marbled Murrelet (rare), and Rhinoceros Auklet. Scoping here can produce hundreds of Pacific Loons, Brant, and scoters per hour in spring (especially April and May). Local birders pay closest attention to MDO (as they call the park) from late August through November when it becomes another classic California coastal migrant and vagrant trap. The cypresses at park headquarters, and especially the pines in the campgrounds and the adjacent willow-lined creek, host migrating warblers and other passerines in fall. The list of eastern and Mexican/southwest vagrants that has been found here is impressive. All species typical of California coastal chaparral can be found on the hillsides. Rufous-crowned Sparrow (uncommon) is resident on the south-facing chaparral hillsides. MDO has the virtue of being "birdable" at any time of the day.

To reach Montaña de Oro from Highway 101 take the Los Osos Valley Road offramp in San Luis Obispo (5.9 miles north of Spyglass Drive), and drive west toward the ocean. Pass through the small community of Los Osos (10.0), following the signs to MDO as the road sweeps to the south and uphill, affording spectacular views of Morro Bay and the coastal dunes. Park at the white headquarters-building (5.1). To hike the bluffs, walk uphill from the parking spot to the obvious trail which skirts the cliffs south of jewel-like Spooner's Cove, and continue walking down-coast for about three miles. The beauty of this walk is such that it almost makes any birds found an unnecessary bonus.

Anna's and Allen's (except in winter) Hummingbirds, Nuttall's Woodpecker, Chestnut-backed Chickadee, Wrentit, California Thrasher, and Hutton's Vireo are all common here, and Pacific-slope Flycatcher is a common breeder, but it is the migration seasons which make this park most interesting. Aside from the cliff-top pelagic-birding possibilities, during migration (especially fall) the willows along the creek behind and below park headquarters can be very productive for western and, occasionally, vagrant eastern migrants. The most predictably active birding locations, however, are the pine groves in the campgrounds. After birding the cypresses near park headquarters, walk inland from your car about one-quarter of a mile, birding the fringe of willows on one side and chaparral on the other, to the campground pines, and sort through the western species for the odd eastern vagrant. Bird numbers vary depending on month (September, October, and to a lesser extent May are best) and flight conditions, but on some days the numerous mandible-snaps of feeding warblers quicken the heartbeat.

The campground is also a very good location for visitors from other states to bird some typical California chaparral. Simply watch the edges along the road above the campground (pishing helps), or walk through the campground to its easternmost point where a trail continues east through chaparral with the willows below eye-level to one's left.

If visiting in winter, a side trip to Sweet Springs on an inlet of Morro Bay is called for when leaving MDO. Retrace the route taken into the park (the only entrance/egress) from headquarters 4.2 miles, then turn left next to a church onto Pine Street. Turn right at the bottom of the gentle hill onto Ramona Avenue and park in front of a mobile-home park, 0.7 miles from where you turned off Los Osos Valley Road. Walk through the cypress and eucalyptus to the *Salicornia*-edged bay where hundreds of ducks and Brant feed daily. Occasionally, Greater Scaup (rare) may be seen here among the Lessers and other diving and puddle ducks, but the major attraction is the opportunity to see Eurasian Wigeon. For at least eight years, one or more male Eurasian Wigeons have wintered here amidst a flock of several hundred American Wigeons. Other birds here (depending on the tide) at this time of year typically include Willet, Long-billed Curlew, Marbled Godwit, Sanderling, Western and Least Sandpipers, and Long-billed and Short-billed Dowitchers. Peregrine Falcon and Merlin are occasionally seen making air strikes here.

After birding Sweet Springs, return to Los Osos Valley Road. To continue on to Morro Bay, turn left and drive to South Bay Boulevard (1.1), where you turn left, drive 3.3 miles, and turn left onto State Park Road, which skirts the estuary and takes you toward Morro Bay Campground.

The environs of the picturesque town of **Morro Bay** provide worthwhile birding year-round, although winter offers the most variety. Morro Bay's primary industry is tourism (fishing is second). Famous Morro Rock (El. 581 ft) guarding the bay hosts spring-nesting colonies of Brandt's and Pelagic Cormorants, Western Gull, and Pigeon Guillemot—but it is the Rock's status as a Peregrine Falcon nesting-site that brings it its most publicized avian distinction. Although Peregrines are resident here, the best time to see them is typically in May and June, when they are feeding and fledging young. The spectacle of Peregrines winging about to the accompaniment of crashing Pacific rollers, mingled with the cries of gulls, songs of the enigmatic resident Canyon Wrens, and the dash of White-throated Swifts, makes the Morro Rock experience dramatic indeed. As likely as not, all the above will be attended by a dozing pod of Sea Otters, wrapped in kelp, floating just off the parking area next to the Rock.

Winter brings loons (Common and Red-throated are common, Pacific uncommon), grebes, cormorants, Brown and American White Pelicans, flocks of shorebirds, Brant, and ducks to the bay. Caspian Terns may be seen year-round, although they are decidedly uncommon in winter. Royal Terns are present from September through March, while Elegant Terns, most abundant from July through early October, are not found here in winter. A mixed flock of wintering gulls, terns, and shorebirds on a sandy beach across the bay inlet from Coleman Drive is best scrutinized with the aid of a spotting scope. The extensive *Salicornia*-marsh in the upper bay supports thousands of wintering and migrant shorebirds, and Morro Bay

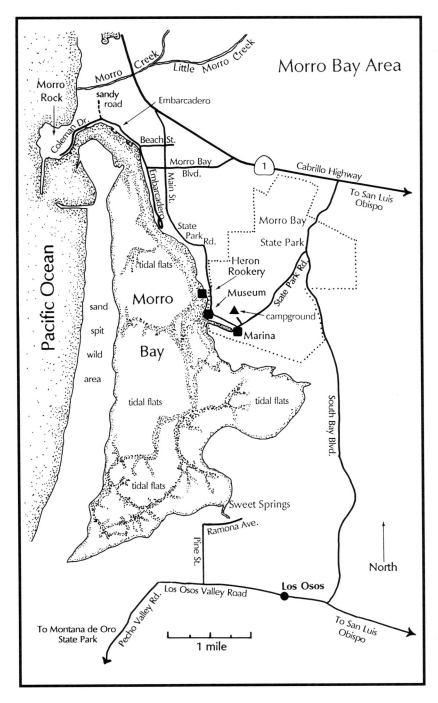

Morro Bay Area

State Park campground, under the pines on the bay's margin, is regularly birded in fall for the vagrant warblers sometimes found among mixed flocks of Chestnut-backed Chickadees and western migrants.

To reach Morro Bay from Highway 101, turn west at the Highway 1 Morro Bay exit (Santa Rosa Street in San Luis Obispo). Turn right (west) on Highway 1 and proceed to the South Bay Boulevard exit (11.2). Turn left onto South Bay Boulevard, continue to the sign for Morro Bay State Park (0.7), turn right onto State Park Road, and proceed to the campground entrance (0.9).

Park next to the campground and bird the pines. In fall the canopy contains migrant flocks mingling with the resident birds. This area is most easily birded in the morning, when the sun strikes the pines lining the road. Walk across the street opposite the campground to look for shorebirds in the *Salicornia*. About 200 yards past the campground entrance, on the opposite side of the street, you will see a parking lot behind eucalyptus trees, with a small marina beyond. Take the path past the marina across a *Baccharis*- and willow-covered peninsula, then follow the peninsula's shoreline, scoping the shorebird concentrations. The hour before and after high tide is best, but any time can be good.

Continue driving on beyond the campground entrance to visit the Morro Bay Museum of Natural History (0.3), where the displays, information, and bay overlook are all worth the traveler's attention. (You can buy the worthwhile SLOCo checklist here.). When you leave the museum, continue on toward the town of Morro Bay. An interesting stop in spring and early summer is the active heron rookery (0.3). Double-crested Cormorants, Great Blue Herons, Great Egrets, and Black-crowned Night-Herons nest here, with the attendant clamor, sights, and smells associated with these elegant birds.

Continue north on Main Street to Beach Street (1.5), and turn left to reach Embarcadero and the waterfront (0.2). Turn right on Embarcadero toward the Rock, keeping your eyes open for Coleman Drive (0.4). Here Embarcadero becomes a sandy/dirt road. If you are here in fall, drive about one-tenth of a mile to this sandy street's dead end on Morro Creek and park. Walk the creek (almost always dry in fall), looking for mixed chickadee/warbler flocks. Continue your drive to the Rock on Coleman Drive, and work anywhere along its base. Look for Peregrines here, and the resident White-throated Swifts, Black Phoebes, Bewick's and Canyon Wrens, and Nuttall's White-crowned Sparrows while at the same time watching the surface of the bay for waterbirds.

Retrace your steps to Morro Bay Boulevard either to return to Highway 1 and then Highway 101, or to continue up-coast on Highway 1 beyond the scope of this book to the beautiful Big Sur Coast in Monterey County via the equally beautiful San Luis Obispo County coast.

To hook up with the Carrizo Plain-Maricopa-Mount Pinos trip, see the instructions at the beginning of the next chapter for starting this route from Morro Bay.

There are plenty of campgrounds in the areas covered in this chapter (e.g., Lopez Lake, Oceano, Montana de Oro, and Morro Bay State Park). Motel accommodations in most price-ranges abound in such areas as Pismo Beach, Shell Beach, San Luis Obispo, and Morro Bay.

Wrentit
Charles H. Gambill

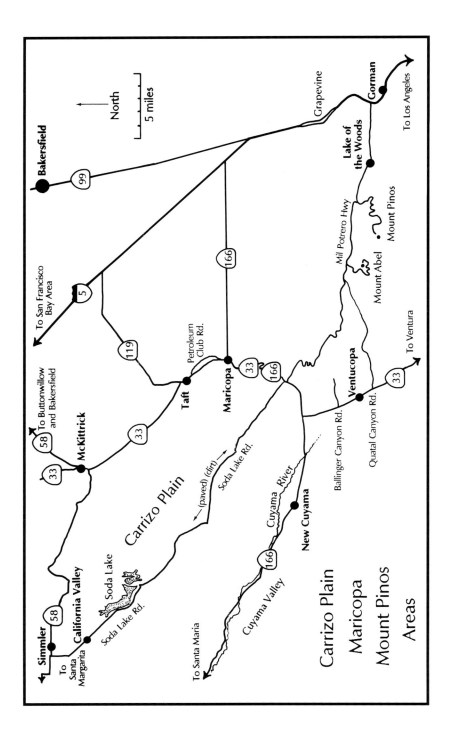

North

5 miles

Bakersfield

99

To San Francisco
Bay Area

5

119

To Buttonwillow
and Bakersfield

58

McKittrick

33

33

Simmler

58

California Valley

To
Santa
Margarita

Soda Lake Rd.

Soda Lake

Carrizo Plain

Soda Lake Rd.

(paved) (dirt)

Taft

Petroleum
Club Rd.

166

Maricopa

33

166

Grapevine

Gorman

To Los Angeles

Lake of
the Woods

Mil Potrero Hwy

Mount Pinos

Mount Abel

To Ventura

Ventucopa

33

Quatal Canyon Rd.

Ballinger Canyon Rd.

New Cuyama

Cuyama River

166

Cuyama Valley

To Santa Maria

Carrizo Plain
Maricopa
Mount Pinos

Areas

CARRIZO PLAIN—
MARICOPA—MOUNT
PINOS AREAS

Several quite different yet productive birding areas lie along a roughly linear route between coastal San Luis Obispo County and Interstate 5 north of the Los Angeles Basin. According to Brad Schram, who helped with this chapter, the route you choose will depend on weather conditions and the time of year.

From Morro Bay, take Highway 1 to its junction with Highway 101 in San Luis Obispo and drive north on Highway 101. At the El Camino Real exit (8.8), leave the freeway and go east toward the town of Santa Margarita. Drive through this small community until you reach the right turn across the railroad tracks onto Highway 58 (1.6). For the next 35 miles you will traverse oak savannah (and some chaparral) with an avifauna especially interesting to out-of-state visitors. Acorn (abundant) and Nuttall's (common) Woodpeckers, Plain Titmouse (common), and Western Bluebird (common) are among the most characteristic birds here year-round. Yellow-billed Magpies are very conspicuous along the route. When you reach Pozo Road (35.3), turn right and park opposite the first oak tree in the pasture on the right. A small resident population of Lewis's Woodpeckers can be found here (best in the morning). Look for them on the fenceposts and flying from tree to tree in the immediate vicinity. This is also a good area for close-up looks at Yellow-billed Magpies. Check out the stock tanks for Lawrence's Goldfinch, and watch for Prairie Falcon, often seen here. Return to Highway 58 and travel eastward over some low hills to Soda Lake Road (46.0) on the **Carrizo Plain**.

One can also reach the Carrizo from the east via Highway 58 west from Bakersfield, or, if coming from Yosemite or the northern Central Valley, via Bitterwater Road off Highway 46. To reach the Carrizo from Highway 46, turn south on the Bitterwater Road 2.2 miles west of the junction of Highways 46 and 41, just west of Cholame (Sha-LAM) (gasoline, restaurant, post office). This is cattle range, and wintering raptors are sometimes seen along this road in substantial numbers. At 9.3 miles south of the turn, take the right fork in the road, following the "To Highway 58" sign for another 22.8 miles to its end at Highway 58. Turn left 6.3 miles to Soda Lake Road.

The best time for birders to visit the Carrizo is from November through March, fortuitously also the most comfortable months climatically. Summer on the Carrizo is hot, very dry, and relatively birdless. This remote, desolate, inland desert-like valley is separated from the San Joaquin Valley by the Temblor Range running along the infamous San Andreas Fault. Historically home to extensive grain, cattle, and sheep ranches, the Carrizo is now also home to The Nature Conservancy's largest project in California (ultimately over 200,000 acres), designed to preserve this largest-remaining undeveloped slice of the southern San Joaquin Valley topography, flora, and fauna. California birders building their "county lists" make the Carrizo Plain a regular birding spot (it's part of San Luis Obispo County).

In winter months the Carrizo hosts a wide variety of raptors, often in large numbers, including Black-shouldered Kite (uncommon), Ferruginous Hawk (common), Rough-legged Hawk (uncommon), and Golden Eagle

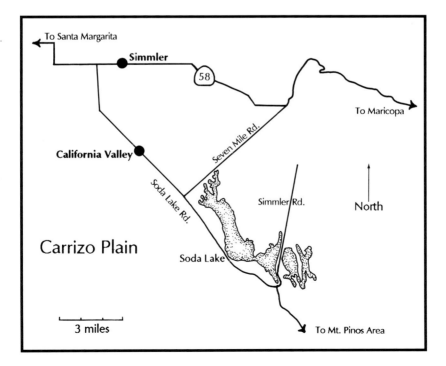

Sandhill Cranes
Charles H. Gambill

(uncommon). The resident Prairie Falcon (uncommon) is seldom missed, and, like the Rough-legs, Merlin numbers vary from winter to winter between uncommon to rare status. Burrowing Owls (uncommon) can best be seen along the dirt road south of Soda Lake, and Short-eared Owls (rare) sometimes winter in small numbers in the grass and sage near Soda Lake. Characteristic birds of the Carrizo in winter include Northern Harrier, Red-tailed and Ferruginous Hawks, American Kestrel, Say's Phoebe, Horned Lark, Common Raven, Savannah Sparrow, and House Finch. Mountain Plover (uncommon) and Mountain Bluebird (uncommon) are regular, if local, wintering species, as is the bird most often asked about—the Sandhill Crane. The cranes arrive in October and are gone by the end of March, feeding wherever the year's grain crops take them. The one predictable place to see the Sandhills, providing there is water in the lake, is in and around Soda Lake in mid- to late afternoon, as this is their roosting site through the night. The sight and sound of hundreds, or thousands, of cranes flying in toward the lake for a night's roost is one of the great sensory experiences in nature.

Turn south from Highway 58 onto Soda Lake Road toward the little settlement of California Valley. The California Valley Motel and Restaurant (Phone: 805/475-2363) tends to open on an as-needed basis and has been very accommodating to birding groups in the past. If one wishes to stay overnight here, a call in advance is recommended. The Carrizo Plain is over fifty miles from the nearest service station, and one should plan accordingly. (You can sometimes purchase some gas on an emergency basis at the California Valley Motel and Restaurant, or it is usually available at Flanagan's Pit Stop east of California Valley at the intersection of Highway 58 and Seven Mile Road.) If it has rained recently, the dirt roads are not recommended, and it is best to ask local advice before you attempt to drive on them. Although winter daytime temperatures in the Carrizo will typically be in the 70s, night-time temperatures drop to the teens, and early mornings are best described as "crisp".

Soda Lake Road is paved until well south of **Soda Lake**, and is drivable whatever the weather conditions. As you drive south, you will pass dirt roads going off to the right and to the left and gigantic high-tension-line towers transecting the valley west to east. Sometimes the sagebrush north of the towers is productive for Sage Thrasher (uncommon to rare here) and Short-eared Owl in winter among the White-crowned and Sage Sparrows. A winter drive on the dirt roads to the west of Soda Lake Road, where plowed fields are seen, sometimes produces Mountain Plovers and Mountain Bluebirds. After crossing under the high-tension lines, one eventually comes to a sign proclaiming "Carrizo Plains Natural Area" (8.0). Across the road from this sign a large pasture stretches east to the edge of Soda Lake, approximately one-half mile distant. Park anywhere along the road to watch Sandhill Cranes fly in to the lake in the afternoon. Sometimes cranes can be seen feeding, resting, or engaging in mini-displays in the pasture.

Soda Lake is a shallow, mineral-encrusted pan several thousand acres in extent in the middle of the Plain. Surrounding the lake is the most-vegetated area of the Carrizo, and Sage Sparrow is resident here. All of the birds mentioned above can be found within a few miles of Soda Lake, while the reintroduced Tule Elk and Pronghorn range anywhere within hundreds of square miles.

If you continue farther south on Soda Lake Road, you will reach Simmler Road (6.4), a dirt track running east. It will take you south of Soda Lake and to a north-south dirt track traversing much of the Plain's east side. You may wander this and similar dirt tracks, when they are dry, with a chance of seeing any bird mentioned for the Carrizo, although the birds' locations will vary from year-to-year and sometimes from day-to-day. As you drive south on Soda Lake Road, watch weed-stalks and fence-lines for Mountain Bluebirds in winter. Burrowing Owls (uncommon) are best seen along this road, usually around California Ground-Squirrel colonies. Also check the huge Horned Lark flocks for longspurs (Chestnut-collared and McCown's). Wintering Vesper Sparrows (uncommon) are usually found by checking out birds perched on the barbed-wire fences and foraging on the ground near the fence-line. South of Simmler Road a few miles, Soda Lake Road changes from all-weather paved to dirt and continues south for approximately 32 miles to its intersection with Highway 33/166 just south of Maricopa. (At this intersection, you will be 65.4 miles east of Highway 101 at Santa Maria via Highway 166.)

After you visit Soda Lake, if the weather does not seem favorable for dirt-road driving, retrace your way through California Valley to the junction of Soda Lake Road and Highway 58 and turn right. This highway traverses the Temblor Range and joins Highway 33 just south of the town of McKittrick (27.2). Turn right to Taft (15.1) and stay on Highway 33 a little farther to Petroleum Club Road (0.2). Turn left and take Petroleum Club Road south to Cadet Road (3.7) in **Maricopa**. This is a good area for LeConte's Thrasher.

LeConte's Thrashers prefer the light-colored terrain of desert flats and washes and are usually seen on the ground running between the low and widely-scattered bushes. While they are found in nearly all of the low deserts of Southern California, nowhere are they more common than here at the south end of the San Joaquin Valley. Even in this favorable habitat, LeConte's is a shy, unapproachable bird, usually found only with difficulty. Prepare to walk up and down a number of washes before flushing one.

The LeConte's are most active mornings and evenings, when they will respond well to a taped recording of their song. They often sing while perched right on top of the higher vegetation and can be easily observed, but only from a distance. A good strategy for seeing one is to walk slowly through suitable habitat, scanning the bushes far ahead. Your best chance is to look for them during the breeding season (February-April), and to arrive early in the day before it warms up and the birds become less active.

Other species to look for in LeConte's habitat are Burrowing Owl, Mourning Dove, Horned Lark, Rock Wren, Loggerhead Shrike, Sage Sparrow, House Finch, and San Joaquin Antelope Ground-Squirrel.

If you do not find LeConte's Thrasher at Cadet Road, continue south on Petroleum Club Road to Kerto Road (0.8). Park and check the flat northeast of this intersection, walking north to the wash, and in the wash east to and beyond the railroad tracks.

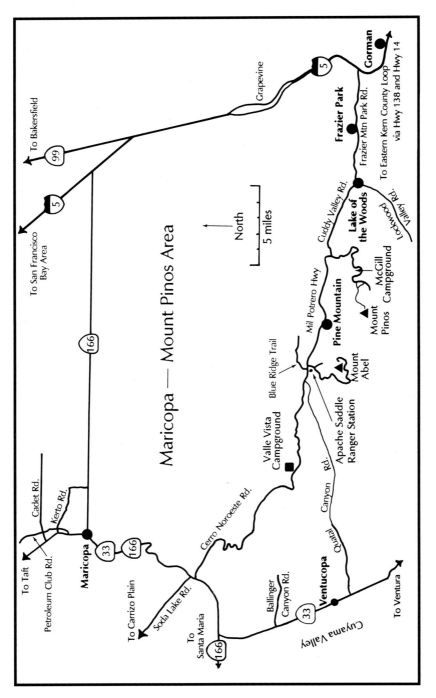

Maricopa — Mount Pinos Area

Drive one block west on Kerto Road to Highway 33 and turn south to the small town of Maricopa (1.3). *If you are headed for Los Angeles and wish to bypass the Mount Pinos section of the route, turn left onto eastbound Highway 166 and drive 22.6 miles to its intersection with Interstate 5.*

To continue the route, bear right and follow combined Highway 33/166 south past the intersection where Soda Lake Road leads off west onto the southeastern end of the Carrizo Plain (9.3). Continue on Highway 33/166 until Highway 33 splits off southward to Ventura and the coast (4.6); turn left onto it. (Highway 166 splits right [west] at this intersection to follow the Cuyama Valley, a great agricultural valley in the four-county corner of San Luis, Santa Barbara, Ventura, and Kern counties. Alfalfa, carrots, grapes, and other crops are raised in this arid country in the shadow of the rainy coastal ranges.)

Drive south on Highway 33 (through the southeast arm of the Cuyama Valley) to Ballinger Canyon Road (3.5), turn left onto it, and drive to the road's end at a campground (3.3). The hillsides in the canyon are at the northwestern limit for the ranges of a number of desert species. Some of the breeding birds you may find from mid-April to mid-July are Mountain Quail, Greater Roadrunner, Lesser Nighthawk, Costa's Hummingbird, Rock Wren, Brewer's, Black-throated, and Sage Sparrows, Scott's Oriole, and Lawrence's Goldfinch.

When finished here, continue to **Quatal Canyon** (4.7), about a mile beyond Ventucopa. This canyon (like Ballinger Canyon) is most productive from mid-April to early June, when nesting birds are in full song and migrants contribute to the diversity. Summer residents you might expect to find, in addition to those species mentioned for Ballinger Canyon, are Common Poorwill, Ash-throated Flycatcher, Common Raven, Phainopepla, Black-chinned and Lark Sparrows, and Lesser Goldfinch. At the higher elevations look for Cooper's Hawk, Olive-sided Flycatcher, Western Wood-Pewee, Violet-green Swallow, Black-throated Gray Warbler, Western Tanager, Black-headed Grosbeak, Chipping Sparrow, and Cassin's Finch. Many other species common in Southern California are also present in the canyon.

A good dirt road, marked with mileposts, leads up the canyon 14.8 miles to join the Mil Potrero Highway. The unfenced land in the upper part of the canyon belongs to the U.S. Forest Service and is open to the public. Sage Sparrows prefer the low, brushy areas with a few scattered bushes between miles 3 and 8. Brewer's Sparrows are generally limited to the pure sage areas, particularly around mile 3.8. Scott's Orioles and Black-chinned Sparrows (common) range throughout most of the canyon from mile 3 to mile 12.

A disjunct population of several pairs of Gray Flycatchers has been breeding in the canyon (1989 and 1990). Look for them between mileposts 9 and 11.

If you have not driven completely through Quatal Canyon to Mil Potrero Highway, retrace your route to the junction and turn right onto Highway 33/166 to Cerro Noroeste Road (4.6). Turn right and begin climbing to the **Mount Pinos** area. Bear right at the junction with Klipstein Canyon Road (2.8).

On the way up the mountain, the long high ridge on your left is Blue Ridge, topped by Brush Mountain to the east. In the afternoons Golden Eagles often circle over the mountain or in the valley below. When you have climbed to 4,600 feet, you will be at the Los Padres National Forest Sign (8.3). For many years this was one of several good observation points for seeing California Condors, now no longer found anywhere in the wild, largely because of pesticides, lead poisoning, and habitat destruction. A captive breeding program (the last wild California Condor was captured April 19, 1987) has plans to eventually return birds to the wild. This is an excellent area for spring wildflowers.

Continue to the Valle Vista Campground (2.4). The campground is good in summer for Black-headed Grosbeak, Lazuli Bunting, Rufous-sided and California Towhees, and Brewer's, Black-chinned, and Lark Sparrows. In winter, look for Fox, Lincoln's, Golden-crowned, and White-crowned Sparrows.

At Apache Saddle Ranger Station (7.5) either continue straight downhill through Jeffrey Pines to Mil Potrero Highway, turn left down the mountain on the Blue Ridge Trail, or, if you have time, turn right to drive to the top of Mount Abel. The birding on this mountain is about the same as that described for Mount Pinos (see next paragraph). A store and other services are available at Pine Mountain (2.6).

Continue southeast to Mount Pinos Road (5.7) and turn right onto it. As you ascend through the wooded areas, watch for Clark's Nutcracker, Cassin's and Purple Finches, and, in fall when the pinyon nuts are ripe, Pinyon Jays (rare). **McGill Campground** (5.3) (El. 7,500 ft) has good facilities and enticing birding possibilities. One of the best areas is below the group campsite on the back side of the campground. Look for Band-tailed Pigeon, White-headed Woodpecker, Williamson's Sapsucker (rare), Steller's Jay, Clark's Nutcracker, Pygmy Nuthatch, Red Crossbill, and Yellow-rumped Warbler. At night, you may find Northern Pygmy-Owl, Flammulated Owl, and Northern Saw-whet Owl.

As you continue up the mountain, you will see several old logging roads; all are dirt, dead-end, and about a mile long. Their names are more impressive than the roads themselves, but they do allow you to get off the main road. Iris Point Road (1.6) on the left leads to the warm south side, where Violet-green Swallow and Western Bluebird abound. Fir Ridge Road (0.2) on the right ends on the shaded north side of the mountain in a stand of White Fir, an indicator of the Canadian Life Zone. This is a good spot for Williamson's Sapsucker (rare) and Golden-crowned Kinglet.

At the end of the paved Mount Pinos Road (1.7) is a large parking lot. The little swale (named Iris Meadow) just beyond is usually good for Mountain Quail, Calliope Hummingbird (breeds mid-May to late June), Dusky Flycatcher, Green-tailed Towhee, and Fox Sparrow.

Just as you enter the parking area, turn onto a small dirt road (if it is not blocked by a locked gate) which takes off to the left and continues up the mountain. Bear to the left at the first fork and continue to the west end of the summit of Mount Pinos (El. 8,832 ft) (1.2 miles). If you cannot drive this old road, it still makes a good hiking trail to the top. Along the way you could find many of the above-mentioned species and more in this beautiful forest.

The most common mammals here are Gray Squirrel and California Ground-Squirrel, although you may find others, particularly at night. Look for Black Bear, Long-tailed Weasel, Gray Fox, Coyote, Bobcat, Lodgepole Chipmunk (in forested areas), Merriam's Chipmunk (in brush), and Northern Flying-Squirrel.

Return to the bottom of the mountain and turn right onto Cuddy Valley Road (8.8). At this intersection you might stop to check the patches of wild rose in spring and summer for nesting Brewer's and Black-chinned Sparrows and Lazuli Bunting.

At Lake of the Woods (5.2) the road forks. The right-hand road (Lockwood Valley Road) takes you to the Chuchupate (Chu-chu-PAH-tay) Ranger Station (Phone: 805/245-3731). The left-hand road is the Frazier Mountain Park Road, leading to the Golden State Freeway (Interstate 5) (7.0).

If you wish to bird the Eastern Kern County Loop, southbound I-5 connects with eastbound Highway 138, which will take you to northbound Highway 14 and Mojave, the loop's starting point. This routing will also take you through parts of Antelope Valley, right by the Lancaster Sewage Ponds (see Miscellaneous Areas section).

There are motels in California Valley (see text), Taft, Bakersfield, and Gorman. Campgrounds can be found on Mount Pinos, in Lockwood Valley, and along the Blue Ridge Trail. The best camping area for birding is McGill Campground on Mount Pinos.

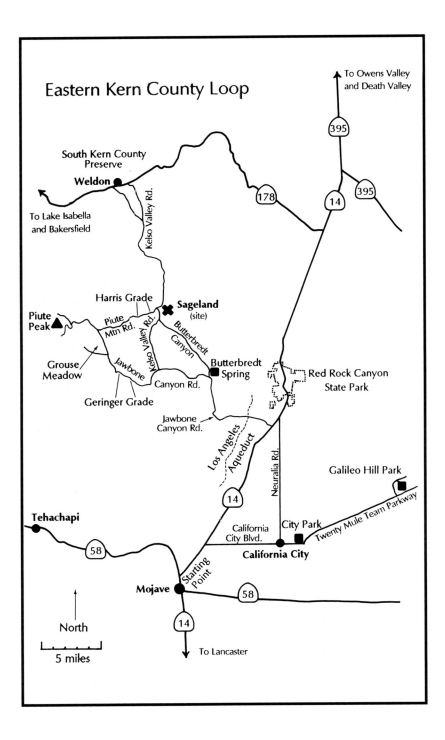

Eastern Kern County Loop

EASTERN KERN COUNTY LOOP

Over 230 species of birds have been observed within this loop, and a visit during spring migration in particular promises a good variety. Start your trip quite early in the morning for best results.

To begin this adventure, drive north from the town of Mojave along Highway 14 to the intersection of Jawbone Canyon Road (19.9). Turn left (west) here and drive to where the Los Angeles Aqueduct crosses under the road (2.9). (This is a *black* pipe; you will already have passed a white aqueduct pipe which is a more recent addition.) Stop here to check the trees around the house *from the road* (good migrant trap). Chukars are occasionally seen on the steep slopes on the opposite side of the canyon from the house.

The pavement ends at about 4.1 miles. You are now in the middle of a BLM-designated Off-road Vehicle Open Area. Bear right (north) up and out of Hoffman Canyon. The turnoff to Butterbredt Canyon (5.2) is easy to find. At the intersection, a white range sign still stands, but shooting has obliterated its former message. Across the cattle-guard on the right, however, is the **Butterbredt Spring Wildlife Sanctuary** sign. Butterbredt Spring (0.9) is down the rough, sandy road to the right. At the lower end of the road you will see the spring directly ahead. (Low-clearance vehicles should avoid this last stretch of road.)

The spring and canyon were named after Frederick Butterbredt, who settled here as a *ranchero* in the 1860s. The Geological Survey crew that mapped the Mojave quadrangle in 1912-13 misspelled his name as Butterbread. The spelling has now been corrected.

There are no facilities of any kind at the sanctuary, and the area is considered primitive. Observe all desert precautions such as having sufficient water, gasoline, and proper clothing. The land is "checkerboarded" with private and public land, and camping is *not* permitted at or near the spring. The spring remains private land, but through an agreement with the Onyx Ranch, Keith Axelson (who helped greatly with this chapter), Santa Monica Bay Audubon Society, and the

Bureau of Land Management, the Butterbredt Spring Wildlife Sanctuary was created and fenced. Do not close any gates found open. Butterbredt Canyon is included within the largest Area of Critical Environment Concern (ACEC) administered by the BLM. All vehicle travel within Butterbredt Canyon is now restricted to Butterbredt Canyon Road and Gold Peak Road. There are no designated motorcycle trails. A letter from you to the BLM, 1695 Spruce Street, Riverside, CA 92597, in favor of continued motorcycle closure will help keep it this way.

Butterbredt Spring Wildlife Sanctuary and the immediate vicinity offer a diverse variety of habitat. Marsh vegetation surrounds the pond, and typical desert plants such as Joshua Tree, cholla cactus, sage, and Rabbitbrush dot the hillsides. Cottonwoods and willows follow the water east as it resurfaces down the wash.

Most birders spend their time at the main spring. After wet winters, water trickles through the area, attracting numerous birds. At all times the large cottonwoods play host to birds, as well as giving a much-needed windbreak to those who watch them. A "lookout" on the east side of these trees offers you a great vantage point. After the morning sun hits the Mulefat below you, the birds often feed there, offering you wonderful views of them as well as photographic opportunities from a distance of only twenty to thirty feet. In addition, this spot allows you a clear view of the canyon as it heads east, letting you see what is flying up the canyon toward you. Because most of the birds will fly past close to the spring, you will be able to test your ability to identify passerines on the wing.

Butterbredt Spring is one of the desert's best localities in spring. Western migrants are best from mid-April to mid-May, although the vagrants are what draw many birders at this season. To date, at least 24 species of warblers have been seen, all at the main spring. While vagrants may show up at any time, mid-May to early June is best. This doesn't mean that spring is the only time to visit Butterbredt. Fall, while less spectacular, also has its share of migrants and vagrants.

It is worth your effort to hike down the canyon to check out the numerous seeps supporting willows and cottonwoods that hold birds. In some years Calliope Hummingbirds have been common (early May). Scott's Orioles nest in the area and are usually seen, as are the ever-so-popular Chukars. Other birds to look for are Ladder-backed Woodpecker, Cactus Wren, LeConte's Thrasher (Be careful—California Thrashers breed at and near the spring.), and Brewer's, Sage, and Black-throated Sparrows.

After you have birded the spring, a leisurely walk/drive up Butterbredt Canyon can reward you with excellent high-desert scenery and add to your bird list. The canyon opens into a broad, bowl-like valley filled with Joshua Trees. Scott's Orioles nest throughout the area, as do Blue-gray Gnatcatchers. Golden Eagles and LeConte's Thrashers are seen regularly. A few Bendire's Thrashers have also been reported from this area. You might hear their distinctive song if you drive along slowly with your windows rolled down. (Nesting Bendire's were reported one time from near the end of this road in Kelso Valley.)

If road conditions allow (and they usually do), continue on through Butterbredt Canyon to the summit (El. 5,220 ft) (5.0), where you will be able to see the Piute Mountains in front of you, due west. Pressing on, about one mile below the summit, stop to listen for Pinyon Jays—they are often found working their way through the Joshua Trees. Down the hill you will come to paved Kelso Valley Road (2.6). Turn right toward the site of Sageland (1.3). Only a concrete historical marker still stands at this intersection.

At this point, you may choose one of two routes to reach the summit of Piute Peak (El. 8,432 ft). Piute Mountain Road, climbing up the Harris Grade, departs from Sageland. Jawbone Canyon Road (with the Geringer Grade) departs 7.7 miles south of Sageland where Kelso Valley Road intersects with Jawbone Canyon Road. This latter route is described several paragraphs hence.

If you have chosen to follow Piute Mountain Road, turn left (west) onto it for a 16-mile trip to the summit of Piute Peak. **Piute Mountain Road** can be productive for montane species such as White-headed Woodpecker, Williamson's Sapsucker (rare), Clark's Nutcracker, and Rufous Hummingbird. Take time to investigate some of the side roads you pass—as long as they lead uphill. Once you have traveled 9.7 miles from the Sageland intersection, you will come to Jawbone Canyon Road leading left. Turn left onto it to reach Grouse Meadow (3.1). You might be lucky enough to see Blue Grouse here, but it is very doubtful. The area has been heavily logged recently.

Return to Piute Mountain Road and continue on to Piute Peak. The last 400-yard stretch requires a four-wheel-drive vehicle, but if you don't have one, park and walk—the view is worth it. (It may help you to have a Kern County map because the Piute Peak turnoff road is no longer clearly signed—although there is a USFS sign that reads "28S17".).

To reach Piute Peak if you have not driven all the way through Butterbredt Canyon, return to Jawbone Canyon Road (where you entered the canyon) and turn right (west). At the intersection with Kelso Valley Road (6.9), you could continue straight ahead on Jawbone Canyon Road taking the Geringer Grade route to the summit of Piute Peak. However, the

Geringer Grade is a difficult road with many switchbacks, and is not recommended for passenger cars. Even with four-wheel drive it should not be attempted during or after bad weather. Snow and mud often block the road.

To reach the smoother route (Harris Grade/Piute Mountain Road) to Piute Peak and the good birding previously described, turn right (north) on Kelso Valley Road. As you approach a house (1.5) among some willows and cottonwoods, watch on the left about 100 yards below the road for three ponds where, in season, you may find shorebirds, ducks, and many passerines. Please observe from the road and do not trespass or agitate the cattle—this is private land. Farther up the valley watch for nesting Brewer's Sparrows. As you near the pass, stop and listen for Black-chinned Sparrows which nest on both sides of the pass.

From the summit of the pass (El. 4,850 ft) (4.0), there is a fine view. To the west you will see the Piute Mountains and a portion of the southern Sierra Nevada to the north. To the south you can see the northern part of the Tehachapi Mountains. Continue driving north and you will pass, on your right, the north end of the Butterbredt Canyon Road (1.2). At the Sageland site (1.3), described earlier, a left turn will send you up the Harris Grade and Piute Mountain Road. A right turn (north) will take you to a massive cottonwood/willow riparian area along Kelso Creek on your left (2.0). Park and walk into the trees and along the creek to look for warblers, vireos, flycatchers, and woodpeckers. You are now in different habitat as evidenced by the nesting birds, which include Scrub Jay, Rufous-sided Towhee, and Western Bluebird. Nuttall's Woodpeckers, found throughout the riparian area, are known to hybridize with the Ladder-backed Woodpeckers in nearby areas.

Continue north on Kelso Valley Road to the town of Weldon (15.2), site of The Nature Conservancy's **South Kern River Reserve**. Turn left on Highway 178 and look for the sign marking their headquarters on the right-hand side of the road. Stop in and pick up a map of the Preserve's trail systems. Some of the trails are partly under water. Birding on the Preserve is best in June; it is generally hot there during the summer. You can contact the Preserve in advance to arrrange a tour (PO Box 1662, Weldon, CA 93283; Phone: 619/378-2531).

Species you might expect to find include the California Yellow-billed Cuckoo (endangered), Bell's Vireo, Blue Grosbeak, Lazuli and Indigo Buntings, Summer Tanager, Willow Flycatcher, and other riverine-type species such as orioles and kingbirds. The cuckoos, the last migrants to arrive, come in late June.

When you are ready to continue the loop, drive east on Highway 178 to its junction with Highway 14 (33.0), where you turn right. After passing through Red Rock Canyon State Park (check for Verdin and, with lots of luck, LeConte's Thrasher by the campground), bear left onto Neuralia Road (21.2). At California City Boulevard (12.2), turn left (east) to **California City**. This community exists largely for people from Edwards Air Force Base. North of the main road at the east side of town is the large Central Park. It has a nice lake surrounded by planted trees and bushes and a golf course. Park in the main parking lot and walk south to the hill that often has a waterfall which is attractive to a large number of birds. Walk around the lake as far as possible (avoid the private property). The islands of vegetation on the north side of the park serve as the most reliable spots for migrants and vagrants (spring is best). Large numbers of flycatchers, thrushes, and warblers are found. The best months are April and May in spring, and late August to the end of October in fall.

Twenty Mule Team Parkway borders the northeast side of the park. Follow it east 10.6 miles and turn left at Galileo Hill. Turn right onto North Columbia (1.3) and then right (0.8) into tiny **Galileo Hill Park** (0.6). Here you are almost guaranteed Chukar as these birds cross the open grassy park on their way to the water. Late afternoon is best, but you may see one or more Chukars almost any time of day.

Retrace your route to Central Park in California City. You may want to stop at the Desert Deli in town. They have always been receptive to birders and allow us to leave notes of recent findings. Take a look at the notes and add any of your own significant finds. Continue on California City Boulevard to Highway 14 and turn left toward Mojave.

If you wisely decide to spend more than one day on this loop, you will find motels in Mojave and Lake Isabella (13 miles west of Weldon on Highway 178).

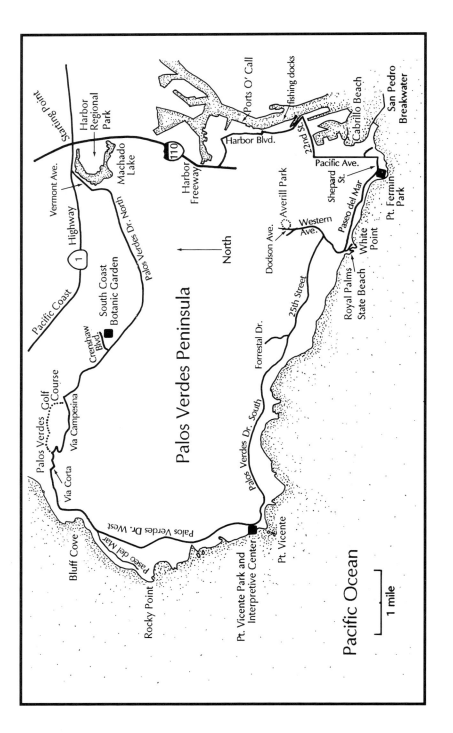

Palos Verdes Peninsula

Pacific Ocean

North

1 mile

Starting Point

Vermont Ave.

Harbor Regional Park

Machado Lake

Palos Verdes Dr. North

Highway

Pacific Coast

1

South Coast Botanic Garden

Crenshaw Blvd.

Golf Course

Palos Verdes

Via Campesina

Via Corta

Palos Verdes Dr. West

Paseo del Mar

Bluff Cove

Rocky Point

Palos Verdes Dr. South

Pt. Vicente Park and Interpretive Center

Pt. Vicente

Forrestal Dr.

25th street

Dodson Ave.

Western Ave.

Averill Park

Royal Palms State Beach

White Point

Paseo del Mar

Shepard St.

Pacific Ave.

Pt. Fermin Park

San Pedro Breakwater

Cabrillo Beach

22nd St.

fishing docks

Ports O' Call

Harbor Blvd.

110

Harbor Freeway

PALOS VERDES
PENINSULA LOOP

The Palos Verdes Peninsula is famous for its scenic coastline and beautiful homes. Most of the original native habitat of low coastal sage shrub has been replaced by extensive plantings of exotic plants and trees, which has greatly increased the number and variety of small landbirds. This is an inspiring trip at any season, but the birding is better in winter and during migration.

The starting point is the intersection of Pacific Coast Highway (Highway 1) and Harbor Freeway (Interstate 110). Go northwest on Pacific Coast Highway and turn left at the traffic light onto Vermont Avenue (0.5) to **Harbor Regional Park** on the left. There are always a few ducks, grebes, gulls, and shorebirds here, particularly in winter. Check the tules for Marsh Wren, Sora, Tricolored and Red-winged Blackbirds, and other marsh birds. In summer look for Least Bittern in the tules along the east shore. During migration, this can be an excellent spot for warblers, especially in the willows bordering the north end of the lake. [Note: Although the park is a good place for birds, it is also a good place for some of the infamous L.A. gangs. Birding and safety are best in the morning. Use caution; avoid going there alone or in the evening.]

Continue on Vermont Avenue to Anaheim Street (0.7). At this multiple intersection, bear west onto Palos Verdes Drive North (PAH-lows VAIR-days). At the traffic light on Crenshaw Boulevard (3.5) turn right and proceed to the **South Coast Botanic Garden** (0.3) (fee). The large variety of trees and plants attract a large number (to date 249) of bird species. The place is particularly good for hummingbirds—the resident Allen's and others. Ask for the checklist of birds at the Lake Gift Shop.

Return to Palos Verdes Drive North and continue west to Via Campesina (1.2); then turn left. During migration and in winter it is worthwhile to check the lush vegetation around the edges of the Palos Verdes Golf Course for small landbirds. At the stop sign on Via Corta (1.7), turn right to the business district. Go one block, and then turn left on Palos Verdes Drive West, which will take you to the ocean side of the peninsula.

Where Palos Verdes Drive West divides (1.7), stop at the small parking lot on the right at Paseo del Mar. From this high vantage point, you can get a sweeping view of Bluff Cove and the ocean. With a scope, you might even pick out a shearwater or other pelagic bird.

Continue on to Point Vicente Park and Interpretive Center (4.0), where you can again look over the ocean. This park was built in 1985 and serves mainly as a whale-watching area. (Gray Whales can be seen offshore between December and April.) In fall, winter, and early spring, check for Black-vented Shearwaters just offshore. Also look for Northern Fulmars (winter), Sooty Shearwaters (May-September), loons, grebes, cormorants, and terns in season. For hikers, there is a steep trail to the rocky beach below, a good spot in winter for Wandering Tattler, Black Turnstone, and Surfbird. As you pull out of the driveway of the Interpretive Center, turn right. The name of the road will change to Palos Verdes Drive South.

You have now entered the range of the California Gnatcatcher. This bird, until recently, was considered a subspecies of the Black-tailed Gnatcatcher. But there are some clear differences. The California is darker overall than the Black-tailed (especially when considering the underparts). The California's shiny black cap extends slightly farther back than that of the Black-tailed Gnatcatcher, and its undertail pattern has less white. Female or cap-less winter males might superficially resemble Blue-gray Gnatcatcher. The California Gnatcatcher, however, can always be told from the Blue-gray by the undertail; in the California, the underside is almost entirely black, while in the Blue-gray, the underside is almost all white. (For details on the tails of these three species, see the illustration.) Best of all, listen for the California's call, a rising then dropping kitten-like *mew*, clearly different from the Black-tailed Gnatcatcher's wren-like call, and less assertive than the *speeeee* call of the Blue-gray Gnatcatcher.

The Palos Verdes Peninsula represents the northwesternmost limit of the California Gnatcatcher's range (and is many miles away from the nearest Black-tailed Gnatcatcher in the interior). The California Gnatcatcher inhabits arid, sage scrub in gullies, canyons, lower slopes, and washes, often with *Opuntia* cactus in coastal Southern California. This habitat seems to be decreasing almost everywhere—giving way to housing tracts—and the isolated Palos Verdes population is under continued pressure. The area between Point Vicente and Western Avenue (see below) contains the remaining California Gnatcatcher habitat on the Peninsula. (Some 49 birds were censused in this stretch in late July, 1990.)

Continue on Palos Verdes Drive South until you reach **Forrestal Drive** (3.8), and turn left onto it. Park at the gate at the end of the road. If the gate is open, do not drive through; you may get locked in. This area, along

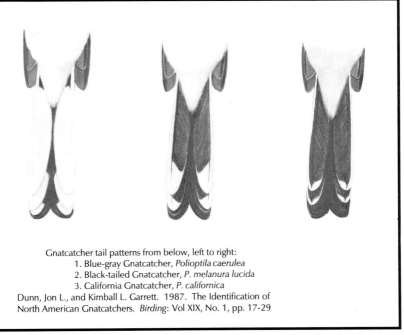

Gnatcatcher tail patterns from below, left to right:
1. Blue-gray Gnatcatcher, *Polioptila caerulea*
2. Black-tailed Gnatcatcher, *P. melanura lucida*
3. California Gnatcatcher, *P. californica*
Dunn, Jon L., and Kimball L. Garrett. 1987. The Identification of
North American Gnatcatchers. *Birding*: Vol XIX, No. 1, pp. 17-29

Jonathan Alderfer

with the South Coast Botanic Garden, is one of the best spots on the peninsula. It is about the only spot that still has large areas of native vegetation and, as a result, a lot of native birds. It is best to visit in early spring and early in the morning.

About 100 feet past the gate walk up a dirt road to the right. One of two year-round springs is located at the end of this canyon. The spring is about one-half mile from the road. This is a good area for California and Blue-gray Gnatcatchers, Allen's Hummingbird, Bewick's, Cactus, and Rock Wrens, Rufous-crowned Sparrow, and California Towhee. Walk back to the road and continue walking away from the gate. Where the road turns left, go straight onto a dirt path. This area and the top of a hill to your left are also good spots for the previously-mentioned species. The city of Palos Verdes has started to accept bids from developers for this area, making its immediate future uncertain.

Continue on Palos Verdes Drive South which soon splits (0.6). Palos Verdes Drive East goes left, but you should bear to the right on 25th Street and continue to Western Avenue (1.5). Turn left onto Western Avenue, then turn right onto Dodson Avenue (0.4). In three blocks you will come

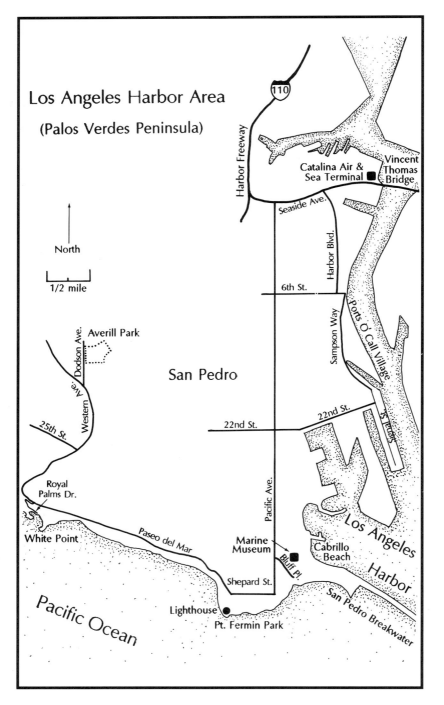

Los Angeles Harbor Area

(Palos Verdes Peninsula)

North

1/2 mile

110

Harbor Freeway

Catalina Air &
Sea Terminal

Vincent
Thomas
Bridge

Seaside Ave.

Harbor Blvd.

6th St.

Dodson Ave.

Averill Park

Western Ave.

25th St.

San Pedro

Sampson Way

Ports O' Call Village

22nd St.

22nd St.

S. Terms.

Pacific Ave.

Royal
Palms Dr.

White Point

Paseo del Mar

Marine
Museum

Bluff Pl.

Cabrillo
Beach

Los Angeles

Shepard St.

San Pedro Breakwater

Harbor

Lighthouse

Pt. Fermin Park

Pacific Ocean

to **Averill Park**, another good spot for Allen's Hummingbird and other local species. The park can be very good during migration.

Retrace your route to 25th Street and Western Avenue and continue on Western Avenue toward the ocean. When Western Avenue ends (0.5), bear left onto Paseo del Mar. Go one block and make a sharp right turn down the hill to the Royal Palms State Beach on White Point. (There is a fee for parking on weekends, but you can walk in for free.) If you arrive at high tide, you can find many birds along the rocky beach—Black Oystercatcher, Surfbird, Wandering Tattler, and both turnstones..

Farther along Paseo del Mar is **Point Fermin Park** (1.6). This has been a favorite spot of local birders during migration, although recent "park maintenance" has trimmed the vegetation excessively. Anna's and Allen's Hummingbirds are common all year. Don't be surprised if you see some exotic parrots flying around. On the cliffs below the lighthouse, you may find Double-crested, Brandt's, and Pelagic (in winter) Cormorants. Black Oystercatchers are frequently seen although they do not nest here.

From the park, go right on Shepard Street to Pacific Avenue and jog right to Bluff Place, which leads down the hill to **Cabrillo Beach** (Cah-BREE-yo) (0.6) (fee for parking, although, once again, you can walk in for free). The free museum has a fine marine exhibit and a few stuffed birds. The main attraction here is the **San Pedro Breakwater**. By walking to the end in the early morning, you can find nearly all of the birds which frequent the inshore ocean and bays. Later in the day the crowds and jet-skis may disperse the birds. At dawn there is a good chance of seeing a few pelagic birds. They often come close to shore at night, but move out to sea as the boats leave the harbor.

On leaving the beach, bear right to Pacific Avenue and turn right. At the traffic light on 22nd Street turn right. At Signal Street (0.8), jog left for a block and then right to the fishing docks. When the fishing boats return at noon and night, they are followed by swarms of gulls seeking a free fish-dinner. You can buy yours at one of the seafood restaurants at Ports O' Call Village, a half-mile up on your right.

After checking the docks, continue north or left to the end of the dock area. Jog left to Harbor Boulevard and turn right. Follow the signs to the Harbor Freeway and back to the starting point (4.0).

From here you can detour to the El Dorado Nature Center (see Miscellaneous Areas section) or link up with the Coastal Orange County trip. Boats for Santa Catalina Island are also available nearby (see Pelagic Birding Trips chapter and Miscellaneous Areas).

There are no campgrounds on this loop. Motels are common along the Pacific Coast Highway.

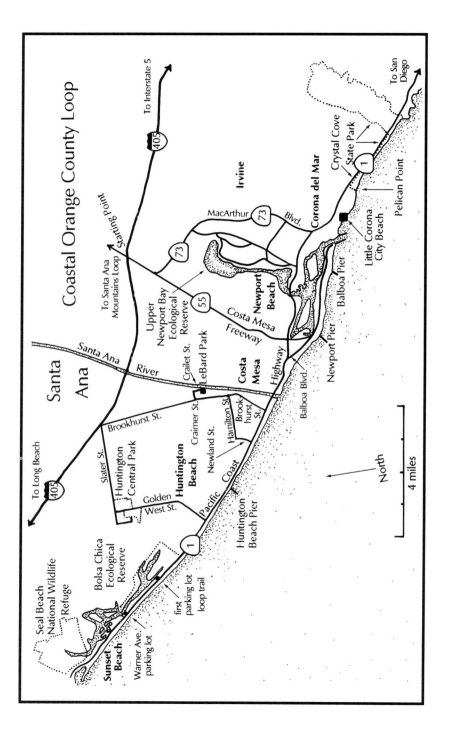

Coastal Orange County Loop

To Interstate 5

405

To Long Beach

405

Santa Ana

Santa Ana

River

Brookhurst St.

Slater St.

Huntington Central Park

Golden West St.

Huntington Beach

Crailet St.
LeBard Park

Craimer St.

Newland St.

Hamilton St.

Brookhurst St.

Costa Mesa

Highway

Balboa Blvd.

Newport Pier

Balboa Pier

Little Corona City Beach

Pacific

Coast

Huntington Beach Pier

1

first parking lot
loop trail

Bolsa Chica Ecological Reserve

Sunset Beach

Warner Ave. parking lot

Seal Beach National Wildlife Refuge

North

4 miles

Upper Newport Bay Ecological Reserve

To Santa Ana Mountains Loop

Starting Point

73

55

73

MacArthur

Blvd.

Irvine

Newport Beach

Costa Mesa Freeway

Corona del Mar

Crystal Cove State Park

Pelican Point

1

To San Diego

COASTAL ORANGE
COUNTY LOOP

By Sylvia Ranney Gallagher

Surprisingly, some excellent birding spots in Southern California are found right in the middle of the urban sprawl of coastal Orange County. Two coastal saltmarshes, Upper Newport Bay and Bolsa Chica (BOL-sah CHEE-cah) State Ecological Reserves, are choice places to visit. That they are there at all is to the credit of some doggedly-determined Orange County environmentalists—Friends of Upper Newport Bay and Amigos de Bolsa Chica. The third location which no one should skip is Huntington Central Park. Since the birding world discovered its potential a few years back, it has proven to be the best place in the county for rare-to-accidental landbirds.

The starting place for this tour is the junction of Interstate 405 and Highway 55, located where the cities of Irvine, Santa Ana, and Costa Mesa come together, just north of the John Wayne Airport.

Drive northbound (actually nearly westbound here) on I-405 to the Brookhurst Street exit (4.7). At the end of the off-ramp, turn right, then immediately turn left onto Slater Street. Follow Slater Street west 2.9 miles. About 100 yards short of the traffic light at Golden West Street, turn left into the parking lot for **Huntington Central Park**.

This large city park is one of the few public parks in urban Orange County which has not been trimmed to within an inch of its life. It has lots of shrubs, willow clumps, weedy patches, and other places where birds can find cover. That is not to say that the City of Huntington Beach hasn't tried to "tidy up" the place, but public pressure keeps them from going too far in this endeavor.

This park is good just about any time of year, except perhaps in the heart of the summer. Spring and fall migrations bring all sorts of unusual

63

species for a few days of rest and recuperation. Each winter a number of choice rarities will stay several months. The official park bird list contains well over 200 species, including 16 flycatchers, 8 vireos, 33 warblers—and counting! Although good birds turn up in all corners of the park, there are a few places that have proven to be better than others.

As you leave your car and walk south into the park, you will come to a large area choked with willows. In wet years, you will walk on the outskirts peering in. In dry years, when the water-table is low, you can enter the area and wander around. Here sparrows, finches, and other seed-eaters are especially likely. Continue walking south, beyond the alder trees near the restaurant (good for warblers), to Lake Talbert, although it may look more like "Talbert Green" in dry years. If there is lots of water in the lake, ducks and possibly even a loon or a grebe may occur here; if there is just a little bit, expect shorebirds. Look over the trees on the opposite side of the lake for warblers, then continue walking eastward. (The city library will be on your right.) The trees in the large southeast quarter of the park have yielded many of the choicest birds over the years. Be sure to check the bits of marsh wherever they exist. Common Moorhens and Pied-billed Grebes nest in wet years, and you might spot a Sora or a Virginia Rail.

To take in the rest of the park, get into your car and turn left out of the parking lot. Drive west on Slater Street to Edwards Street (0.6) and turn left. Watch on your right for the small green "Huntington Central Park" sign, and turn left (0.4). Park in the lot at the end of the street (0.3).

At the north end of the parking lot is a well-marked trail leading to the Shipley Nature Center (usually opens at 9). This is worth a visit, especially if you're looking for Tricolored Blackbirds. Around the parking lot itself and the area just north of it, flowering eucalyptus trees attract Allen's Hummingbirds. The area also attracts insects, which in turn attract warblers and other insectivorous species. Birders haunt this area during migration.

Another good site is the pines east of the parking lot. Here Red-breasted Nuthatches are often found in winter. Some winters Mountain Chickadees, Golden-crowned Kinglets, or Varied Thrushes are present.

At the south end of the parking lot is Lake Huntington, which usually has water even when Lake Talbert is dry. Check it over for ducks; Wood Ducks are sometimes found. The cattails around the edge might harbor Yellow-headed or Tricolored Blackbirds.

If you haven't found Tricolored Blackbirds by now, you may wish to take a quick side-trip up to tiny Carr Park. Retrace your route via Edwards Street to Slater Street and turn left to Springdale Street (0.5). Turn right and go just short of 1 mile; the park will be on your right. The Tricolored

Blackbirds are around all year and nest on the minute island in the middle of the tiny lake. You'll probably see them out on the grass eating handouts from the park visitors.

The next important place to visit is **Bolsa Chica State Ecological Reserve**. Return via Springdale and Slater Streets almost all the way to your first stopping place at Huntington Central Park, but turn right as you reach the park onto Golden West Street. Continue south on Golden West Street to the Pacific Coast Highway (Highway 1) (3.0). Turn right and drive up the coast to the first signal light (2.5). Just past it turn right into the little parking lot. (A second parking lot is located 1.5 miles farther north—just around the corner to the right on Warner Avenue—but the best birding is usually from the first lot.)

The Bolsa Chica is an estuary with saltmarsh, mudflats, and open water. It is excellent at any time of year, but what has really put the place on the map is the colonization, starting in 1985, by hundreds of terns and Black Skimmers. Before that year only a few Least Terns (endangered) nested there. Then, over a period of just four years, it became the breeding ground for Elegant, Forster's, Caspian, and Royal (rare) Terns, plus Black Skimmer. So far the influx of these other species has not hurt the Least Terns; they are doing better than ever before at this location.

Bolsa Chica is also the home of a large number of Belding's Savannah Sparrows. This endangered subspecies (California list only) is a permanent resident of the pickleweed (*Salicornia*) of the saltmarsh.

The best way to tour the Bolsa Chica is to take the 1.5-mile loop trail which starts in the parking lot. Most of the typical birds of a coastal estuary can be found. Many are the same ones that may be seen more easily at Upper Newport Bay, but a few that are more easily seen here should be mentioned. During the winter it is usually possible to find Clark's and Horned Grebes among the more common Western and Eared. Red-throated and Pacific Loons are sometimes present, although most loons will be Common. Rarely, a Greater Scaup is found in the large raft of Lessers. Other rare, but somewhat regular, waterfowl are Brant, White-winged Scoter (Surf is common), Common Goldeneye (Barrow's is accidental), and Common Merganser (Red-breasted is common). A wide variety of shorebirds is also present. Bolsa Chica may be somewhat better than Upper Newport Bay for Wilson's and Red-necked Phalaropes in July and August and for Red Knot and Lesser Yellowlegs (both rare) most of the year.

Beyond the previously-mentioned Bolsa Chica parking lot on Warner Avenue (1.5) is Sunset Beach and the Seal Beach National Wildlife Refuge (2.0). There are lots of birds here, but access is currently restricted, and it's hard to find a place from which to observe the birds. At present your best bet is to bird from the highway. A few Pacific Golden-Plovers are found here most winters.

Turn around and drive southeast on Pacific Coast Highway past the Huntington Beach Pier (3.5 miles south of the first Bolsa Chica parking lot). (The pier was damaged in recent winter storms and is currently closed for reconstruction, but will be worth a visit when it is rebuilt.) Even if you can't walk out on the pier, you'll get an eyeful of the latest thing in Southern California architecture—mile after mile of peach-colored buildings with red tile roofs.

Turn left on Newland Street (1.6), go to Hamilton Street (0.5), and turn right. Just beyond the signal at Brookhurst Street (1.5) turn right and park behind the gas station for access to the mouth of the **Santa Ana River**. The river here is tidal, and depending on the arrangement of silt in the riverbed, there is usually a good assortment of gulls and shorebirds. There is also a flood-control channel entering the ocean here which provides deeper water.

From the parking area, walk up onto the bridge-approach, then right onto the public bicycle trail. Look out for the bikes! They can be more dangerous than cars, because you can't hear them coming. It is possible to walk (or bike) 1.5 miles to the ocean from here. (You can also bike in the opposite direction for about 32 miles to the Riverside County Line.) In the fall, rare gulls sometimes are found; Franklin's is most likely, but Common Black-headed and Little have also been seen. There are usually Bonaparte's. (The willow riparian area across the river looks inviting, but birding there may be dangerous because of its transient *human* population.)

Another access point to the Santa Ana River is reached by driving north on Brookhurst Street. Just past the signal at Indianapolis Street, turn right onto Crailet Street (1.1). At the end of the street (0.2), turn right onto Craimer Street. Shortly you will come to tiny LeBard Park. A bicycle bridge crosses the river here and allows you to bird both sides easily. The area across the river will become the new Fairview Park. How the city of Costa Mesa will choose to develop it remains to be seen. Now it is worth checking for field and brushland birds. One or two pairs of Burrowing Owls nest on the dike between the main river channel and the flood-control channel, located between the bike bridge and Brookhurst Street.

A walk north along the bike trail or the foot trail just east of it is sometimes productive. Intermittently there are mud, marsh, and small ponds, both in the main river channel and in the flood-control channel.

Return to Brookhurst Street, drive south to Pacific Coast Highway (2.4), and turn left. Turn right onto Balboa Boulevard (1.7) and follow it out onto

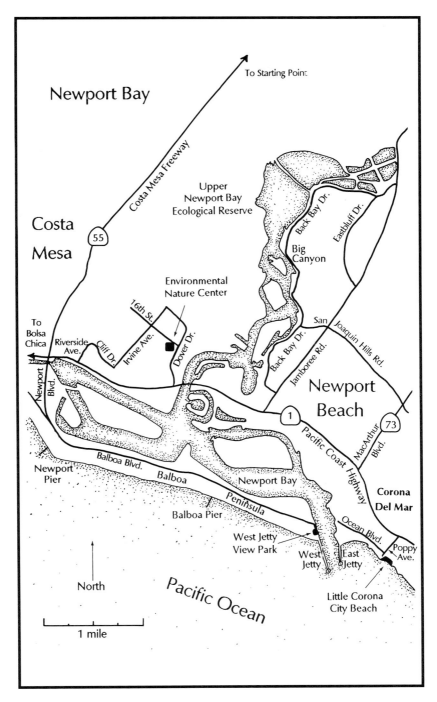

Newport Bay

To Starting Point

Costa Mesa Freeway

Upper
Newport Bay
Ecological Reserve

Costa
Mesa

55

Back Bay Dr.

Eastbluff Dr.

Big
Canyon

Environmental
Nature Center

16th St.

To
Bolsa
Chica

Riverside
Ave.

Cliff Dr.

Irvine Ave.

Dover Dr.

San Joaquin Hills Rd.

Back Bay Dr.

Jamboree Rd.

Newport Blvd.

Newport
Beach

1

73

Balboa Blvd.

Pacific Coast Highway

MacArthur Blvd.

Newport
Pier

Balboa

Balboa
Peninsula

Newport Bay

Corona
Del Mar

Balboa Pier

Ocean Blvd.

West Jetty
View Park

West
Jetty

East
Jetty

Poppy
Ave.

North

Pacific Ocean

Little Corona
City Beach

1 mile

the Balboa Peninsula. Here there are two piers, the **Newport Pier** (1.1) and the **Balboa Pier** (1.6 farther). Signs direct you to each one. Continue on to the end of the peninsula (1.3 farther), bearing left at every Y-intersection. Park wherever you can on the street and walk to West Jetty View Park. From there you can view the entrance to Newport Harbor.

The entire peninsula should be avoided like the plague during the summer, especially on weekends, but the birding is best in the winter anyway. From the piers you can look for loons (Common, Pacific, and Red-throated are possible), scoters (mostly Surf, but White-winged and rarely Black are possible), and Western and Clark's Grebes. Among the rarities which turn up once in a while are Oldsquaw and Black-legged Kittiwake—sometimes even Northern Fulmar or Black-vented Shearwater.

Retrace your route along Balboa Boulevard, and at the Newport Pier fork right onto Newport Boulevard. At Pacific Coast Highway (0.7 farther), turn right (sign reads: "To San Diego"). Turn left at the first signal light onto Riverside Avenue (0.4). At the stop sign at the top of the hill, continue straight ahead—now on Cliff Drive—to Irvine Avenue (0.5 from the highway). Turn left and go to 16th Street (0.6). Turn right and park in the second parking lot past the stadium (0.3). It belongs to the Newport-Mesa School District. Here you have access to the Environmental Nature Center, a gem of a spot established by the biology teachers at Newport Harbor High School. Well-hidden in the bushes near the street, behind the sign for the nature center, is the entry turnstile. This area is always worth a walk-through.

To continue the tour, turn right out of the parking lot, then make an immediate right onto Dover Drive (0.1). At Pacific Coast Highway (0.4) turn left. Turn left again at Jamboree Road (1.0), then left once more onto Back Bay Drive (0.2). This mostly *one-way* road meanders along the shore of **Upper Newport Bay** for 3.3 miles.

Upper Newport Bay (sometimes called Back Bay) is the largest estuary in Southern California, and one of the easiest to bird. It is a *must* on any birding tour. It is most famous as a wintering ground for shorebirds and waterfowl, but should not be overlooked in the summer. Fall migration for shorebirds starts almost as soon as the last of them have gone north in June, and by the latter half of July is in full-swing. From then until the end of October is a wonderful time to study the birds in their breeding and juvenile plumages and in various stages of molt to their winter garb.

The most famous bird here is the Light-footed Clapper Rail. Well over half of the members of this subspecies residing north of the Mexican border are found right here. Listen for their loud choruses, and look for them along the shores of the channels. They are most easily seen at low tide or when the highest high tides force them up out of the marsh. Other rails at the bay include Virginia and Sora. Black Rails are reported with much more regularity than their numbers here warrant. All too many birders, whose judgment is distorted by too much wishful thinking, mistake Soras, Clapper Rail chicks, and even Song Sparrows for these birds. Marsh Wrens, Common Yellowthroats, and Belding's Savannah Sparrows are here—and elsewhere along the drive, too.

At the junction with San Joaquin Hills Road (1.0 from Jamboree Road) stop to look over the ducks. In the winter there are usually a few Blue-winged Teal and occasionally a Eurasian Wigeon among the flocks of other more common dabbling ducks, which include Green-winged and Cinnamon Teal, Mallard, Northern Pintail, Northern Shoveler, and American Wigeon.

The road now circles a large area of open water. Here you can expect the diving ducks, the most common being Lesser Scaup, Surf Scoter, Red-breasted Merganser, Bufflehead, and Ruddy Duck. Other deep-water birds which are regularly seen here are Pied-billed, Eared, Western, and Clark's Grebes, Brown Pelican, and Double-crested Cormorant.

Rounding the point with a high cliff on the right, you will come to an open, flat area with a scruffy, dirt parking lot on the left. This is the mouth of Big Canyon. As you came around the point, you passed under the cliff-face nests of resident White-throated Swifts.

Near the Big Canyon parking lot, masses of shorebirds can be found all winter. About an hour after a good high tide is the best time to arrive to study them. The most regular wintering species are American Avocet, Willet, Long-billed Curlew, Marbled Godwit, Western and Least Sandpipers, Dunlin, and Short-billed Dowitcher (with perhaps a few Long-billed). Other common-to-uncommon shorebirds at the bay, which you may find here or elsewhere, are Black-bellied and Semipalmated Plovers, Killdeer, Black-necked Stilt, Greater Yellowlegs, Spotted Sandpiper, Whimbrel, Ruddy Turnstone, and Common Snipe. Fourteen additional shorebird species have made an appearance at one time or another.

Terns of several species are often found here. In the winter, they will most likely be just Caspian and Forster's, but the spring, summer, and fall months bring the possibility of Elegant, Common (not in mid-summer), and Least—plus Black Skimmer. Royal Terns are possible in fall and spring, rare in winter. Gulls of several species are also likely. Ring-billed and California are most common, but Bonaparte's, Herring, Western, and Glaucous-winged (rare) would not be unexpected. You will also see Great Blue and Green-backed Herons, and Great and Snowy Egrets.

Across the street a little boardwalk leads to a freshwater pond. Here you will find many of the same ducks you encountered at the foot of San Joaquin Hills Road, but also some new ones. Canvasbacks are almost a sure thing in winter, but you might also see Gadwall, Redhead, Ring-necked Duck, or something more exotic. Present all year are American Coot, Common Moorhen, and Black-crowned Night-Heron. Swallows of several species are likely to be swooping over the pond. In the summer, expect to see Barn, Northern Rough-winged, and Cliff; in winter you might find Tree.

The brush on the south side of the pond is a likely location for California Gnatcatcher. If you don't find these birds here, walk either direction along Back Bay Drive and listen for them. They can be found in the brush along the cliff face anywhere. *Please avoid using a taped call.*

If your taste for land birds has been piqued by the gnatcatcher, continue up the Big Canyon trail on the south side of the pond. In the open area where the California Gnatcatchers reside, you may also find birds like the Mourning Dove, Say's Phoebe (winter), Loggerhead Shrike, and Savannah (*nevadensis*) Sparrows. These are also quite likely in similar habitat anywhere along Back Bay Drive.

In the willows farther up the trail, the most-likely species found all year are Spotted Dove, Anna's Hummingbird, Northern Flicker, Black Phoebe, Bushtit, Bewick's Wren, Northern Mockingbird, California Towhee, Red-winged and Brewer's Blackbirds, Brown-headed Cowbird, House Finch, and Lesser and American Goldfinches.

Winter visitors include Ruby-crowned Kinglet, Blue-gray Gnatcatcher, Hermit Thrush, Orange-crowned and Yellow-rumped Warblers, Rufous-sided Towhee, and Lincoln's, Golden-crowned, and White-crowned Sparrows. Some likely summer visitors are Black-chinned Hummingbird, Cassin's and Western Kingbirds, and Hooded and Northern Orioles.

Spring and fall migrations bring the possibility of Rufous and Allen's Hummingbirds, Olive-sided Flycatcher, Western Wood-Pewee, Willow, Hammond's, Pacific-slope, and Ash-throated Flycatchers, Swainson's Thrush, Solitary and Warbling Vireos, Nashville, Yellow, Black-throated Gray, Townsend's, MacGillivray's, and Wilson's Warblers, Yellow-breasted Chat (rare), Western Tanager, Black-headed Grosbeak, and Lazuli Bunting.

Return to your car and drive the remainder of the road. There are no new habitats to be found, but you may still find additional species. Park along the road wherever you can and scope the mudflats and marsh, or beat the bushes along the roadside for landbirds.

One group of birds, the raptors, has been left out of the preceding Upper Newport Bay lists. These mobile birds can be found anywhere. The most frequently observed are Turkey Vulture, Osprey (rare), Black-shouldered Kite (rare), Northern Harrier, Sharp-shinned (winter), Cooper's, Red-shouldered, and Red-tailed Hawks, Golden Eagle (rare), American Kestrel, Peregrine and Prairie Falcons (both winter, rare). No owls are observed commonly, but the list of possibilities includes Barn, Great Horned, Burrowing (on the opposite side of the bay, rare), and Short-eared (winter, rare).

The road finally climbs the bluff to Eastbluff Drive. Although it is difficult to do so without making an illegal U-turn, there is one last area which should be checked—the view north from the top of the bluff to your left. Here you can scope man-made islands which were established to encourage nesting Least Terns. So far, predation has kept the area from living up to its potential, but small numbers of terns (Least plus other species) and Black Skimmers have nested there, and their numbers seem to be increasing. The area also seems to serve as a high-tide resting area for just about all the gulls and shorebirds of the bay.

This concludes the tour of Upper Newport Bay. Access to the opposite shore is possible at a number of spots. You may wish to get a street map and figure it out. Several of the access points present the possibility of lovely walks away from the traffic.

From the north end of Back Bay Drive, turn right onto Eastbluff Drive and go to Jamboree Road (1.1) Turn right and return to Pacific Coast Highway (1.6). Turn left and go to the signal light at Poppy Avenue in Corona del Mar (2.1). (The streets are in alphabetical order by flowers.) Turn right and go to where the street ends at Ocean Boulevard (0.3) Park wherever you can and walk back to the corner and down the hill to the beach at **Little Corona City Beach**. This area is better covered on weekdays or early in the morning on weekends. At other times, people and dogs scare the birds away. Avoid it also at high tide or in the early summer, when the number of bird species is minimal.

Corona del Mar marks the dividing line between sandy and rocky coastline in Orange County. An earthquake fault nearby accounts for the sharp transition.

A number of shorebirds prefer the ocean front, especially southward where there are rocks, too. Some which are uncommon to missing at Upper Newport Bay are Wandering Tattler, Spotted Sandpiper, Whimbrel, Ruddy and Black Turnstones, Surfbird, and Sanderling.

Because water from Buck Gully enters the ocean at Little Corona, large numbers of wintering gulls gather here to drink. It is perhaps the best place in the county for Herring, Thayer's, and Glaucous-winged Gulls. In addition, you should find Heermann's, Ring-billed, California, and Western. The Western Gulls will mostly be of the darker *wymani* subspecies, but occasionally a paler *occidentalis* comes down from northern California. To compound the problem, Western x Glaucous-winged hybrids are also just as likely. The nice thing about this spot is that the birds will usually stand there patiently while you figure them out—or frustrate you until you give up!

Out in the water of the little cove, you can expect Red-throated, Pacific, and Common Loons. (The Red-throated Loons are the most likely ones right in the breaking surf.) Other birds which you looked for from the Newport and Balboa Piers should also be expected here. From the beach you can scope Arch Rock (better in the afternoon) and sometimes see three cormorant species—Pelagic, Brandt's, and Double-crested.

If you have not found all the birds listed above, you may wish to drive toward the other end of Ocean Boulevard (0.6) and explore the rocks around the Newport Harbor jetty. Unfortunately, there are usually more fisherfolk than birds on the jetty.

Return via Poppy Avenue to Pacific Coast Highway and turn right. As soon as you leave Corona del Mar, you will come to **Crystal Cove State Park** (day use only; fee). There are a number of parking areas along the ocean side of the highway where you can park and walk down to the beach. The birds here are much the same as at Little Corona—and the state-park parking fee is steep. The only good thing about it is that once you've paid it, it's good all day at *any* state park. Sometimes early in the morning or midweek during the winter season, there is no attendant at the gate, so you get in free! So far no one has started collecting on the way out.

If you do decide to sample Crystal Cove, enter the first parking lot—Pelican Point (1.2 from Poppy Avenue). California Gnatcatchers are common in the area. The point is a fairly good place from which to observe migrating seabirds (March-May, August-October). Loons, shearwaters, scoters, and Brants are possible.

Crystal Cove State Park (2,791 acres) also has an inland portion, El Moro Canyon, where you can hike for miles through coastal sage scrub, grassland, and willow/oak/sycamore riparian habitats. The parking lot for this hike is on your left 3.1 miles from Poppy Avenue, just before a school.

Some of the more interesting land birds seen throughout the year in Crystal Cove State Park are Northern Harrier, Cooper's Hawk, California Quail, Greater Roadrunner, Barn Owl, White-throated Swift, Costa's Hummingbird (rare winter), Allen's Hummingbird (rare), Nuttall's Woodpecker, Cassin's Kingbird (uncommon winter), Cactus Wren,

California Gnatcatcher (possible near El Moro Canyon parking lot, but more common on the ocean side of the highway), Wrentit, California Thrasher, Hutton's Vireo, Rufous-sided and California Towhees, and Rufous-crowned Sparrow. A few summer visitors, most of which are confirmed or possible breeders, are Common Poorwill, Western Wood-Pewee, Ash-throated Flycatcher, Phainopepla, Blue Grosbeak, Lazuli Bunting, Black-chinned and Grasshopper Sparrows. This area has not proven to be a "hot-spot" during migration, despite its proximity to the coast.

To return to the loop's starting point from Crystal Cove State Park, take Pacific Coast Highway northward to Highway 73 (MacArthur Boulevard) at the north end of Corona del Mar (0.8 miles past Poppy Avenue). Turn right and stay on Highway 73 when it parts company with MacArthur Boulevard (3.6). After 1.9 miles on this freeway make the transition to the northbound Costa Mesa Freeway (Highway 55). You will be back to its junction with I-405 in about 1.5 miles.

If you wish to connect with the Santa Ana Mountains Loop, continue up Highway 55 to Highway 91 (11.7), which you take 2.3 miles to the junction of Highways 90 and 91, the starting point.

There is camping at the Newport Dunes Aquatic Park and plenty of motels along the route.

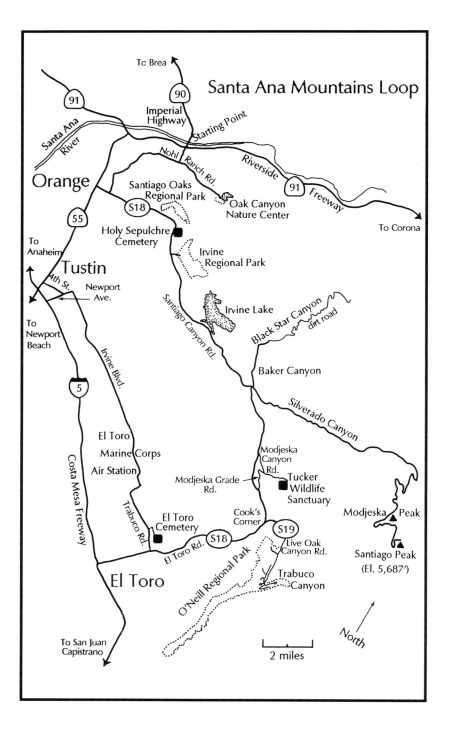

Santa Ana Mountains Loop

To Brea

91

90

Imperial Highway

Starting Point

Santa Ana River

Nohl Ranch Rd.

Riverside

91 Freeway

Orange

55

S18

Santiago Oaks Regional Park

Oak Canyon Nature Center

To Corona

Holy Sepulchre Cemetery

Irvine Regional Park

To Anaheim

Tustin

4th St.

Newport Ave.

Santiago Canyon Rd.

Irvine Lake

Black Star Canyon

dirt road

To Newport Beach

5

Irvine Blvd.

Baker Canyon

Silverado Canyon

Costa Mesa Freeway

El Toro Marine Corps Air Station

Modjeska Canyon Rd.

Modjeska Grade Rd.

Tucker Wildlife Sanctuary

Trabuco Rd.

El Toro Cemetery

Cook's Corner

Modjeska Peak

S18

El Toro Rd.

S19

Live Oak Canyon Rd.

Santiago Peak (El. 5,687')

El Toro

O'Neill Regional Park

Trabuco Canyon

To San Juan Capistrano

2 miles

North

SANTA ANA MOUNTAINS LOOP

Saddleback, the most prominent feature of the Santa Ana Mountains, can be seen from almost any point in Orange County. Not only do its twin peaks (Modjeska and Santiago) dominate the skyline, but also its presence is reflected in the names of many schools, motels, and other buildings. Its numerous canyons, ridges, and peaks are fun to explore. This trip will take you to a few of them.

The starting point is the intersection of the Riverside Freeway (Highway 91) and Imperial Highway 90 northeast of the city of Orange.

Go south on Highway 90 to Nohl Ranch Road, turn left, and follow past the golf course to Walnut Canyon Road (1.7) on the left. Turn here to **Oak Canyon Nature Center** (0.5) (open 9-5 daily). This 58-acre park offers six miles of trails through a variety of habitats of chaparral and oak woodlands with a small stream, all set in the Anaheim Hills.

A partial list of the birds commonly seen here is Red-tailed Hawk, Western Screech-Owl,Costa's and Anna's Hummingbirds, Acorn and Nuttall's (uncommon) Woodpeckers, Black Phoebe, Ash-throated Flycatcher (summer), Scrub Jay, American Crow, Common Raven, Plain Titmouse, Bushtit, Cactus, Bewick's, and House Wrens, Ruby-crowned Kinglet (winter), Wrentit, Northern Mockingbird, California Thrasher, Phainopepla, Orange-crowned, Yellow-rumped (winter), Black-throated Gray (migration), and Townsend's (migration) Warblers, Western Tanager (migration), Black-headed Grosbeak (migration), Rufous-sided and California Towhees, Song Sparrow, Dark-eyed Junco (winter), Brown-headed Cowbird (summer), Northern Oriole, House Finch, and Lesser Goldfinch. This site also has a long list of accidentals.

To continue the route, return to Nohl Ranch Road, go past Imperial Highway 90, and turn left on Meats Avenue (1.2 miles past Imperial). Then turn left onto Santiago Boulevard (1.7). Bear right onto Wanda Road (0.6), and turn left onto Villa Park Road (0.3). This soon becomes Santiago Canyon Road (Route S18). Turn left onto Windes Drive (2.6) to **Santiago**

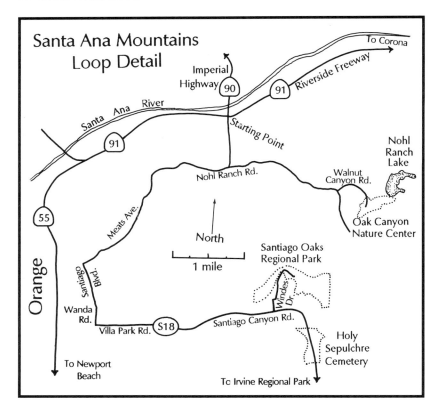

Santa Ana Mountains
Loop Detail

Oaks Regional Park (fee) on the left. Santiago Creek, lined by California Sycamore, Coast Live Oaks, and coastal sage scrub, runs through the park.

This park may be the finest spot in the county for finding the regular land birds of coastal Southern California. It has many of the same birds as the Oak Canyon Nature Center, although, with the habitats in close proximity here, the birder can sample them all in a two-mile walk. Besides the various riparian habitats and coastal sage scrub, there is a large area dotted with exotic trees, once planted in conjunction with plans for a mansion that never materialized. From the parking lot walk up the trail to the interpretive center and pick up a bird list. Among the permanent residents in the park are Black-shouldered Kite, California Quail, Greater Roadrunner, Western Screech-Owl, Acorn and Nuttall's Woodpeckers, Western Bluebird, California Thrasher, Hutton's Vireo, California Towhee, and Rufous-crowned Sparrow. Summer visitors include Black-chinned Hummingbird, Pacific-slope and Ash-throated Flycatchers, Black-headed

Grosbeak, Black-chinned Sparrow (rare), and Hooded Oriole. Winter visitors include Red-breasted Sapsucker, Blue-gray Gnatcatcher, Hermit Thrush, Cedar Waxwing, and Golden-crowned Sparrow.

When leaving, turn left onto Santiago Canyon Road. In a short distance you will see Holy Sepulchre Cemetery (1.1) on the left. It may be worth a stop in winter for sparrows. From the far edge of the cemetery you can also scope the reservoir behind Villa Park Dam for ducks and cormorants. At Chapman Avenue (0.7) turn left to **Irvine Regional Park** (fee), which is just around the bend. The park is alive with Acorn and Nuttall's Woodpeckers, California Quail, Plain Titmouse, and, on the weekend, people. Check for Blue Grosbeaks near the entrance in summer. Barn and Great Horned Owls and Western Screech-Owls can all be found. Look for Lesser Nighthawks over the parking lots at dusk in summer. Try birding the Nature Area along the hillside on the south edge of the park across the road from the little lake. First check the trees around the lake for Black-crowned Night-Heron and Purple Martin. Then follow the trail past the huge Coast Live Oaks and up the hill through the chaparral. Watch for California Thrasher, Bushtit, Wrentit, Rufous-sided and California Towhees, and, in winter, Fox, Golden-crowned, and White-crowned Sparrows. Warblers are sometimes common here in migration. Rufous-crowned Sparrows can usually be found in the dry, sparse brush along the very crest of the hill.

Return to Santiago Canyon Road and continue east toward Irvine Lake. Black-shouldered Kites may be seen along the foothills or over the low areas to the right as you climb the long hill. Beyond the summit and near the forestry headquarters (2.2), you will find open grasslands, which are good for Western Kingbird in summer and for Say's Phoebe and Mountain Bluebird in winter. At the bottom of the hill, check the patches of wild roses and willows for Blue Grosbeak and Lazuli Bunting in the spring.

Irvine Lake (1.4) is always crowded with fishermen or hunters, but not birds. Beyond the lake the fence lines are often lined with Western Bluebirds, while at night, Barn Owls often sit on the fence posts.

At the next intersection (3.0) you have a choice of three roads. The road to the left goes up Black Star Canyon and is worth exploring for the first 2 or 3 miles. You can park your car at the gate and walk through (unless the area has been closed by the fire marshal). A side road, Baker Canyon, can yield Rufous-crowned Sparrows along the slopes.

The road straight ahead goes up Silverado Canyon, which is well settled and rather poor for birds. However, from the end of the paved road, a rocky, dirt road winds 13 miles to the top of Santiago Peak (El. 5,687 ft). This road is closed in summer because of the fire hazard and in winter by the snow. In March and April, however, it can make a great trip with lots of birds, flowers, and magnificent views. Plan to go on a weekday, or get a very early start. On a Sunday afternoon, you will think that you are caught up in a motorcycle race on the Hollywood Freeway during rush-hour traffic.

To continue the loop, turn right and continue along Santiago Canyon Road. The next few miles traverse an area of scattered Coast Live Oaks and Western Sycamores mixed with patches of brush. Stop anywhere to look for California Quail, Scrub Jay, Bushtit, Wrentit, Bewick's Wren, American and Lesser Goldfinches, California Towhee, and sparrows. In summer, check for Ash-throated Flycatcher, Phainopepla, Northern Oriole, Black-headed and Blue Grosbeaks, and Lazuli Bunting.

Bear left onto Modjeska Canyon Road (2.7). You will soon enter a stand of olive trees, which can be filled with Western Tanagers in early May. The trees were planted on the estate of the great Polish actress Madame Modjeska. Turn left at the next intersection (0.9) to visit the lovely canyon where she lived. There is a historical marker (0.6) on the right, but her home is not visible from the road nor is it open to the public.

The **Dorothy May Tucker Wildlife Sanctuary** (El. 1,350 ft) (0.4) (open 9-4; donation requested) is farther up the canyon. This spot is worth a visit at almost any season. From the porch of the cabin, you can watch in comfort as a wide assortment of birds come to the feeders. Some of the more common species are California Quail, Band-tailed Pigeon, Mourning Dove, Northern Flicker, Acorn and Nuttall's Woodpeckers, Scrub Jay, Plain Titmouse, Wrentit, House and Bewick's Wrens, California Thrasher, Orange-crowned Warbler, House Finch, Rufous-sided and California Towhees, and Song Sparrow. In summer, there are also Hooded and Northern Orioles and Black-headed Grosbeak. In winter you should find White-breasted Nuthatch, Hermit Thrush, Ruby-crowned Kinglet, Yellow-rumped Warbler, Purple Finch, Dark-eyed Junco, and Chipping, White-crowned, Golden-crowned, and Fox Sparrows.

The major attraction, and the one for which the refuge is famous, is the hummingbirds. There are always a number of Anna's about, augmented by Black-chinned and Costa's in summer, and by Rufous and Allen's in migration. During the peak of the migration season in late July and August, literally hundreds of hummingbirds swarm like bees around the feeders. It is a fantastic show.

Across the road is the office, and behind it, across from the parking lot, is a large tract of chaparral and a well-marked nature trail on the hillside, where you may be able to pick up a few things that do not come to the feeders. In April and May, Black-chinned Sparrows sing all over the place, but are very hard to see. Except during the fire season, you can walk up the fire break beyond the gate to explore this habitat better. It is a pleasant walk, and you will get a good view of Flores' Peak, where a notorious gang of outlaws was captured in 1854.

Return to the mouth of the canyon (1.0) and turn left on Modjeska Grade Road toward O'Neill Park. After going over the steep ridge, you will rejoin Santiago Canyon Road (1.3), where you should bear left. At Cook's Corner (1.2), turn left onto Live Oak Canyon Road (Route S19) toward O'Neill Park. As you climb the hill, check the brush for Wrentit and other chaparral birds. Beyond the summit, you will enter Live Oak Canyon, a good area for Hutton's Vireo. In winter, the Hutton's Vireo is often confused with the more abundant Ruby-crowned Kinglet. If it flashes its wings regularly, it is probably a kinglet.

O'Neill Regional Park (fee) (3.2) is a very popular spot, where there are often too many people for good birding. During the week or in off-seasons, you may find Red-shouldered Hawk, Band-tailed Pigeon, Acorn Woodpecker, Purple Martin (spring and summer), Plain Titmouse, Western Bluebird, and Bushtit. It is a nice place to camp.

Return to Cook's Corner and continue straight ahead on El Toro Road. After a couple of miles, you will come to a row of Blue Gum Eucalyptus which serves as a windbreak. Cassin's Kingbirds can be found in these trees at any season.

Continue to Trabuco Road (3.0) and turn right. At Lake Forest Drive (0.8) turn right, go one block, and turn right onto Old Trabuco Road to the entrance of the **El Toro Cemetery** (0.5). California Gnatcatchers can often be coaxed from the little ravine along the right side of the entrance road, or from the brushy hillsides behind the cemetery. This bird is often hard to find, but will sometimes respond to squeaking or tapes.

Return to Trabuco Road. *If you wish, you can end the tour loop here, go back to El Toro Road, and take it south to Interstate 5 and San Juan Capistrano so you can hook up with the Lake Elsinore Loop.* If you prefer to return to the starting point, drive west on Trabuco Road. For the next 10 miles you will pass through agricultural areas, citrus groves, and the El Toro Marine Corps Air Station (where the road's name changes to Irvine Boulevard), and you will travel through more and more housing tracts. To get back to Orange, turn north onto the Costa Mesa Freeway (I-55) in Tustin, bear right onto the Riverside Freeway (Highway 91), and return to its intersection with Highway 90. You may wish to extend your trip in Orange and Anaheim by checking sites along the Santa Ana River (see *Miscellaneous Areas*).

There are campgrounds in O'Neill Park. Motels can be found along the freeways, but not in the canyons.

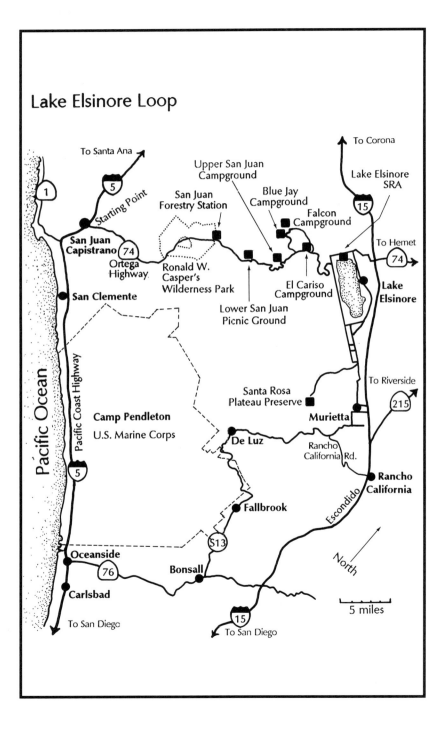

Lake Elsinore Loop

To Santa Ana

To Corona

1

5

Starting Point

Lake Elsinore SRA

San Juan Forestry Station

Upper San Juan Campground

Blue Jay Campground

Falcon Campground

To Hemet

15

San Juan Capistrano

74

74

Ortega Highway

Ronald W. Casper's Wilderness Park

El Cariso Campground

Lake Elsinore

San Clemente

Lower San Juan Picnic Ground

Pacific Coast Highway

To Riverside

Santa Rosa Plateau Preserve

215

Pacific Ocean

Camp Pendleton U.S. Marine Corps

Murietta

De Luz

Rancho California Rd.

5

Rancho California

Escondido

Fallbrook

North

Oceanside

S13

76

Bonsall

Carlsbad

15

5 miles

To San Diego

To San Diego

LAKE ELSINORE LOOP

On a clear day after a heavy rain or a "Santa Ana" wind, the view from the Elsinore Escarpment is magnificent. From this high vantage point you can see the boats and swimmers on the lake a thousand feet below. The skyline is a ring of mountains. Nearly all of the major mountain peaks of Southern California are visible, especially in winter when their snow-capped summits stand out like huge bird-rocks in the sea. A certain tune will surely come to mind: "On a clear day, you can see forever".

A clear day is now a rare occurrence in California. You may find the smog so thick that even the lake will not be visible from the escarpment. However, you should still find numerous birds and (in spring) blankets of wildflowers. Birding is at its best in winter; the flowers, in March and April.

The starting point is the junction of the San Diego Freeway (Interstate 5) and the Ortega Highway (Highway 74) in San Juan Capistrano. The mission is one block to the west and well worth a visit (open 9-5; fee). Cliff Swallows have not nested here in recent years, but the beautiful grounds abound with Anna's Hummingbirds.

Go east on the Ortega Highway toward Lake Elsinore. For the first few miles, the road is bordered by houses, and birds are few. At San Juan Creek (2.3) the water attracts Lesser and American Goldfinches, California Towhees, and sparrows. Black Phoebes often nest under the bridge, and Northern Orioles nest in the Western Sycamore at the end of it. A Black-shouldered Kite can sometimes be seen hovering over the grassy hillsides.

Farther inland, stands of Coast Live Oaks become common. Check here for Acorn Woodpecker, Plain Titmouse, Bushtit, Hutton's Vireo, Black-headed Grosbeak (summer), and at night, Great Horned Owl and Western Screech-Owl. At the start of the rainy season in November, you may find the woods alive with California Newts, dull-red salamanders.

The dry hillsides are covered in places with Prickly-Pear cactus, which often shelter a Cactus Wren or a covey of California Quail. In winter, here as elsewhere in California, White-crowned Sparrows are abundant. If you look hard enough, however, you may find other kinds of sparrows. Stop at all of the windmills to check for birds around the water tanks, particularly during the dry season.

Casper's Wilderness Park (5.2) (fee; picnicking and camping) is an excellent place to bird, for it has a wide variety of habitats, 5,500 acres of fertile valleys, and running streams. It also has a visitors' center and trails. (Some camping areas may be closed because of a Mountain Lion scare.)

During the rainy season, when the roads in the Cleveland National Forest are open, you will want to drive up the one behind the **San Juan Forestry Station** (5.1) on the left. Not only is the birding good, but also this road will enable you to get away from some of the traffic. Along this short road you will find a variety of habitats ranging from chaparral-covered hillsides to stream-side woodlands. Some of the birds to expect are Anna's Hummingbird, Northern Flicker, Acorn and Nuttall's Woodpeckers, Scrub Jay, Plain Titmouse, Bushtit, Wrentit, House and Bewick's Wrens, California Thrasher, Blue-gray Gnatcatcher, Hutton's Vireo, Orange-crowned Warbler, House Finch, American and Lesser Goldfinches, Rufous-sided and California Towhees, and Black-chinned (hard to find) and Song Sparrows. In spring look for Black-chinned and Costa's Hummingbirds, Ash-throated Flycather, Western Wood-Pewee, Swainson's Thrush, Phainopepla, Warbling Vireo, Yellow Warbler, Hooded and Northern Orioles, Black-headed and Blue Grosbeaks, and Lazuli Bunting. In winter you may find Red-naped Sapsucker, White-breasted Nuthatch, American Robin, Hermit Thrush, Ruby-crowned Kinglet, Yellow-rumped Warbler, Purple Finch, Dark-eyed Junco, and Chipping, White-crowned, Golden-crowned, Fox, and Lincoln's Sparrows.

Beyond the forestry station on Highway 74, the canyon walls become steeper and rockier—a good habitat for Canyon Wren. **Lower San Juan Picnic Ground** (3.8) and **Upper San Juan Campground** (2.4) are worth checking. The birdlife is about the same as behind the forestry station.

If you like to hike, try the San Juan Loop Trail (0.8) or the Main Divide Truck Trail (2.4). The latter is open to motor vehicles at times during the non-fire season. It is an exciting road that runs along the crest of the mountains, but it may be rough and muddy or dusty.

El Cariso Campground (Cah-REE-so) (1.2) near the summit of this highway is worth checking. Varied Thrushes sometimes winter here. Beyond this point, the chaparral is very lush and productive. Check for any birds that you might have missed in this habitat. The bright-orange vine you will see is Dodder, a parasite.

Turn left (0.2) onto a paved road to the Falcon (4.3) and Blue Jay (0.5) Campgrounds. (These can also be reached by taking this loop road from its other end, the Main Divide Truck Trail, mentioned previously.) These are well off the highway, and during the week they are not crowded. They also boast the best oak-woodland habitat along the Ortega Highway.

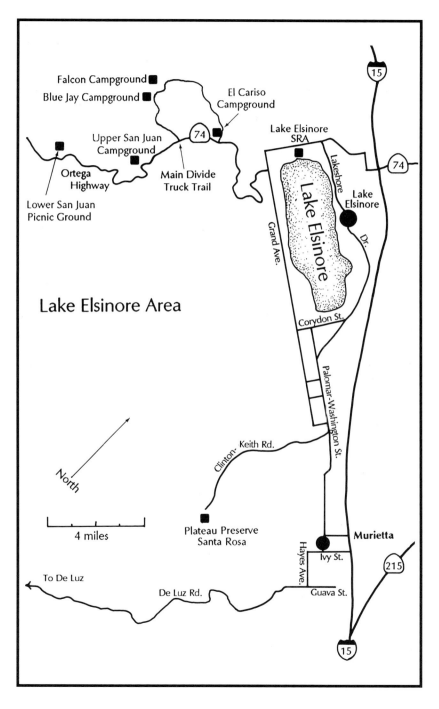

Falcon Campground

Blue Jay Campground

El Cariso Campground

Upper San Juan Campground

74

Lake Elsinore SRA

Lake Elsinore

Lakeshore

74

Lake Elsinore Dr.

Ortega Highway

Main Divide Truck Trail

Lower San Juan Picnic Ground

Grand Ave.

Lake Elsinore Area

Corydon St.

Palomar-Washington St.

Keith Rd.

Clinton-

North

4 miles

Plateau Preserve Santa Rosa

Murietta

Ivy St.

Hayes Ave.

215

To De Luz

De Luz Rd.

Guava St.

15

15

Western Bluebird and White-breasted Nuthatch nest here, as do most of the birds listed for the lower elevations.

Return to the Ortega Highway and continue toward Lake Elsinore. After you pass the summit, look on the left for a viewpoint (1.2) from which you can see a good part of Southern California on a clear day. Most of the major mountain peaks are visible. On the far left is Mount San Antonio or Mount Baldy (El. 10,064 ft) in the San Gabriel Mountains. The next peak to the right is San Gorgonio or Grayback (El. 11,502 ft) in the San Bernardino Mountains. This large, bare, rounded mass is the tallest peak in Southern California. San Jacinto Peak (El. 10,786 ft) in the San Jacinto Mountains is nearly due east. Almost hidden from view to the right of this is Santa Rosa Mountain (El. 8,046 ft). In the distance to the far right, you can see the Laguna and Palomar Mountains. The shiny dome of the Palomar Observatory is visible if you look hard enough. A thousand feet below is Lake Elsinore (El. 1,274 ft).

Wind your way down the mountain to Grand Avenue (4.4). The north end of the lake is accessible at **Lake Elsinore State Recreation Area** (camping; fee). To get there, turn left and follow Highway 74 (1.7). American Coots and Ring-billed Gulls are common all year. Ducks may be numerous in winter, when you may also find Western, Clark's, and Eared Grebes, American White Pelican, and Common Merganser.

Continue to the traffic light at Lakeshore Drive (0.7) and turn right. At a public parking lot (1.6) stop and scan the lake. Keep right at the fork (0.2). At Elm Grove Park (0.5) you can get a general view of the south end of the lake. As you continue south to Corydon Road (4.3), the dry lake bed on the right may have Horned Larks in winter. Check for McCown's, Lapland, and Chestnut-collared Longspurs (all three very rare) among the Horned Larks. Turn right on Corydon Road and look in the fields for these birds as well as for Vesper and Savannah Sparrows. At Grand Avenue (2.0) turn left. The street trees here are olives and California Pepper (fern-like leaves).

Turn left where the pavement on Grand Avenue ends (2.9), then right onto Palomar-Washington Street (0.5) to Clinton-Keith Road (0.9). If you have plenty of time, turn right at Clinton-Keith Road to visit the **Santa Rosa Plateau Preserve** (3,100 acres acquired in 1984 by The California Nature Conservancy). Park at the locked gate (4.6). The Preserve is not a park, but visitors are welcome. Just walk through the turnstile and take a map showing the area trails. There are varied habitats of grassland, chaparral, and oak woodland of Coast Live Oak and the rarer, threatened Engelmann Oak. There are also some riparian zones of sycamore and willow. Birds to be expected in the oak woodlands are Band-tailed Pigeon, Acorn

Woodpecker, Phainopepla, and Red-shouldered Hawk. The chaparral produces such birds as California Quail, California Thrasher, and Wrentit. In the grassland look for Black-shouldered Kite, American Kestrel, Western Bluebird, and Grasshopper Sparrow, among others.

The creekbeds throughout the Preserve contain deep holes called tenejas (ten-AY-has) which hold water throughout the rainless summer months. Some of California's last vernal pools are found on top of the level mesas; they support some wintering waterfowl.

Return to Palomar-Washington Street and turn right. You will soon come to the little (but rapidly growing) settlement of Murrieta (Mur-ree-ET-ah) (4.0). At the southern edge of town, turn right on Ivy Street (3.7), go just beyond the flood-control channel, and turn left onto Hayes Avenue (0.5). You will come to De Luz Road (1.1) where you turn right (if you turn left, the road is named Guava Street). This road (which starts out paved for 0.6 miles but becomes gravel for the last 1.6 miles) leads up the escarpment and becomes good, paved De Luz Road (2.2). (De Luz Road can be reached, avoiding the gravel part, by taking the Rancho California Road right [west] from Interstate 15 at the Temecula-Rancho California exit.) This is an excellent road to explore if you have the time. It leads 11.3 miles to De Luz and then on another 11.0 miles to Fallbrook (see *Miscellaneous Areas* section). During very wet weather, the road may not be passable, for it fords the stream several times. When it is open, this is a beautiful drive through grasslands, chaparral, and oak woodlands. It is excellent in spring for wildflowers, in fall for autumn colors, and at all seasons for birds. Phainopeplas, in winter, are often found in large numbers, and during migrations the area can be alive with birds. But the biggest thrill is to be among the White Alders along the stream at De Luz on a spring evening and listen to the song of the Swainson's Thrush. From Fallbrook continue south on S13 to Highway 76 at Bonsall and turn right to Oceanside.

If you do not go to De Luz, turn left on Ivy Street to I-15 and consider several choices. You can return to San Juan Capistrano by taking I-15 north to Highway 74 (13.0) and driving back over the Ortega Highway. Or turn right on I-15 to Highway 76 (12.0) and right to Oceanside, following the San Luis Rey River down. Return to the starting point at San Juan Capistrano, *or turn left to the start of the Palomar Mountain Loop, which starts at Oceanside.*

You may camp at the Forest Service campgrounds on the Ortega Highway or at Lake Elsinore State Recreation Area.

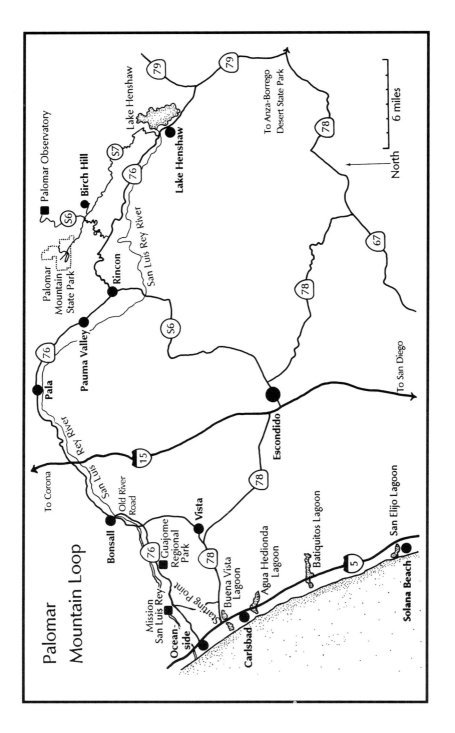

Palomar
Mountain Loop

Palomar Observatory
Birch Hill
S6
Palomar Mountain State Park
Rincon
Lake Henshaw
79
79
To Anza-Borrego Desert State Park
78
North
6 miles
S7
76
Lake Henshaw
San Luis Rey River
67
78
Pauma Valley
76
S6
Pala
San Luis Rey River
Escondido
To San Diego
To Corona
15
78
Old River Road
San Luis Rey River
Vista
78
Bonsall
76
Guajome Regional Park
78
Buena Vista Lagoon
Agua Hedionda Lagoon
Batiquitos Lagoon
San Elijo Lagoon
Mission San Luis Rey
Starting Point
Ocean-side
Carlsbad
5
Solana Beach

PALOMAR MOUNTAIN LOOP

M ost people first visit here to see the Palomar Observatory telescopes. Until recently many would return to enjoy rural California as it used to be. However, the housing booms, freeways, and shopping centers that are so typical of Southern California are beginning to overwhelm the western half of this loop. You can still enjoy some coastal lagoons, rolling foothills, meadows, and certainly the forested mountains. Although not as productive as the mountains farther north, this route is convenient for San Diego-based birders. You should be able to compile an impressive list of birds here at any season.

The starting point is the intersection of the San Diego Freeway (Interstate 5) and the Vista Freeway (Highway 78) just south of Oceanside. Drive east on the Vista Freeway toward Vista. At the first exit, get off on Jefferson Street (0.6) for a drive around **Buena Vista Lagoon**. As soon as you leave the freeway, and before crossing the bridge, turn right onto the little road along the north side of the lake.

Large flocks of ducks and a few shorebirds winter on the lagoon. Most leave in summer, but a few stay to nest. You should be able to find Mallard, Gadwall, American Wigeon, even an occasional Eurasian Wigeon, Northern Pintail, Green-winged and Cinnamon Teal, Northern Shoveler, Redhead (nests), Ring-necked Duck, Canvasback, Lesser and Greater (rare) Scaup, Common Goldeneye, Bufflehead, Ruddy Duck (nests), and Red-breasted and Common (rare) Mergansers. In winter you should also see Great Blue and Green-backed Herons, Black-crowned Night-Heron, Great and Snowy Egrets, American Bittern, Double-crested Cormorant, and numerous gulls and terns. Check the patches of tules for Common Moorhen, Marsh Wren, Common Yellowthroat, Song Sparrow, and, in summer, Least Bittern.

To check the western section of the lagoon, return to Jefferson Street and turn right across the little bridge. Go over the freeway (0.8) and turn right onto Laguna Drive (0.5) and right again onto State Street (0.3). This will take you back to the lagoon at Carlsbad Boulevard. The patch of tules

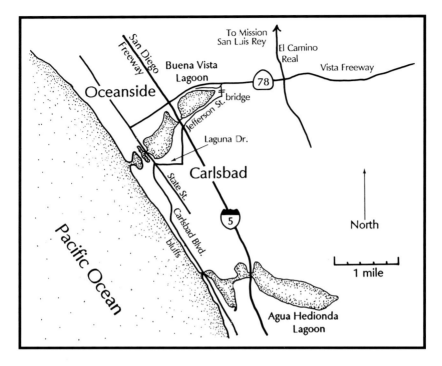

at the south edge is very good for Least Bittern, although you may have to use a tape-recording of their calls to get them up. Redheads, Ruddy Ducks, and Eared Grebes nest in this section of the lagoon.

If you cross the lagoon and turn right at the light on Vista Way (0.6), you will return to the starting point. However, you may want to look over the ocean before heading for the mountains. If so, turn around and go south on Carlsbad Boulevard. After passing through the town of Carlsbad, you will come out on the bluffs overlooking the ocean (0.8). A little farther along is Agua Hedionda Lagoon by the power plant (1.0). This salt-water inlet is sometimes full of scoters, loons, and grebes, primarily in winter.

You may also wish to check the Batiquitos (4.5) and San Elijo Lagoons for species you may have missed at the Buena Vista Lagoon. Besides, the area around the San Elijo Lagoon is good for California Gnatcatcher.

To bird the San Elijo Lagoon area, turn right on Lomas Santa Fe Drive in Solana Beach (6.7) and right at the traffic light onto Rios Avenue (0.7). At the end of this street (0.8) is the **San Elijo Lagoon Sanctuary**. A good trail leads east along the lagoon. Check for waterbirds and shorebirds on the lagoon and, along the trail, for Anna's Hummingbird, Nuttall's

Woodpecker, Canyon Wren, California Gnatcatcher, Wrentit, California Towhee, and Rufous-crowned Sparrow.

Retrace your way back to the starting point and head inland on the Vista Freeway (Highway 78). Get off at the second exit and go left (north) on El Camino Real (1.5) toward Mission San Luis Rey. Turn right onto Mission Avenue (Highway 76) (3.0). The mission (0.8) is on the left. Farther along on the right, you will see some ponds (3.0) which are part of Guajome Regional Park. This can be a good spot. It was once part of an exotic bird farm, and you may still find something rather strange here. A Black-shouldered Kite often hunts over the marsh. As you climb the hill, watch for Cassin's Kingbirds in the Canary Island Pines. Vermilion Flycatcher has been found here several times, too.

Just past the turnoff to Vista (3.0), Highway 76 turns left across the San Luis Rey River, but you should make a little jog and continue straight ahead on the **Old River Road** along the south side of the river. Rufous-crowned Sparrows frequent the brushy hillsides here, and you may find hummingbirds in the patches of flowering Tree Tobacco. (This is a tall, somewhat willow-like plant with yellow tubular flowers about an inch long.) Anna's Hummingbirds are common all year; Black-chinned and Costa's Hummingbirds are present in the spring and summer. Blue Grosbeaks like the Mexican Elderberry along the stream in summer, where you may also find Hooded and Northern Orioles, Yellow-breasted Chat, and Bell's Vireo (rare).

At Country Club Road (2.2), turn left, cross the river to Bonsall, and rejoin Highway 76 going east. Beyond I-15 (5.3) the hills become steeper and the chaparral thicker. Watch on the left for the Pala Mission (6.6), which is small but interesting. It is worth a visit.

One-half mile beyond the mission, there is a series of dry washes where Lazuli Buntings are fairly easy to find in spring and summer. Also watch for California Quail, Bewick's Wren, California Towhee, and Western and Red Diamond-backed Rattlesnakes. Next, you will pass a nice farming area known as the Pauma Valley (Pah-oo-mah) (El. 840 ft) (2.0). At Rincon (1.8) bear left with Highway 76. The road climbs rapidly now and is bordered by groves of lemons and avocados. While most orchards are barren of birds because of the heavy use of pesticides, these particular orchards abound with birds. Everything from Red-shouldered Hawks to California Thrashers may be found here.

The road next enters an area of Coast and Mesa Live Oaks. The Mesa Live Oak has light-gray bark and bluish leaves. Watch here for Acorn Woodpecker and Plain Titmouse. At the top of the grade, check the open area for Western Bluebird, Lark Sparrow, and Lawrence's Goldfinch.

Turn left onto Highway S6 (South Grade Road) (5.3) toward Palomar Mountain. (If you have a trailer, continue on 10 miles to less-steep Highway S7, East Grade Road.) The road now climbs rapidly through oak groves and tops out at Summit Grove (6.8) (El. 5,202 ft). You are suddenly in a different world. Here, on top of the mountain, the principal tree is the Yellow Pine of the Transition Zone. You will also find White Fir, Incense Cedar, Black Oak (deciduous), Canyon Live Oak, and White Alder.

Some of the birds that might be encountered are Mountain Quail, Band-tailed Pigeon, Northern Flicker, Hairy and White-headed Woodpeckers, Steller's Jay, Common Raven, Mountain Chickadee, White-breasted and Pygmy Nuthatches, Brown Creeper, American Robin, and Dark-eyed Junco. In summer there may also be Olive-sided Flycatcher, Western Wood-Pewee, Violet-green Swallow, Hermit Thrush, Solitary Vireo, Western Tanager, Black-headed Grosbeak, Lawrence's Goldfinch, and Chipping Sparrow. In winter Purple Finch and Fox Sparrow are to be expected. If you work hard enough at night and use a tape, you should find Great Horned, Spotted, and Northern Saw-whet Owls, Western Screech-Owl, and possibly Northern Pygmy-Owl.

There are three main areas on top of the mountain, and you should explore them all. **Palomar Mountain State Park** (fee for day use, camping,

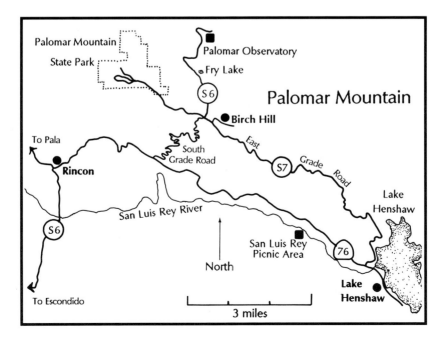

or hot showers) is 3 miles to the left on Highway S7. This is a great area with meadows, forests, and a few little lakes. Spotted Owls have been found right in the campground. The view from Boucher Lookout on a clear day is magnificent.

The Palomar Observatory (open 8-5) is 5 miles straight ahead on Highway S6. You get to only look at, not through, the telescope, but there are many exhibits. It is well worth a visit. There is excellent birding all along this road, so you can stop almost anywhere and find something. One of the better spots is tiny **Fry Lake**. It is about 2 miles ahead on the right, just before the entrance to the Observatory Campground. Birds often come here to drink, and it is a good area for Spotted Owls at night. Check the picnic grounds below the parking lot at the telescope.

Many of the cabins in the housing area on **Birch Hill** have feeders, where you can occasionally find White-headed Woodpeckers. To reach the hill, turn right onto Highway S7 and then left onto the first little road.

After exploring the mountain-top, return to Summit Grove and go east on Highway S7 for the trip down the mountain. Traffic is not as heavy on this road, so you can stop almost anywhere to bird. In a couple of miles you will reach the grasslands. Mountain Bluebirds often winter here along with the more numerous Westerns. Also watch for Horned Lark, Lark Sparrow, and hawks.

Eventually, Lake Henshaw (El. 2,727 ft) (9.0) will come into view. It often has too many fishermen and too few birds, but sometimes, in fall and winter, there are large numbers of ducks and some geese. Use your scope. A little area below the dam has water that attracts birds during the dry season. In winter you may wish to explore areas to the north and east of the lake, great for Ferruginous Hawks and Bald Eagles. You have a reasonable chance of seeing Rough-legged Hawk, Golden Eagle, Merlin, and Prairie Falcon some winters.

Turn right at Highway 76 (2.3) and follow the San Luis Rey River, a good birding area at any season. In winter it is alive with Hermit Thrushes and sparrows, and in summer with Yellow-breasted Chats and Lazuli Buntings. The woods around the **San Luis Rey Picnic Area** are especially productive.

From the junction of Highway S6 (9.8) you can retrace your route to Oceanside. Or you may want to follow one of the other roads back to the coast and hook up with the San Diego Loop. All of the roads down to the coast are beautiful, particularly in the spring. Yet another alternative is to drive through on Highway 79 to the Anza-Borrego Desert State Park trip, or hook up with the Laguna Mountains Loop.

There are campgrounds on Palomar Mountain and two private ones along the San Luis Rey River. There are no motels in the recreational area.

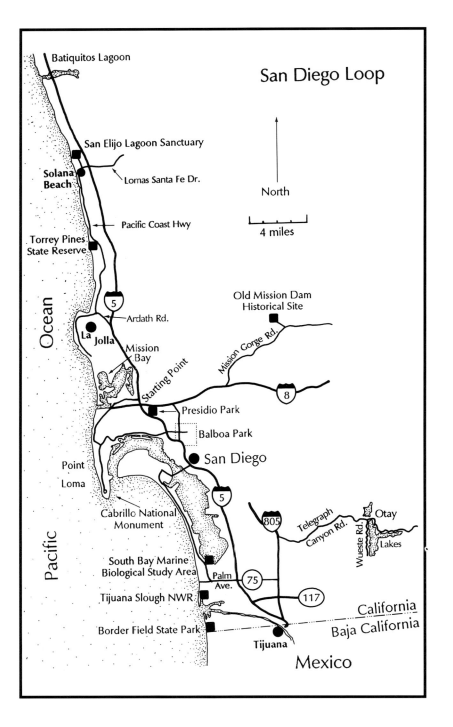

San Diego Loop

Batiquitos Lagoon

San Elijo Lagoon Sanctuary

Solana
Beach

Lomas Santa Fe Dr.

Pacific Coast Hwy

North

4 miles

Torrey Pines
State Reserve

Old Mission Dam
Historical Site

5

Ardath Rd.

La Jolla

Mission
Bay

Mission Gorge Rd.

Ocean

Starting Point

8

Presidio Park

Balboa Park

San Diego

Point
Loma

5

Cabrillo National
Monument

805

Telegraph
Canyon Rd.

Otay

Wueste Rd.

Lakes

Pacific

South Bay Marine
Biological Study Area

Palm
Ave.

75

Tijuana Slough NWR

117

California

Baja California

Border Field State Park

Tijuana

Mexico

SAN DIEGO LOOP

No other major city in the United States offers such outstanding opportunities for birding as does San Diego. A rare combination of year-round ideal weather and a variety of habitats in very picturesque settings makes this community a favorite of both birds and people. While a few other areas may top San Diego on the Christmas Bird Count, they are hardly a match on a year-long basis. There is *always* something to see in San Diego.

If you come into San Diego from the north on Interstate 5, the starting point is the intersection of the San Diego Freeway (I-5) and the Sea World Drive exit. Take Sea World Drive to the San Diego River (0.7) and exit onto the old road on the north side of the river. Here you can look over shorebirds, gulls, and terns in the estuary and on the marsh.

If you are coming from the south on I-5 or from the east on I-8, go north on I-5 to Sea World Drive and follow the directions above.

Continue to Ingraham Street and take it north about one-quarter mile to the next exit, where it makes a loop and crosses over Ingraham Street. You are now on West Mission Bay Drive. After making the loop, take the first left turn, which is Quivira Road (0.5). Then immediately turn left again and follow this road as its name changes to Quivira Way until it ends on the banks of the channel. This is Hospitality Point, where a walk out on the jetty could be productive. Also check for birds in Mission Bay Channel and in the Quivira Basin. This area is good in winter for Red-throated, Pacific, and Common Loons.

For eons the **San Diego River** meandered across this area, etching out Mission Bay on the north and San Diego Bay on the south. Now it has been strait-jacketed along this canal and can only flow meekly out to sea. However, the backwater along the channel is still an excellent refuge for waterbirds. Gulls, terns, shorebirds, herons, and ducks are common in winter. You should also see Black Brant. By looking hard enough, you could find a Eurasian Wigeon among the numerous Americans.

When you leave the river, go back up Quivira Way and take the first little road to the right, which is unnamed. Immediately turn right again onto Sunset Cliffs Boulevard going south across the river. After passing the Ocean Beach Freeway (I-8), bear right toward Ocean Beach. Turn right

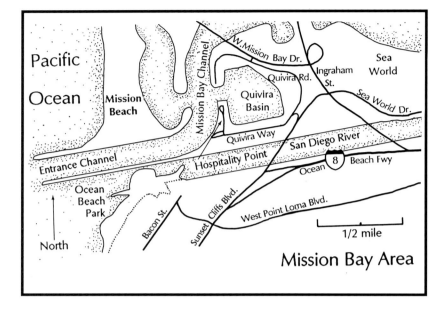

Mission Bay Area

(west) onto West Point Loma Boulevard (2.0) and right on Bacon Street to parking areas at Ocean Beach Park. Check the grassy areas for Tricolored Blackbirds and the beach for shorebirds. This is an excellent place to see terns, including Royal, Elegant, Common, and Least. Return to Sunset Cliffs Boulevard and drive south until you reach the rocky cliffs (1.3).

By stopping at all of the little turnouts along the cliffs, you should find Western and Heermann's Gulls, Double-crested Cormorant, and a few shorebirds. In winter there should also be other kinds of gulls, Brandt's and Pelagic Cormorants, Black Turnstone, Surfbird, and Wandering Tattler.

At Hill Street (0.6) turn left and follow the scenic-route arrows toward Cabrillo National Monument. Turn right onto Catalina Boulevard (Highway 209) (0.7), which leads down the ridge of **Point Loma** (best migrant landbird locality in the area, and one of the best in the state). Because of the extensive plantings of conifers, you may find American Robins, Red-breasted Nuthatches, and other mountain birds nesting here. Bird along any street or on the grounds of the **Point Loma Nazarene College** (to the right at the end of Dupont Street) (0.6). Park and walk the trails running both north and south. This area is best in migration with large numbers of western migrants in late April and the first half of May, and an interesting variety of vagrants from the East during September and October.

To reach the monument, you must cross a military reserve (0.4), which

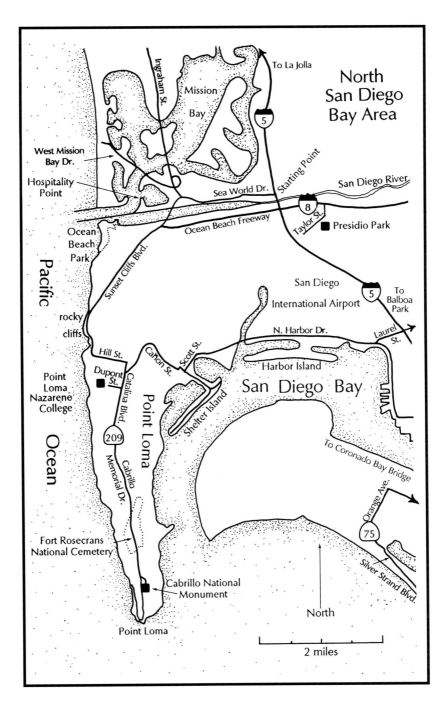

North
San Diego
Bay Area

To La Jolla

Ingraham St.

Mission

Bay

West Mission
Bay Dr.

Hospitality
Point

Starting Point

San Diego River

Sea World Dr.

Ocean Beach Freeway

Taylor St.

Presidio Park

Ocean
Beach
Park

Pacific

Sunset Cliffs Blvd.

San Diego

International Airport

To
Balboa
Park

rocky

cliffs

N. Harbor Dr.

Laurel
St.

Hill St.

Cañon St.

Scott St.

Harbor Island

San Diego Bay

Point
Loma
Nazarene
College

Dupont
St.

Catalina Blvd.

Point Loma

Shelter Island

Ocean

209

Cabrillo
Memorial Dr.

To Coronado Bay Bridge

Fort Rosecrans
National Cemetery

Orange Ave.

75

Cabrillo National
Monument

Silver Strand Blvd.

North

Point Loma

2 miles

is open only from 9-5 in winter and 8-7 in summer. On the base is **Fort Rosecrans National Cemetery** (1.4), an excellent migrant trap (April 15 to May 15 in spring, September 1 to November 15 in fall) and worth checking at any season. Many rare birds (mostly eastern vagrants) have shown up here over the years. For migrants the area is best in the morning and when the skies are overcast or foggy.

Continue on to the old lighthouse (1.0) of the **Cabrillo** (Cab-BREE-yo) **National Monument** (fee). (Stop at the visitors' center for maps, pamphlets, and books.) This viewpoint is one of the official observation stations for monitoring the migration of Gray Whales from December to March. Check the ornamental plantings around the parking lot and visitors' center for migrants in spring and fall. Flowering Bottlebrush attracts many hummingbirds in April, including Calliope. Another good birding spot is the cliffs north of the new lighthouse, which can be reached by turning left on Cabrillo Memorial Drive about a block after leaving the visitors' center. Go down the hill and then bear right to the end of the road (2.0).

Along this rocky shore in winter, you can find Black Turnstone, Surfbird, and Wandering Tattler. Double-crested, Brandt's, and Pelagic Cormorants frequent the cliffs. Black-vented Shearwaters can be seen off the point. Check the brush along the hillsides for California Quail, California Thrasher, Bewick's Wren, Wrentit, Bushtit, California Towhee, and several kinds of sparrows.

As you leave the monument, retrace your way north on Catalina Boulevard to Cañon Street (3.2) and turn right. At the end of the street, turn left onto Anchorage Lane. Go one block to Shelter Island Drive and turn right for a loop around the island. Stop and check the fishing pier. You will probably see more naval ships than birds, but there are loons, grebes, mergansers, and scoters on the bay in winter. Check the gulls and terns for a possible Black-legged Kittiwake or some other rarity, and the lawns for Whimbrel and Black-bellied Plover (winter). Return to Shelter Island Drive and turn right at the light on Scott Street (0.4). You will pass the Point Loma Sport Fishing Pier, where you can go on a fishing or whale-watching boat and see some pelagic birds. (See *Pelagic Birding Trips* chapter.) Turn right on North Harbor Drive (1.1) for a scenic look at the bay and its various tourist attractions.

After checking out the harbor area, continue on around the bay on North Harbor Drive until you reach Laurel Street at the end of the San Diego International Airport (3.2). Bear left onto Laurel Street and follow it east, as its name changes to El Prado, and until it ends at Balboa Park. The birding in the park can be excellent in winter. You may want to visit the Museum of Natural History and the San Diego Zoo (open 9-5, fee). Each is excellent. Moreover, the blooming eucalyptus and other plantings at the zoo have turned up some interesting wintering passerine rarities in recent years such as Greater Pewee and Dusky-capped Flycatcher.

When you are ready to leave Balboa Park, go south on Highway 163 (Cabrillo Freeway) to southbound I-5 and follow it about 12 miles to the Palm Avenue (Highway 75) exit in South San Diego. Follow Palm Avenue to Seacoast Drive (3.0) and turn left. Watch on the right for the **Imperial Beach Pier** (0.3), an excellent observation station for birds of the inshore ocean. Loons, grebes, gulls, terns, scoters, and California Sea Lions are usually common in winter. A King Eider spent part of one winter with the scoters here.

Continue south on Seacoast Drive past Imperial Beach Boulevard (0.2) to the **Tijuana Slough National Wildlife Refuge**, one of the best saltmarshes remaining in Southern California. Numerous herons, egrets, and shorebirds can usually be seen here. Clapper Rails can be seen, particularly at high tide. Walk on past the end of the road southward along the beach to the outlet of the Tijuana River. Look across to a sandbar where gulls and terns are usually resting. Elegant Terns and an occasional Gull-billed Tern are often in this group in summer. Next, walk over to the ocean to check for Sanderling, Whimbrel, and Willet. On the way back, walk along the beach. Stay below the high-tide line (April through August) to protect nesting Snowy Plovers and Least Terns.

If you could not find a parking place on Seacoast Drive, try the usually less-crowded south end of 5th Street, which is accessible from Imperial Beach Boulevard. By walking south along the fence-line to Ream Field (helicopter airport), you will reach the river mouth, where large numbers of American Wigeon can be found in winter, including an occasional Eurasian Wigeon. This may also be the best place in the state to still find a stray Reddish Egret or even a Tricolored Heron. Little Blue Herons are regular.

Return to Imperial Beach Boulevard (which soon becomes Coronado Avenue) and turn right. At Hollister Street (2.3), turn right toward the **Tijuana River Valley**, a famous (but declining) area for rare and unexpected birds. By closely checking all of the habitats, you can nearly always find something unusual in this valley, especially during fall migration (September and October).

The best birding is on the farms, which cover the less than five square miles of riverbottom. The best thing to do is to drive up and down as many of the roads as you can and check every field, weed-patch, and row of trees. Tanagers, orioles, and other medium-sized birds are usually found in the tamarisk trees and orchards. The warblers, vireos, and other small birds also like the trees, but are often found in stands of Tree Tobacco, Fennel, and Bladderpod. Mountain Plovers, Mountain Bluebirds, pipits (including an occasional Red-throated in October), larks, and rarely longspurs show a preference for newly-plowed fields, especially those covered with manure. Finches, buntings, sparrows, and other seed-eaters like the weed-patches and tomato fields.

At the south end of Hollister Street is Monument Road (2.3), which parallels the Mexican border. To the right is **Border Field State Park**. The weedy fields between Hollister Street and the park are usually good for Lesser Goldfinch, California Quail, and, in winter, Short-eared Owl. You should be able to spot a Black-shouldered Kite somewhere in the area. Check the brushy hillsides along the road to the park for California Thrasher, Wrentit, California Gnatcatcher, and Golden-crowned Sparrow (winter) and the patches of Tree Tobacco and Bladderpod for Anna's, Black-chinned, Costa's, Allen's, and Rufous Hummingbirds. Lawrence's Goldfinches are regularly found here in March and April.

As you enter the park, you can make only a left turn. Drive as far as you can to the extreme southwest corner of the continental United States. This is an excellent place from which to view the marshland at the south end of the Tijuana Slough and look out over the ocean to the Los Coronados Islands (Mexico).

After you have worked the valley from one end to the other, go east on Monument Road until you come to Dairy Mart Road (2.8). Turn left to the Montgomery Freeway (I-5) (1.2). Just before you reach the interstate, check the usually very good ponds and riparian growth along the river on both sides of Dairy Mart Road. Least Bitterns and Great-tailed Grackles both nest here, and Northern Waterthrushes have been found here in winter. Then take Interstate 5 north toward San Diego.

At this point you may want to take a side trip to visit the **Otay Lakes** east of here. The drive to the lakes and beyond is a pleasant tour through a rural part of San Diego County. To get there, turn east on Highway 117 (1.0) to I-805 (2.0), north to Telegraph Canyon Road (4.0), and right (east) to the lakes (8.0).

Turn right on Wueste Road (3.6) to Lower Otay Lake, which usually has more fishermen than ducks. However, you should be able to compare the Western and Clark's Grebes since both occur here. You should also be able to find Western and Cassin's Kingbirds and Northern Oriole in the eucalyptus trees and Lark Sparrow along the fence-line. The Otay Lake County Campground is located at the end of the road (3.0). Return to the junction and turn right. In one-half mile the road curves back south between the two lakes, and at milepost 4.5 you will find a pulloff where

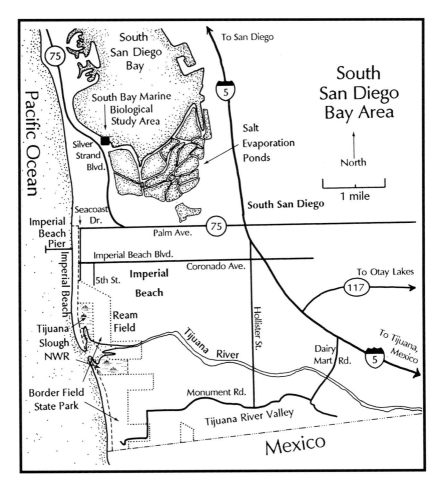

you should stop and park. Walk carefully through the chaparral toward the lake on your right. This entire area has numerous California Gnatcatchers. Also check the reeds at the lake for Virginia Rail and Sora.

When you are ready to continue the loop, return to northbound I-5, and exit at Palm Avenue (Highway 75) (1.4). Drive west and north to the best birding spot on the Silver Strand, the **South Bay Marine Biological Study Area** (3.5). Elegant Terns can be found here nesting on the dikes. Other birds to look for in migration or winter are Semipalmated and Black-bellied Plovers, Ruddy Turnstone, Long-billed Curlew, Whimbrel, Willet, Greater Yellowlegs, Red Knot, Dunlin, Short-billed Dowitcher,

Marbled Godwit, American Avocet, Black-necked Stilt, and Least and Western Sandpipers. Black Skimmers are year-round residents.

Continue north on Highway 75 along the Silver Strand. The State Beach (2.0) (camping; fee) is kept too clean for birds, but there are often resting flocks of gulls. You should be able to pick out Glaucous-winged, Heermann's, and Mew Gulls in winter, or even a Thayer's.

You will see the Coronado City Hall on your right (4.0). Stop in its parking lot and walk behind the National Guard building. In winter there are usually loons and grebes. It is always worth checking through the large numbers of Surf Scoters on San Diego Bay for an occasional White-winged or Black, or even an Oldsquaw. Check the rocky fill for Black Turnstone and Spotted Sandpiper. Three blocks north is the very ornate Hotel del Coronado (built in 1888) on the left. Follow Highway 75 across the San Diego-Coronado Bay Bridge (toll) and turn north onto I-5 (4.2).

At the junction of I-5 and I-8, you have several options. The closest birding area is **Presidio Park** in San Diego's Old Town. To reach it turn east onto I-8. Exit immediately at Taylor Street, which skirts the park. Turn left on Juan Street and follow the signs for the Serra Museum. If you wander around among the beautiful trees and down the hill behind the museum, you should find lots of birds (early morning is best).

Your second choice from the intersection of I-5 and I-8 is to explore **La Jolla and Torrey Pines**, which can be extremely productive. The rocky shoreline at La Jolla is not only very scenic, but also can be good for shorebirds and gulls in winter. To reach La Jolla, drive north on I-5 and exit at Ardath Road (6.8). By following the arrows for the scenic route, you can easily find the rocks and coves near the downtown area. Park at the lifeguard station just south of Point La Jolla; from the rocks there you may be able to see pelagic birds flying by offshore.

Deep water just off the La Jolla coast makes it the best location in the county for observing seabirds. In winter you can regularly see large numbers (up to 1,000) of Black-vented Shearwaters from here along with occasional Northern Fulmar, Sooty and Short-tailed Shearwaters, Red Phalarope, Pomarine and Parasitic Jaegers, Black-legged Kittiwake, Common Murre, and Rhinoceros Auklet. All three San Diego County records for Fork-tailed Storm-Petrel were seen from here. All three species of loons, along with all three species of cormorants and Royal Terns, are common at the appropriate times of year, and the rocky shore attracts Wandering Tattlers, Black Turnstones, Surfbirds, and even an occasional Black Oystercatcher. Magnificent Frigatebirds have been seen around the boats fishing close to shore in July and August. Sabine's Gulls are somewhat regular here in September.

When you get to Torrey Pines Road, drive east until you can turn north onto La Jolla Shore Drive, again following the scenic-route arrows. There is an interesting aquarium at the Scripps Institute of Oceanography (1.3) on the left, and also a very good bookstore. Bear left onto North Torrey Pines Road (1.2) and left again onto the Pacific Coast Highway (S21) (1.2).

Torrey Pines State Reserve (4.3) (fee) was set aside to protect the rare pine that grows only here and on Santa Rosa Island. It is a good area for chaparral birds. You should be able to find Scrub Jay, Wrentit, California Towhee, and California Thrasher. The latter is particularly abundant around the picnic area and along the trails. Rufous-crowned Sparrow is resident around the lower parking lot and visitors' center. Down the beach to the south and out of the park is one of the few clothes-optional beaches in the nation. Judging from the number of binoculars seen in use along the cliffs, this must be a popular area for birders.

Time permitting, another option is a visit to the riparian woods at the **Old Mission Dam Historical Site** on the San Diego River about 14 miles to the east. Here, among the Western Sycamores and Fremont Cottonwoods, you should find Nuttall's Woodpecker, Red-shouldered Hawk, and American and Lesser Goldfinches. In summer, also look for Bell's Vireo, Ash-throated Flycatcher, Yellow-breasted Chat, and Hooded and Northern Orioles. Rufous-crowned Sparrows are found on the rocky hillsides. During migration, you might find anything.

To reach the dam site, go east on I-8 and exit at Mission Gorge Road (5.7). Go under the freeway and follow Mission Gorge Road for about 7 miles. As you descend a long hill, you will see some ponds ahead. At the bottom of the hill turn left onto the Father Junipero Serra Trail and proceed to the dam-site parking lot on your left (1.5). A breeding colony of Grasshopper Sparrows is located in the rolling grasslands on the far side of the river. You can locate them by their buzzing song, which is heard from April into June. To reach the far side of the river follow the trail downstream from the parking area to the foot-bridge crossing the river.

If your next birding stop is the Laguna Mountains area, retrace your route to I-8 and get onto the freeway eastbound. To return to the starting point in San Diego, westbound I-8 and northbound I-5 will take you there.

There is one public campground on this loop at Silver Strand State Beach; motels are numerous. Check at the Mission Bay Information Station, call the Chamber of Commerce, or look in the Yellow Pages or the AAA Camping Guide for the location of private camping and trailer facilities. One such facility that has camping for tents, trailers, and RVs is located on the north side of Mission Bay.

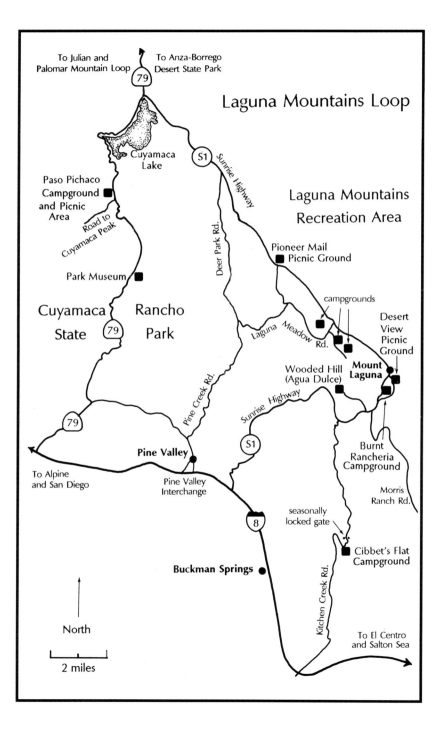

To Julian and
Palomar Mountain Loop

To Anza-Borrego
Desert State Park

79

Laguna Mountains Loop

Cuyamaca
Lake

S1

Sunrise Highway

Laguna Mountains
Recreation Area

Paso Pichaco
Campground
and Picnic
Area

Road to
Cuyamaca Peak

Deer Park Rd.

Pioneer Mail
Picnic Ground

campgrounds

Desert
View
Picnic
Ground

Park Museum

Cuyamaca

State

79

Rancho

Park

Laguna Meadow Rd.

Wooded Hill
(Agua Dulce)

**Mount
Laguna**

Pine Creek Rd.

Sunrise Highway

79

S1

Burnt
Rancheria
Campground

Pine Valley

Pine Valley
Interchange

Morris
Ranch Rd.

To Alpine
and San Diego

8

seasonally
locked gate

Cibbet's Flat
Campground

Buckman Springs

Kitchen Creek Rd.

North

2 miles

To El Centro
and Salton Sea

LAGUNA MOUNTAINS LOOP

Two major north-south mountain ranges separate the Pacific coast from the deserts of interior San Diego County, both just over 6,000 feet in elevation. The Laguna Mountains, the easternmost of the ranges, has a more arid climate since cool, wet air coming from the Pacific Ocean loses much of its moisture to the westernmost range, the Cuyamaca Mountains (quee-yah-MAH-cah).

Predominant vegetation types in the Laguna Mountains are chaparral, oak pine woodland, and grassy meadows. Rocky outcroppings, intermittent streams, and scattered marshy and lake areas add variety and punctuate the landscape. Summers are pleasant, mostly sunny, and warm, except when monsoon winds bring clouds, lightning, and some rain. In autumn the nights turn cooler, and winter brings snow—mostly after November—and most of the year's rain.

Begin at the junction of Interstate 8 and Route S1 (Sunrise Highway), 41 miles east of San Diego. Go north on S1 and stop at the Meadow Information Station (6.0), located where the road climbs into the woodlands. Birds typical of this habitat include Western Bluebird, Steller's Jay, White-breasted and Pygmy Nuthatches, and Dark-eyed Junco. Drive on, and when you reach open meadow, stop to look for Western Meadowlark, Western Bluebird, Lark Sparrow, and Lawrence's Goldfinch. In winter it is possible to find Lewis's Woodpecker and Cassin's and Purple Finches here. You will soon reach Kitchen Creek Road (1.5).

You may start this tour differently, depending on the time of year and whether you want to search for the elusive breeding Gray Vireo. The alternate route is not open the entire distance from late fall through early spring, but the drive might still be productive.

To take the alternate route, leave the freeway 6.5 miles east of the Sunrise Highway exit and go north on **Kitchen Creek Road**. The lower, more-open areas will have typical grassland birds, while the middle section of the road traverses rocky, chaparral habitat. At Cibbet's Flat Campground (4.6) there is a running creek, large oaks, and associated shrubs surrounded

103

by thick chaparral. Stop at a parking area (1.7) and walk in either direction along the creek. Mountain Quail can be found here during the winter.

A gate just beyond the end of the tarred road (0.1) is locked from late fall through early spring, but you can walk up the irregularly-maintained dirt road for several miles looking for Mountain Quail, Gray Vireo (April through June), and Black-chinned Sparrow. During April and May the Gray Vireo is singing, and it might be found anywhere in the first two miles above the gate. Its song is said to be sweeter and more liquid than that of the Solitary Vireo. If the gate is open, continue on to the junction with Route S1 (11.8), looking for Sage Sparrows along the way.

The next stop, Wooded Hill (1.2), has two campgrounds and a dirt road leading to Agua Dulce Creek, an area known to have Spotted and Northern Saw-whet Owls. Check out Burnt Rancheria Campground (1.4). The hamlet of **Mount Laguna** (0.2) has a ranger station, a restaurant, and a small market.

The cluster of campgrounds at Mt. Laguna offers a variety of habitats in a small area, increasing the variety of species you might see. Look for Red-shouldered and Red-tailed Hawks, American Kestrel, California and Mountain Quails, Band-tailed Pigeon, Anna's Hummingbird, Acorn, Nuttall's, and Hairy Woodpeckers, Red-breasted Sapsucker, Northern Flicker, Steller's and Scrub Jays, Plain Titmouse, Mountain Chickadee, White-breasted and Pygmy Nuthatches, Brown Creeper, Western Bluebird, Hermit Thrush (winter), Wrentit, California Thrasher, Hutton's Vireo, Ruby-crowned and Golden-crowned Kinglets (winter), Rufous-sided and California Towhees, Fox (winter), White-crowned (winter), and Golden-crowned (winter) Sparrows, Dark-eyed Junco, Purple Finch, and Lesser Goldfinch. In summer you might also see Olive-sided Flycatcher, Western Wood-Pewee, Violet-green Swallow, Black-chinned Sparrow, and Northern Oriole. Several coniferous-forest species (e.g., White-headed Woodpecker, Mountain Chickadee, Pygmy Nuthatch) reach their southernmost limits for California in this area.

The Mount Laguna environs are particularly valued for such species as White-headed Woodpecker, Williamson's Sapsucker (rare, winter), Purple Martin (summer), Pinyon Jay (rare, winter), and Evening Grosbeak (rare, winter).

Desert View Picnic Area (0.3) and nearby Vista Point (0.1) offer wonderful views of the desert to the east. Laguna El Prado Campground (2.4) and the Laguna Meadow Road (left turn) access an area where Evening Grosbeaks and Pinyon Jays have been found in winter. Pioneer Mail Campground is (4.0) is a pleasant picnic area.

Soon the woodland is left behind as the road drops in elevation, first into thick chaparral, and then into the wide and rolling, grassy fields north of Cuyamaca Lake. The landscape is punctuated by large live oaks and criss-crossed by fence-lines. In this habitat you may observe in spring and summer: Turkey Vulture, Red-shouldered Hawk, Golden Eagle, American Kestrel, Acorn Woodpecker, Horned Lark, Violet-green, Cliff, and Northern Rough-winged Swallows, Loggerhead Shrike, Black-headed and Blue Grosbeaks, Lazuli Bunting, Lark Sparrow, Western Meadowlark, and Lesser and Lawrence's Goldfinches. In fall and winter look for Bald Eagle (Cuyamaca Lake), Northern Harrier, Ferruginous and Rough-legged Hawks, Merlin, Prairie Falcon, Mountain Bluebird, Black and Say's Phoebes, American Pipit, Vesper and Savannah Sparrows, and Cassin's Finch.

The Sunrise Highway (S1) ends at Route 79 (7.4). *If you wish to end the loop here, you can reach Anza-Borrego Desert State Park by turning north onto Highway 79 to Julian (5.8), then right onto Highway 78 to Yaqui Well (18.2). Or continue north and west on Highway 79 at Julian, ending up at Lake Henshaw on the Palomar Mountain Loop (18.7).*

To continue this loop, go left onto Highway 79 and skirt the western shore of **Cuyamaca Lake** on your way into Cuyamaca Rancho State Park. The lake (El. 4,635 ft) is good for ducks in winter and for American Robin and Western Bluebird at any season. Check the grassy flats around the lake in winter for American Pipit and Mountain Bluebird.

The state park encloses large areas of chaparral, oak woodlands, and coniferous forests. Birding is good at almost any stop, and, depending on proper habitat, you may expect to find the same species listed previously. Perhaps the best campground for birding is the **Paso Picacho Campground and Picnic Area** (4.9). It is usually reliable for White-headed Woodpecker.

Green-tailed Towhees can be found in the brushlands along the fire road (0.1) leading to Cuyamaca Peak (El. 6,515 ft). Farther up this road (you are not allowed to drive to the summit) you should find Band-tailed Pigeon, Hairy Woodpecker, Olive-sided Flycatcher, Violet-green Swallow, Steller's Jay, Mountain Chickadee, Pygmy Nuthatch, and other mountain birds. Mountain Quail are found in the brushy terrain among Ponderosa Pines on the higher slopes.

Stop at the Park Museum (2.7) on your way back to I-8 (8.0).

If you are heading west toward San Diego, get onto westbound I-8 and go 40.9 miles to the junction of Interstates 8 and 5. If you're on your way to the Salton Sea Loop, travel east on I-8 for 77 miles to El Centro, then north on Highway 86 to Brawley (15.9) to begin that loop. Or drive another 56 miles east to Yuma, Arizona, to do the Imperial Dam Loop.

You have a good choice of campgrounds on this loop.

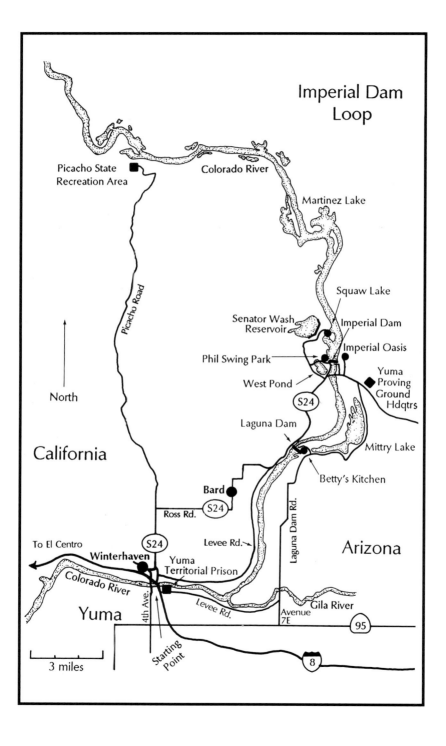

Imperial Dam Loop

Picacho State Recreation Area

Colorado River

Martinez Lake

Picacho Road

Squaw Lake

Senator Wash Reservoir

Imperial Dam

Imperial Oasis

Phil Swing Park

West Pond

Yuma Proving Ground Hdqtrs

North

S24

Laguna Dam

Mittry Lake

California

Betty's Kitchen

Bard

S24

Ross Rd.

Laguna Dam Rd.

Arizona

To El Centro

S24

Levee Rd.

Winterhaven

Yuma Territorial Prison

Colorado River

Yuma

4th Ave.

Levee Rd.

Avenue 7E

Gila River

95

Starting Point

8

3 miles

IMPERIAL DAM LOOP

The long, green oasis created by the Colorado River has been used for countless centuries as a migration route by both men and birds. While men have developed the habit of doing what comes unnaturally and now travel from east to west, many birds still follow their ageless paths up and down the river. Human activity has replaced much of the native vegetation with farmland. Therefore, in addition to the migrants, you will now find many wintering and breeding species.

Many birders come during the cool winters, when there are concentrations of waterfowl. Even more come during the migration periods of April and early May and late August through October. A few hardy souls brave the summer heat, for this area is near the western limit for several breeding birds, such as Lucy's Warbler. In late summer there is always a slim chance of finding a rare straggler from Mexico, such as a booby or a Roseate Spoonbill.

The starting point is Interstate 8 and the 4th Avenue exit in Yuma. Go west toward Winterhaven and turn right at the stop sign (0.4) onto Picacho Road (S24). Cross a canal and then jog left (0.2) under the railroad tracks.

The road now crosses farmlands, usually empty of birds unless the fields are being irrigated. Wherever you find water in the desert, you will find birds. During migration, shorebirds may congregate by the hundreds on irrigated fields. Follow the main road (S24) as it swings right onto Ross Road (3.6) toward Bard.

If you are an adventuresome type, you can follow Picacho Road straight ahead to Picacho State Recreation Area (19.0). The road is sometimes rough and always dusty. It passes through a barren but beautiful land of rocky canyons and multicolored mountains. The park, located on the banks of the Colorado River, is small with few facilities and is a delightful place to camp.

As you travel through the Bard valley you will notice groves of citrus trees and Date Palms. They offer nesting sites for Gila Woodpecker, Gilded Northern Flicker (rare), Barn Owl, White-winged Dove, Hooded Oriole, and the ever-present European Starling and House Sparrow. The side roads in this area are worth exploring at any time of year. Resident species include Common Ground-Dove, Inca Dove, Greater Roadrunner, and

107

Phainopepla. Ruddy Ground-Dove has been seen here twice in recent years. However, if you're in a hurry, stay on S24 as it winds its way toward the river.

Laguna Dam (9.7) was the first of many dams across the Colorado River. The brushy river valley between it and Imperial Dam can be entered by several dirt roads. The conifer-like Salt-cedars or Tamarisks, native trees of Asia, are abundant here, along with palo verde and willow trees. Scan the area for the reintroduced Harris's Hawk (see *Specialties of Southern California* section), Ladder-backed Woodpecker, Crissal Thrasher, Verdin, Black-tailed Gnatcatcher, Phainopepla, Lucy's Warbler, and Abert's Towhee.

At Senator Wash Road (3.7) turn left. After crossing the All-American Canal (0.25), you will see **West Pond** on your right with several dirt roads leading to it. This small lake can be good for Black Rail (a difficult-to-see resident), Least Bittern, other freshwater-marsh species, and sometimes a rarity or two.

At McKinley Road (0.75) turn right toward Imperial Dam. Another entrance to West Pond takes off at 0.5. Imperial Dam is at the end of McKinley Road at Phil Swing Park (0.75), a little spot with tables, restrooms, and drinking water. Part of the lake above the dam is visible from here. Most of it is silted in and supports a vast stand of cattails. If you should happen to be here on a spring evening, you may be treated to the sight of thousands of swallows coming to roost in the marsh. The few Date Palms are also worth checking. The first California records of Great-tailed Grackle (now common) and Rufous-backed Robin were of birds that wintered in these trees. At dawn and dusk listen and watch for Lesser Nighthawks.

After checking the little park, return to Senator Wash Road. Turn right and go past Senator Wash Reservoir and over the dam (2.3). Below the dam is an inlet of the Colorado River known as Squaw Lake. There is a nice campground here, and a few birds.

Return to Imperial Road (3.3), turn left, and cross the Colorado River to the Arizona side. (If you keep state lists, you will have to shuffle them a few times on this loop.) After crossing the river, turn left (0.8) onto a paved road and follow it to where it ends at the base of the dam (0.6). There is a small lake with picnic tables and grills. Check the lake and canals for herons, egrets, and waterfowl. Return to the main road, turn left, and (after crossing another bridge) turn left onto a paved road (0.1). This road ends at Imperial Oasis Concessions (0.9) (store, cafe, and boat rentals). There are always a few Gambel's Quail running around the trailer park, and you may find an active bird-feeder or two.

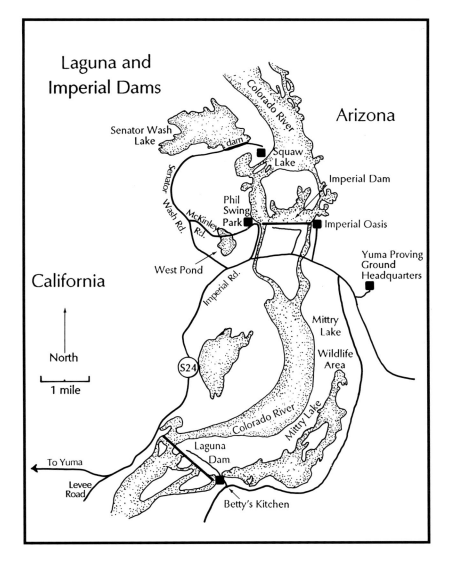

Laguna and
Imperial Dams

Arizona

Colorado River

Senator Wash
Lake

dam

Squaw
Lake

Imperial Dam

Senator Wash Rd.

McKinley Rd.

Phil
Swing
Park

Imperial Oasis

California

West Pond

Yuma Proving
Ground
Headquarters

Imperial Rd.

North

Mittry
Lake

1 mile

S24

Wildlife
Area

Colorado River

Mittry Lake

To Yuma

Laguna
Dam

Levee
Road

Betty's Kitchen

As you leave Imperial Oasis, you will again cross over the Gila Irrigation Canal. After crossing, turn left and drive along the canal levee. Watch for birds on the sides of the canal on the left and in the marsh and the stand of mature cottonwood trees on your right. Cross the paved highway (1.0) near the Yuma Proving Ground Headquarters and continue on the west levee of the canal.

Follow the levee through the **Mittry Lake Wildlife Area**. The extensive marsh on the right contains large concentrations of waterfowl in the winter. At wide points in the road stop and check the tules for Common Moorhen, Red-winged and Yellow-headed Blackbirds, and in summer for Least Bittern. The endangered Yuma race of Clapper Rail can be found here, along with Black and Virginia Rails and Sora. The easiest way to attempt observing them in the thick tule growth is to play a tape of their calls. In summer look for Northern Oriole; Brown-crested (rare), Ash-throated, and Vermilion Flycatchers, Phainopepla, Blue Grosbeak, and rarely Cassin's Kingbird. Check the mesquite for Verdin and Lucy's Warbler. In migration, you may find anything.

As you approach the Arizona side of Laguna Dam, turn right at the sign for Betty's Kitchen Wildlife Interpretive Area (6.1). Follow the signs to the parking area (0.2). There are picnic tables, restrooms, and a nature trail. During migration this is an excellent place to see flycatchers, vireos, warblers, tanagers, buntings, sparrows, and orioles. A dock overlooking the back of the dam can provide good views of Common Moorhen, Least and Spotted Sandpipers, and Green-backed Heron.

Walk or drive west, past the parking area, to some irrigated fields (0.1). Keep going west along the south edge of the fields to a grove of trees surrounding an abandoned house. You are now in California again. Check the area for Harris's Hawk, Hooded Oriole, Abert's Towhee, Greater Roadrunner, and several kinds of sparrows. The river is to the north on the other side of the fields.

Return to Mittry Lake Road and turn right. After 0.4 miles the road is again paved and passes through irrigated farmland. This road is now called the Laguna Dam Road. Stay on this road as it winds to the south. It soon crosses what is left of the Gila River (7.0) and comes to the south levee of the Colorado River (0.2).

If you have had enough of dirt roads, continue south on what is now called Avenue 7E to Highway 95 (2.0). Turn right toward Yuma. At Interstate 8 (4.0) you can turn right and go back to the starting point.

Otherwise, turn right onto the south levee of the Gila River. The river will be on your right, and a concrete-lined canal will be on your left. Shortly (2.5), the road jogs and continues with the canal, now on the right side. With a little luck this can be a rewarding drive. Greater Roadrunner, Burrowing Owl, doves, and quail are plentiful. The levee ends at the Yuma Territorial Prison State Park (6.6). During migration the trees at the park may contain some good birds. A backwater of the river on your right at the end of the levee road often has White-faced Ibis, Clapper Rail, pelicans, egrets, herons, Common Moorhens, and other birds.

Interstate 8 will take you back to the starting point.

To reach Brawley, the starting point for the Salton Sea Loop, drive west on I-8 to the Highway 86 exit in El Centro (56.4), and take it north to Brawley (15.9).

The only improved campground is at Squaw Lake, but there is plenty of open space in which to camp. Motels are abundant in Yuma.

Yuma Clapper Rail
Charles H. Gambill

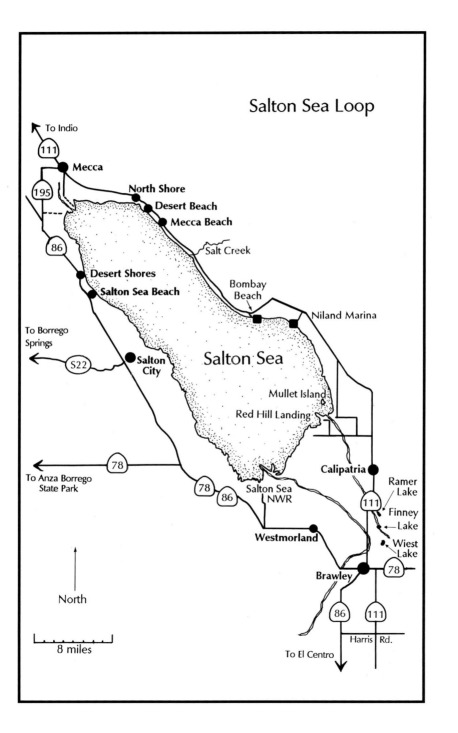

Salton Sea Loop

To Indio

111

Mecca

195

86

North Shore

Desert Beach

Mecca Beach

Salt Creek

Desert Shores

Salton Sea Beach

Bombay Beach

Niland Marina

To Borrego Springs

S22

Salton City

Salton Sea

Mullet Island

Red Hill Landing

78

Calipatria

Ramer Lake

111

Finney Lake

To Anza Borrego State Park

78

86

Salton Sea NWR

Wiest Lake

Westmorland

Brawley

78

North

86

111

Harris Rd.

8 miles

To El Centro

SALTON SEA LOOP

The Salton Trough, extending from Palm Springs south into the Gulf of California, is part of a rift valley created by the uplifting of the mountains. Millions of years ago the delta of the Colorado River created a dam across the gulf, isolating the trough. The basin has since been dry or filled with intermittent lakes, depending on the vagaries of the river. The last great lake to fill the basin was Lake Cahuilla, about 160 miles long and 35 miles wide. It lasted for roughly 450 years until A.D. 1500

In the 1880s, the feasibility of bringing water from the Colorado River to irrigate the dry, fertile (the sediments are 8,000 feet thick!) delta was recognized. By 1901 a 40-mile canal had been opened along an old course of the river. Soon 300,000 acres were being cultivated. In 1905, a flood, one of the many which plagued the river before the dams were built, caused the channel to shift until the entire river was diverted into the canal. Some 63 billion gallons of water a day poured into the dry lake bed. After 18 months, the river was finally turned back, but a lake 35 miles long and 15 miles wide had been formed. The Salton Sea was born!

As excess water from the irrigation projects continued to run into the lake, what had been a land of burning sand became a lush valley filled with birds.

The soil surrounding Salton Sea is very alkaline, and today farmers must continually leach out the salts by allowing fresh water to run over their fields. This salt-laden water runs into rivers such as the Alamo, New, and Whitewater and then into the Salton Sea, which gets saltier every year. This over-abundance of salt plus the pesticides from the farms may eventually make it a dead sea. Of the numerous fish that were introduced, only the Orange-mouthed Corvina, Gulf Croaker, and Sargo have successfully survived, and even they are declining.

The temperatures may be more bearable in winter, but the birding is good all year. At any season you can find herons, shorebirds, gulls, and a scattering of landbirds. Some of the more enticing year-round birds are Western and Clark's Grebes, American White Pelican, Cattle Egret, White-faced Ibis, Cinnamon Teal, Ruddy Duck, Gambel's Quail, Yuma Clapper Rail, American Avocet, Black-necked Stilt, Common

113

Ground-Dove, Greater Roadrunner, Burrowing Owl, Gila and Ladder-backed Woodpeckers, Black Phoebe, Verdin, Cactus and Marsh Wrens, Black-tailed Gnatcatcher, Crissal Thrasher, and Abert's Towhee.

In summer look for Fulvous Whistling-Duck, Gull-billed Tern, Black Skimmer, White-winged Dove, Lesser Nighthawk, Black-chinned Hummingbird, Western Kingbird, Blue Grosbeak, and Yellow-headed Blackbird. In late June and July there is an influx of birds from Mexico, such as Wood Stork (confined to the south end) and Yellow-footed and Laughing Gulls. Magnificent Frigatebirds are seen every year, while Brown and Blue-footed Boobies and Roseate Spoonbill show up sporadically.

In winter up to a half-million ducks of some 15 species are in the valley, as well as some 30 to 50 thousand geese, including Snow, Ross's, and Canada. Shorebirds are common and landbirds easy to find. A few of the more interesting winter visitors are Eared Grebe, Ferruginous Hawk, Sandhill Crane, Mountain Plover, Long-billed Curlew, Costa's Hummingbird, Say's Phoebe, Mountain Bluebird, Orange-crowned Warbler, and Brewer's and Sage Sparrows.

During the migration seasons, particularly in spring, millions of birds pass through the valley. Swallows sometimes line the telephone wires by the thousands. Irrigated fields may be covered by hundreds of egrets,

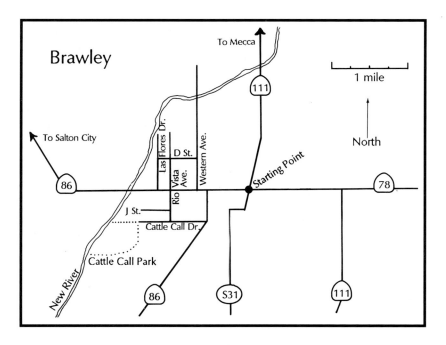

shorebirds, and gulls. American White Pelicans can be seen in large flocks, and Eared Grebes form huge rafts on the sea. If you hit just the right day in spring, every tree and brush-pile may be brightly colored with warblers, tanagers, grosbeaks, buntings, and orioles. Of course, with such a mass of birds, you may find something outstanding.

The starting point is the intersection of Highways 78 and 111 in downtown Brawley (El. minus 113 ft). Birding the Brawley area itself can be very rewarding, especially in winter months (October to March). Go west on Highway 78/86 to Western Avenue and turn right (north) two blocks to D Street. Turn left and continue to Las Flores Drive. Park and walk north. On your right you will see a small Date Palm grove. Here you may find such special birds as Barn Owl, Gila Woodpecker, Verdin, Cactus Wren, Black-tailed Gnatcatcher, and Abert's Towhee along with the more common species. Check the residential area north and east of the grove for Inca Dove and Common Ground-Dove.

Return east on D Street to Rio Vista Avenue and turn right (south), cross Highway 78/86, and go three blocks to J Street, then park and walk. This residential area is always good for Gila Woodpeckers, most easily found by their noise. A number of unexpected birds such as Solitary Vireo, Yellow and Black-throated Gray Warblers, American Redstart, Hooded Oriole, and even Red Crossbill have been known to over-winter here. This is a most productive area in April and early May when flowering Bottlebrush attracts many hummingbirds, including Calliope Hummingbird.

Continue south to Cattle Call Drive and turn right to Cattle Call Park. This area, too, is good for Gila Woodpecker and Common Ground-Dove, and, in summer, Bronzed Cowbird is regular.

A special treat in winter is watching Sandhill Cranes come in to roost. Drive south from Brawley on Highway 86 to Harris Road (7.3). Turn left (east) and go about 3.5 miles to just short of Highway 111. Plan to arrive at least one hour before sunset. The cranes may be feeding in any of the fields in this area and normally fly to the duck club on Harris Road just west of Highway 111, to the north and behind a row of shrubs. Large flocks of White-faced Ibis, egrets, and gulls also fly in.

When you are ready to continue the tour, go west from Brawley on Highway 78/86 through Westmorland (6.7) to Vendel Road (5.0). At this corner you will find a small market on the right with a date grove behind. Barn Owls and, in summer, Hooded Orioles may be found here. Just beyond Vendel is Garvey Road going left over the canal. Take this dirt road as it follows the canal for a half-mile. In the thickets check for Crissal Thrasher, Black-tailed Gnatcatcher, Abert's Towhee, and other birds of the desert scrub.

Retrace your route to Highway 78/86 and turn left onto it. Drive north 2.2 miles to Poe Road and turn right. In 1.4 miles you will reach the southern shore of the Salton Sea. The birding may be good here.

Return on Highway 78/86 to Vendel Road, a good dirt road, and go left (north), watching along the way for Burrowing Owls at any season and in winter for Mountain Plover, Mountain Bluebird, Horned Lark, and Savannah Sparrow. The road ends at the gate to Unit 1 of the **Salton Sea National Wildlife Refuge** (3.5). This area of man-made ponds and fields is open all year (no hunting). Park at the gate and continue north on foot to the sea. This is the most southern tip of the sea, just west of the New River delta. The ponds here were built to shelter and feed the thousands of migrant and wintering waterfowl. The rare Yuma Clapper Rail nests here, along with Least Bittern (uncommon), Cinnamon Teal, Redhead, Ruddy Duck, Black Rail (very rare), and others. Songbirds will be found in the Salt-cedars and cattails. In winter look for Stilt Sandpiper (rare) among the large numbers of Long-billed Dowitchers, and you can expect White-faced Ibis along with many Snow, Ross's, and Canada Geese.

Drive south on Vendel Road to Bannister Road (2.5) and turn left (east) to Kalin Road (7.5), jog right to Rutherford Road (0.2), and left (east) toward Wiest Lake. Just east of Highway 111 you will pass a large cattle pen teeming with blackbirds. Check for Red-winged, Brewer's, and even Yellow-headed. Of course, there will be plenty of Brown-headed Cowbirds, and frequently Cattle Egrets. Great-tailed Grackles, also present, have recently moved into the valley.

Wiest Lake Imperial County Park (fee; camping) (5.0) is usually bare, but sometimes flocks of Black Terns occur in migration. Retrace your route to the cattle pen and turn right by the railroad tracks onto Kershaw Road. Check beside the grain elevators for Common Ground-Doves.

Turn right on Titsworth Road (2.2) and right again on Smith Road (0.2) toward **Finney Lake** (0.6). Bear right at the T-intersection, then left, and continue through the primitive camping area to a high spot from which you can look over the tules. Explore the network of dirt roads and dikes around the numerous ponds. Except during the hunting season (November to January), ducks frequent the site. Fulvous Whistling-Duck, Wood Stork (post-nesting visitor), and Black Rail (rare) may be found here in summer, along with the more numerous herons, egrets, and Common Moorhens. Be sure to work the patches of Saltbush and Honey Mesquite for White-winged Dove, Ladder-backed Woodpecker, Crissal Thrasher, Verdin, Cactus Wren, Phainopepla, Abert's Towhee, and Gambel's Quail. This desert quail resembles the California Quail, but can be separated by the decidedly red cap. Hunters call them "redheads".

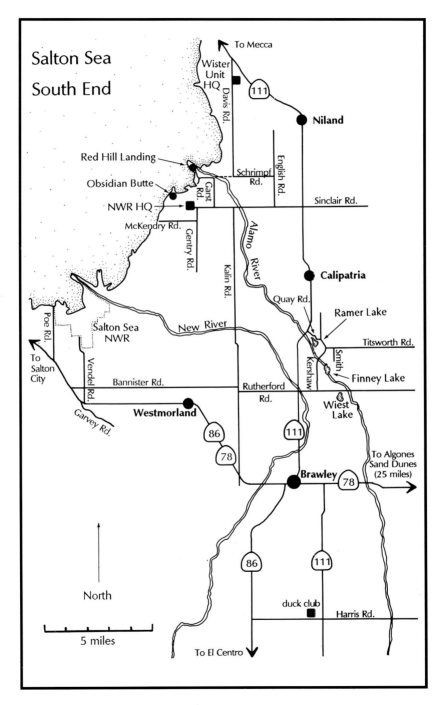

Salton Sea
South End

Return to Kershaw Road, turn right to Quay Road (0.6), then left to **Ramer Lake** (0.2). It used to be more productive than Finney Lake, but it is temporarily quite dry while the area is under reconstruction. To the left is a levee across the lake. When the lake has water again, a walk on this dike will be a good way to see the Fulvous Whistling-Duck. Do not walk here during the hunting season. Continue west on Quay Road to check the rest of the lake. Just before you reach the highway, there is a patch of mesquite that usually has Abert's Towhee and Crissal Thrasher, and is good for Phainopepla in winter.

Turn right onto Highway 111 (0.8) (there is a rest stop to the left just across the river) to Calipatria (2.8) (El. minus 184 ft), "the lowest-down town in the Western Hemisphere." The people of the town built the world's highest free-standing flagpole so the flag would fly above sea level. You can't miss seeing it one block to the left of the highway.

Continue north to Sinclair Road (3.8) and turn left toward Red Hill Landing. The banks of the irrigation ditches along this road are very attractive to the Round-tailed Ground-Squirrel and its guest, the Burrowing Owl.

The **Salton Sea National Wildlife Refuge** headquarters (PO Box 120, Calipatria, CA 92233; Phone: 619/348-5278) are located at the end of Sinclair Road at its intersection with Gentry Road (5.6). The refuge personnel are very courteous and can be helpful in locating the birds of the area (closed on weekends). A checklist and information about which areas are open to birding are available at the bulletin board.

The bushes and trees around the buildings are good for Verdin, Cactus Wren, and Abert's Towhee, and the observation tower is a good place from which to observe the area beyond for waterfowl. In spring migration the area teems with birds. In winter the refuge hosts thousands of ducks and geese. During the hunting season, you can often see great flocks right behind the headquarters, where they are safe.

Walk west past the headquarters for half a mile on Seaside Trail and turn right to the observation station up on Rock Hill. From here you can see a portion of the south end of the sea where there are usually quite a few ducks. Stilt Sandpipers can sometimes be found in the shallow ponds in migration and winter. These freshwater ponds formed naturally behind dikes of washed-up barnacles. The barnacles were introduced accidentally into the Salton Sea by the floats of seaplanes conducting training activities here during World War II. The ponds provide nesting-sites for Clark's and Western Grebes. During July and August watch for Laughing Gull. Gull-billed Terns and Black Skimmers can also be seen from here, but look northeast and you can see Red Hill; both species regularly nest to the east of it. Look to the southeast and you will see Obsidian Butte and cove. You can drive to the cove by taking Gentry Road south from headquarters and turning right on McKendry Road. Both the Alamo River delta at Red Hill and Obsidian Cove are good areas for Yellow-footed Gull in summer, and in winter when it is considered rare.

Retrace your route on Sinclair Road to Garst Road (1.0) and turn left. Follow the signs to **Red Hill Landing** (2.0) ($2.00 fee), one of the best spots on the loop. In the shallows of the causeway ponds and on the sea (El. currently minus 226 ft), you should find numerous ducks, gulls, terns, and shorebirds. The mouth of the Alamo River here is the best area on the sea to find Wood Stork in summer. The campground is not deluxe but is adequate.

When returning from Red Hill Landing, if the water is low and the road is dry, you may be able to take a shortcut to Davis Road by turning left at Garst Road, then turning right immediately across the bridge over the Alamo River onto Schrimpf Road, and then left onto Davis Road (1.0), saving 7 miles. By taking this route you will pass the area where Gull-billed Terns and Black Skimmers regularly nest. If you cannot drive this route, return to Sinclair Road and turn left. Turn left onto English Road (3.0), left onto Schrimpf Road (1.5), and right onto Davis Road (2.0). Up ahead on the right, you will see some old adobe buildings (1.4) that were once part of a mineral-water spa. This area had a number of hot springs, which are now being tapped for thermal energy at several hard-to-overlook facilities. This is an excellent location for studying shorebirds and is where a number of the area's Semipalmated Sandpipers have been found in spring.

White-winged Ring-necked Pheasants have been introduced (and immediately shot; new stock is released every year) in the fields near the headquarters of the **Wister Unit** of the State Imperial Wildlife Area (4.5) (open to the public except during hunting season; camping; fee; pick up checklist). This Unit has over 500 acres of open water, marsh, and desert habitat, with 36 miles of criss-crossing roads. The barren fields should be checked in winter for Mountain Plover, Mountain Bluebird, American Pipit, Horned Lark, and longspurs (rare, and always with Horned Larks). Short-eared Owls can sometimes be flushed from the high weeds along the irrigation ditches. In April and May the Yuma Clapper Rail is heard as it nests. In late summer (July to mid-September) Yellow-footed Gulls are fairly common and Wood Stork is possible. Greater Roadrunners and Gambel's Quail are common residents.

At the intersection of Davis Road and Highway 111 (0.3) turn left (north) toward Mecca. The Warmwater Fish Hatchery on the left (1.6) is good in winter. Park in the parking area next to the buildings and walk the dikes.

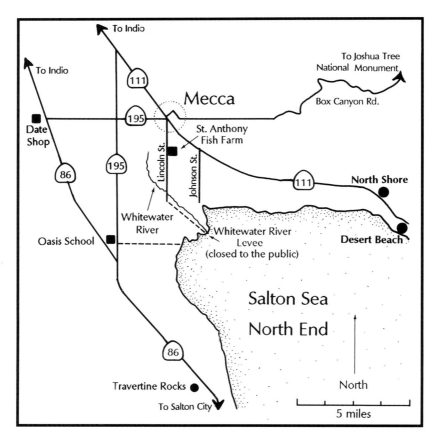

Bird each pond for ducks. This is one of the better places to see diving ducks and is where the area's only Tufted Duck was found. Brewer's Sparrow may also be present in winter. During migration five species of swallows can be seen here.

For the next 30 miles, the road parallels the east shore of the Salton Sea across a very barren stretch of desert. After the first 5 miles, the shore is all part of the **Salton Sea State Recreation Area** (fee), a mecca for swimmers, water-skiers, and boat enthusiasts, but with little to offer birders except a place to camp. If time permits, you can investigate all the side roads down to the beaches and check the shore. The better spots are at Niland Marina (6.4), Bombay Beach (5.5), Salt Creek(10.8) (check the inlet for grebes and ducks, and usually a Snowy Plover can be found), and Mecca Beach (4.9) with its numerous trees. The Recreation Area Headquarters is located at Desert Beach (1.5).

Just before reaching the town of Mecca, check the shallows at the north end of the sea by turning left onto Johnson Street (9.2) and going to where water over the road prevents you from driving farther. Here you will find numbers of ducks, waders, and shorebirds. A ditch, which is good for Green-backed Heron and small landbirds, parallels the road on the right side. Look straight down the road from your stopping point; you can see the delta of the Whitewater River. Scope it. You never know what you might find. This is the North End of the Salton Sea, and anything could show up.

Return to Highway 111, turn left, and turn left again onto Highway 195 (1.3). The highway immediately makes a right turn, but you should continue straight ahead on Lincoln Street. At the St. Anthony Fish Farm (1.0) you will see a number of ponds on your left. This is private property (the owner has been known to be very hostile to birdwatchers), so scan the many ducks and waders from the road. DO NOT TRESPASS.

Continue on Lincoln Street to where the pavement ends at the Whitewater River Levee (2.0). The levee roads are now closed to eliminate possible liability claims. NO TRESPASSING signs are everywhere. The shallow water here is good at any season, but during spring migration ducks and shorebirds often bank up before moving north, giving this area the distinction of being one of the best birding spots for finding rarities in all of Southern California. The dead tree snags provide perches for Osprey, Bald Eagle (very rare in winter), and in late summer, for Brown Booby, Magnificent Frigatebird, and Brown Pelican. Blue-footed Booby, which never perches in trees, has also been seen here. Yellow-footed Gull, a summer visitor from the Gulf of California, may be found here but is much more common along the western shore.

Return to Highway 195 and turn left. The brushy salt-flats in this area are worth checking for Black-tailed Gnatcatcher, Verdin, Crissal Thrasher (rare), and Abert's Towhee. When the highway turns left (2.0), continue straight ahead to Valerie Jean's Date Shop on Highway 86 (4.0), where you can try a date milk shake. It's different. You can also purchase locally-grown citrus and dates.

Turn left onto Highway 86 and proceed southward. At the junction with Highway 195 (7.0) turn sharp left and head back north to the Oasis School on the left (0.5). Across the highway from the school is a ditch with a dirt road on each side ending at the sea (2.0) just south of the Whitewater River delta. This is a good vantage point for viewing the North End of the Salton Sea, and as of this writing it is not posted. Return to Highway 86

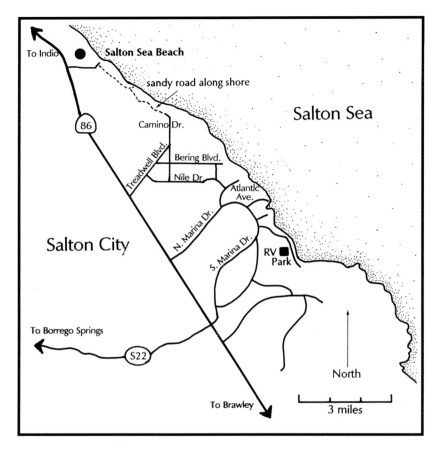

To Indio

● Salton Sea Beach

sandy road along shore

86

Camino Dr.

Treadwell Blvd.

Bering Blvd.

Nile Dr.

Atlantic Ave.

Salton Sea

N. Marina Dr.

S. Marina Dr.

RV Park

Salton City

To Borrego Springs

S22

North

To Brawley

3 miles

and continue southward. Notice the cliffs along the mountain on the right. Traces of the old waterlines of the previous lakes are still visible. You can see them very clearly on Travertine Rocks (6.0), which are near the road.

The next 40 miles of road crosses barren desert, largely out of sight of the sea. However, there are roads leading to developments along the shore. Desert Shores (1.0) and Salton Sea Beach (2.5) both offer good vantage points from which you can look over the shore and the sea. Among the gulls in summer you should be able to pick out the Yellow-footed. Always keep an open mind as to what other waterbirds may occur—Laysan Albatross and Sooty Shearwater have both been seen from Desert Shores.

To visit Salton City, turn left on North Marina Drive (5.5) and drive down to the shore. Explore the many roads leading to the shore and running along the shore. If it has not rained recently, a sandy track leading north from Camino Drive is worth investigating. A small peninsula, marked by a lamp-post with its base underwater, provides a good vantage point from which to scope the sea and the shoreline. Shorebirds, waders, pelicans, and gulls may be numerous here. In Salton City you will notice that many buildings have been abandoned since the water level has risen in recent years. This is a good place to find Yellow-footed Gull in summer, with a few present into early winter. North Marina Drive becomes South Marina Drive, which will take you back to the highway opposite the road (S22) leading west to Borrego Springs. If you are returning to Brawley, turn left and follow Highway 86. *If you wish to visit the Anza-Borrego Desert State Park, take Route S22 to Borrego Springs.*

There are motels in Brawley, El Centro, North Shore, and Indio. Campgrounds range from the primitive one at Finney Lake and the Wister Unit of the Imperial Wildlife Area to the Wiest Lake County Park and the ones at Salton Sea State Recreation Area. The campground at Red Hill Landing may smell of fish, but it is in the best birding area. Also, a good improved campground is located at Salton City.

Blue-footed Booby
Charles H. Gambill

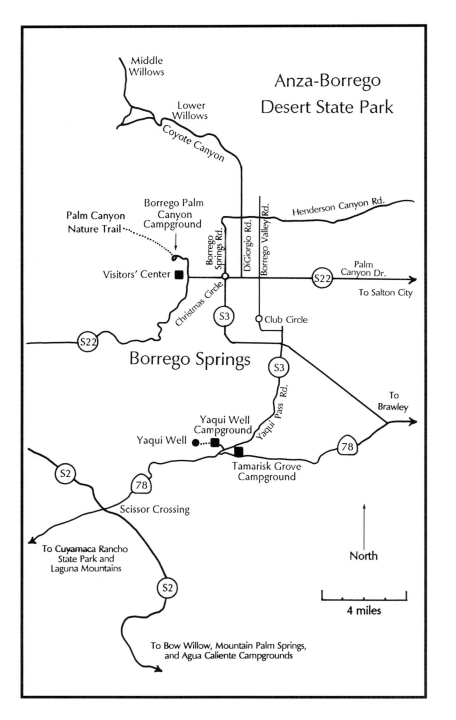

ANZA-BORREGO DESERT STATE PARK

Visitors to California's largest State Park are urged to "...go out into the desert and let the silence, light, and space weave their spells..." Birders are also well-advised to take time to explore this 600,000-acre park, 80 miles east of San Diego and 25 miles west of the Salton Sea. Seventy miles long and 32 miles wide, Anza-Borrego is the largest jewel in the California State Park system. Its varied terrain includes mountains, desert, dry lakes, creosote scrub, palm groves, and a few riparian areas, each with its representative assortment of plant and bird life. Some 230 species of birds have been found here.

Although this short chapter serves as a "bridge" between the Salton Sea and Joshua Tree National Monument loops, it could just as easily link up with the Palomar Mountain Loop, the San Jacinto Mountains Loop, or with the nearby, and short, Laguna Mountains Loop.

If you enter **Anza-Borrego Desert State Park** by way of Highway S2 from Ocotillo on Interstate 8, several campgrounds (all on the south side of S2) offer good birding along the route. Bow Willow has Rock Wren and offers a opportunity for LeConte's Thrasher and Brewer's Sparrow. At Mountain Palm Springs you may find Western Bluebird and Scott's Oriole in winter. The mesquite in and around the campground at Agua Caliente County Park attracts a variety of birds, including White-winged Dove. Ask the county rangers for birding tips.

Anza-Borrego Desert State Park surrounds the town of Borrego Springs, population 2,700, which doubles during the winter season. From whichever direction you enter the park, your first stop should be at the State Park Visitor Center. From Christmas Circle in the heart of the town, go west on Palm Canyon Drive to the end (1.75). Here you can get maps, a bird list, and other information about the park. Some birds found near the visitor center are Costa's Hummingbird, Ladder-backed Woodpecker, Cactus Wren, and Verdin.

Return east on Palm Canyon Drive to the first road on the left (0.3), which leads to **Borrego Palm Canyon Campground.** Here and on the

125

Palm Canyon Nature Trail you should be able to find Gambel's and California Quail (watch for hybrids), Greater Roadrunner, Canyon Wren, and Black-throated Sparrow. In winter there is a good chance for American Dipper above the first California Palm grove. Bell's Vireo and Hooded Oriole nest here.

If you drive north from Christmas Circle on Borrego Springs Road, you can bird the fringes of the citrus groves and vineyards from the road. Greater Roadrunner, Gambel's Quail, Common Ground-Dove, Verdin, and Black-throated Sparrow can be found along the roadsides. In the open desert where the bushes are few and far between, look for the LeConte's Thrasher. Even though the cover is sparse, they are hard to find unless you hike around a bit. A good place to look for the thrashers is the sharp right turn where Borrego Springs Road become Henderson Canyon Road (3.3). They can also be found along the dirt road that leads up Coyote Canyon from the north end of DiGiorgio Road (1.0) (closed to visitors June 16 to September 15 to allow Bighorn Sheep undisturbed use of the water). At Lower Willows along Coyote Creek look for wintering Virginia Rail and Sora. This is a good place for migrating warblers in spring, and you might see White-winged Dove, Yellow-breasted Chat, and Blue Grosbeak as well.

In winter it may be worthwhile to check out Club Circle on Borrego Valley Road about 2 miles south of its intersection with Palm Canyon Drive. Look for wintering Scott's Orioles here; rarities such as Lewis's Woodpecker have been found in this area.

A good spot for Crissal Thrasher is located south of town. Take Highway S3 south from Christmas Circle to its intersection with Yaqui Pass Road (5.0). Keep straight at the intersection rather than bearing right with Highway S2, and turn left (north) onto Yaqui Pass Road. Drive to the dead-end (1.1), where it is possible to find Crissal Thrasher in the mesquite. This is private land, so please remain next to the road. This area may also produce Phainopepla, Brewer's and Sage Sparrows, and migrating warblers. Turn around and follow Yaqui Pass Road (Highway S3) to the Tamarisk Grove Campground (6.8). Long-eared Owls nest here in the trees during some years (February-April). Bewick's Wren may also be present here. Continue one block (just short of Highway 78) and turn right (west) up the dirt road for one-half mile to unimproved Yaqui Well Campground (free) and **Yaqui Well**, the best of the very few wet spots in the park. This road can be soft after a rain, so before entering check for signs of recent travel. If in doubt, walk. You can also reach the spring on a trail leading there from the Tamarisk Grove Campground.

This little spring attracts an unbelievable number of birds, particularly in migration. Look for California and Gambel's Quail, Greater Roadrunner,

Ladder-backed Wookpecker, Rock Wren, California and Sage Thrashers, Black-tailed and Blue-gray Gnatcatchers, Phainopepla (numerous, especially in winter around Ironwood Trees with mistletoe clumps), House Finch, and (in winter) sparrows. In migration, you can expect almost anything. Once, there were even Evening Grosbeaks here. The canyon behind the spring can be very good at times. In February and March, the air is filled with the bullet-like zings of Costa's and Anna's Hummingbirds making their courtship dives about the Chuparosa bushes.

If you want to continue birding in the desert at Joshua Tree National Monument, take Route S22 east from Borrego Springs to Salton City (29.0). Drive north on Highway 86 to Highway 111 (24.7), east to I-10 (8.2), and east to the Highway 62 exit (21.1). If you'd rather cool off on the San Jacinto Mountains Loop, follow these instructions, but continue on Interstate 10 15.4 miles farther west to Banning.

You will find motels in the town of Borrego Springs and a good selection of campgrounds along the birding route.

Costa's Hummingbirds
Shawneen Finnegan

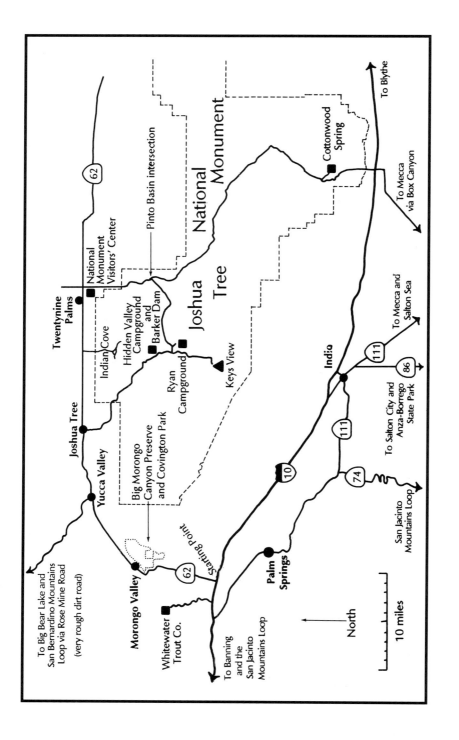

To Blythe

Cottonwood
Spring

To Mecca
via Box Canyon

Joshua Tree National Monument

Pinto Basin intersection

National
Monument
Visitors' Center

Twentynine
Palms

Indian Cove

Hidden Valley
Campground
and
Barker Dam

Ryan
Campground

Keys View

Joshua Tree

Yucca Valley

Big Morongo
Canyon Preserve
and Covington Park

India

To Mecca and
Salton Sea

111

86

To Salton City and
Anza-Borrego
State Park

111

10

74

San Jacinto
Mountains Loop

To Big Bear Lake and
San Bernardino Mountains
Loop via Rose Mine Road

(very rough dirt road)

Starting point

62

Morongo Valley

Whitewater
Trout Co.

Palm
Springs

To Banning
and the
San Jacinto
Mountains Loop

North

10 miles

JOSHUA TREE NATIONAL MONUMENT LOOP

The Joshua Tree National Monument lies sprawled along the San Andreas Fault Line in a wondrous array of rocks, arid slopes, and superb desert vegetation. Its sandy washes reach to sea level in the Colorado Desert, while its austere peaks rise to almost 7,000 feet along the ridge of the Little San Bernardino Mountains in the Mojave Desert. It may look barren and forbidding, as deserts often do, but it has a strange magnetism that will draw you back again and again to explore for its treasures.

Herpetologists and botanists might find more of interest in this 575,934-acre wonderland than birders; however, there are a few streams and oases where birds are fairly numerous. For a greater appreciation of this varied area, read *Lives of Desert Animals in Joshua Tree National Monument* by Miller and Stebbins.

Most birders come during the cooler months, but many of the birds that are peculiar to the area can be found at any season. Bendire's Thrasher, Gray Vireo (rare), and Scott's Oriole are summer residents, best looked for in April, May, and June. Others such as Gray Flycatcher (uncommon), Sage Thrasher (uncommon), and Brewer's Sparrow are winter visitors from October to May. Since this area is on a major migration route, you will find the most birds in April and May and again in September and October.

The starting point is the intersection of Interstate 10 and Highway 62, some 16 miles east of Banning. Go north on Highway 62 toward Twentynine Palms. The road climbs rapidly from the low, barren Colorado Desert (El. 1,000 ft), through the Little San Bernardino Mountains, to the Mojave Desert at Morongo Valley (El. 2,600 ft).

Turn right at East Drive (10.5) and go 3 blocks to San Bernardino County's **Big Morongo Canyon Preserve**, the best birding spot on the loop. This lush oasis has a fine grove of Fremont Cottonwoods, a permanent stream, and fine stands of brush. Over 200 species of birds have been found here, mostly during migration. California birders are particularly attracted to the Preserve because it is one of the few places in the state where one can find nesting Brown-crested and Vermilion Flycatchers,

Lucy's Warbler (uncommon), and Summer Tanager. You may also be attracted by nesting Gambel's Quail, White-winged Dove, Long-eared Owl (rare), Nuttall's Woodpecker, Costa's Hummingbird, California Thrasher, Phainopepla, Yellow-breasted Chat, Scott's Oriole, and Lawrence's Goldfinch. This is an excellent place for migrants and eastern vagrants (April- May and September-early November). It has proven to be a good spot for eastern vagrants.

Adjacent to the preserve is tiny **Covington Park**, which you should also check. Vermilion Flycatchers like this spot, and Brown-crested Flycatchers usually nest in the tall cottonwoods.

Continue to the town of Yucca Valley (8.0), where you may want to visit the Hi Desert Museum, one block left (north) off 29 Palms Highway on Dumosa Street. The next town is Joshua Tree (8.0), gateway to the **Joshua Tree National Monument**. The turnoff to the park is marked by a small sign about midway through this drawn-out town. Watch for a small sign on the right at Park Boulevard, where you will turn right. Check your gas.

As soon as you enter the monument (5.2), the Joshua Trees seem to get bigger and more contorted. To really appreciate these strange lilies, take a walk among them. Some of the 30-foot giants may be over 200 years old. They play host to Ladder-backed Woodpecker, Cactus Wren, Black-throated Sparrow, House Finch, Scott's Oriole, and, in winter, Gray Flycatcher (uncommon). At night, you may find bats feeding about the flowers on Yucca Moths, which are the chief pollinators of the yucca. Even the fallen trees are important, for they provide shelter for rodents and reptiles. The unusual Desert Night Lizard may be found by turning over fallen limbs. Be sure to return the limbs to their original position.

Hidden Valley Campground (9.0) is the first of several dry camps. The garbage cans may attract a hungry Coyote, Desert Cottontail, Antelope or California Ground-Squirrel, or a Merriam's Chipmunk. Scan the massive rocks for Golden Eagles, Red-tailed Hawk, Prairie Falcon, and Rock Wren.

Adjacent to Hidden Valley Campground is Barker Dam, reached by following a dirt road north of the campground (look for the sign near the campground entrance) to the Barker Dam parking lot. The dam, about one-half mile distant, often has water behind it, especially in spring, and the place can be teeming with migrants. Desert Bighorn Sheep come down to the water here to drink.

Return through the campground and continue east on the park road until you reach Keys View Road (1.4), where you turn right. Go one block, and stop for the **Cap Rock Nature Trail**. Here you can learn to identify most of the desert plants. Keys View (El. 5,185 ft) (5.6) offers an excellent look over the Colorado Desert toward the Salton Sea.

Return to the main road and turn right toward Twentynine Palms. The area around Ryan Campground (0.5) has Bendire's Thrasher, which is most easily found in April. Continue east on the park road. At Pinto Basin intersection (9.4), go straight ahead. Desert Bighorn Sheep have been seen crossing the road along this section and climbing around in the heights.

Monument headquarters is located in the **Twentynine Palms Oasis** (8.1) on the left at the bottom of the long hill. After viewing the exhibits, walk the nature trail to see what is left of the original 29 palms. Gambel's Quail, Phainopepla, and Verdin are abundant here all year. This is a good migration trap for small landbirds. Check with the rangers about other birding areas. If you like to hike, ask about the Fortynine Palms Trail.

Retrace your route to Pinto Basin intersection and bear left toward Cottonwood Spring. The Cactus Garden Nature Trail (10.0) will help you to identify the plants of the lower desert. Reptiles seem more abundant here. You might even see a Desert Tortoise. At least, you should see the speedy little Zebra-tailed Lizard, which darts across the road with its banded tail curled over its back. Your chances of seeing snakes are better if you drive the roads at night. You may also see a Black-tailed Jackrabbit, Bobcat, Kit Fox, or Coyote.

Although badly overrun, **Cottonwood Spring** (21.0) still attract numerous birds, but there are usually hordes of people about. The campground here is the most popular in the park. Check the Fremont Cottonwoods for warblers, grosbeaks, tanagers, and flycatchers during migration. The area is also good for wintering birds.

A good birding area is the **Lost Palms Oasis**, a beautiful spot. Here, among the 110 California Fan Palms nestled in a deep canyon, you can find Hooded and Scott's Orioles, Ladder-backed Woodpecker, Ash-throated Flycatcher, and numerous migrants. In recent years, the little pools have dried up, causing a great decline in the number of birds. The oasis can be reached by a rather rough 4-mile trail that starts at Cottonwood Spring. Even if you do not see many birds, it is a nice hike.

Continue south out of the park to Interstate 10 (8.0). To return to the starting point (49.0), turn right and go through Indio. *Beyond Indio, in Banning, is Route 243 and the start of the San Jacinto Mountains Loop. If you want to visit the Salton Sea now, continue straight ahead on Highway 195 to Mecca via Box Canyon.*

There are numerous dry camps in the monument, so be sure to take plenty of water. All of the cities along Highway 62 have motels.

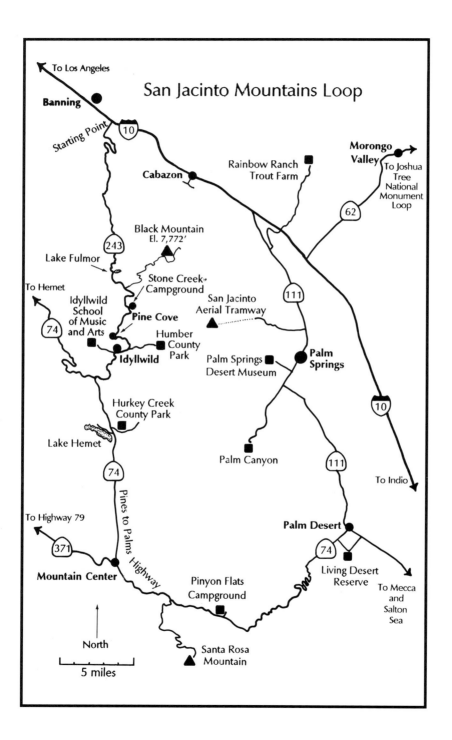

San Jacinto Mountains Loop

To Los Angeles

Banning

Starting Point

10

Cabazon

Rainbow Ranch
Trout Farm

Morongo
Valley

To Joshua
Tree
National
Monument
Loop

62

Black Mountain
El. 7,772'

243

Lake Fulmor

Stone Creek
Campground

San Jacinto
Aerial Tramway

111

To Hemet

Idyllwild
School
of Music
and Arts

74

Pine Cove

Humber
County
Park

Idyllwild

Palm Springs
Desert Museum

Palm
Springs

Hurkey Creek
County Park

Palm Canyon

10

To Indio

Lake Hemet

74

Pines to Palms Highway

111

To Highway 79

371

Palm Desert

Mountain Center

Pinyon Flats
Campground

74

Living Desert
Reserve

To Mecca
and
Salton
Sea

North

Santa Rosa
Mountain

5 miles

SAN JACINTO
MOUNTAINS LOOP

From the summit of Mount San Jacinto (Hah-SIN-toe) at 10,786 feet, one can look almost straight down to Palm Springs at 450 feet. Most birders will never reach the summit, but this trip will take you all the way around it. Because of the great changes in elevation, you will cross four life zones and many habitats. This is one of the most scenic trips in Southern California and is a good trip at any season.

The starting point is the intersection of Interstate 10 and Highway 243 (San Gorgonio Avenue) in Banning (El. 2,250 ft). Leave the freeway at Highway 243 and follow the signs southward toward Idyllwild and the mountain resorts. Very quickly the road begins to climb and presents a magnificent view from every turn.

The chaparral of the Upper Sonoran Life Zone is the dominant vegetation for the next 10 miles. It has been called the *elfin forest*. In spring when every bush bursts into bloom, it is indeed a fairyland. Stop anywhere and do a little squeaking and you should see Scrub Jay, Wrentit, California Towhee, and perhaps a Black-chinned Sparrow. After passing the 4,000-foot marker, the road dips into a stand of Coast Live Oaks where you may find Band-tailed Pigeon, Acorn and Nuttall's Woodpeckers, and Plain Titmouse. The red-stemmed manzanita has now become prominent in the chaparral, in places forming dense thickets. Its little bell-shaped flowers attract hummingbirds, particularly in April, when Calliopes may be abundant.

Near the 5,000-foot level, you will begin to see Coulter (huge cones) and Yellow Pines, and the California Black Oak of the Transition Life Zone. Start watching for Steller's Jay, Hairy Woodpecker, American Robin, and other mountain species. Western Gray Squirrel and Merriam's Chipmunk are also here.

Tiny **Lake Fulmor** (15.0), when not overrun with people, is worth checking. By using a tape-recorder at night, you have a good chance of finding Northern Pygmy-Owl, Northern Saw-whet, and Spotted Owls here and even Whip-poor-wills (May and June), very rare birds in California.

133

As the road climbs beyond the lake, Incense Cedar and Sugar Pine (very long cones) become noticeable. Look for a well-marked dirt road on the left (1.5) to **Black Mountain** (closed in winter). Stop anywhere along the road for good birds, including Mountain Quail, Acorn, Nuttall's, White-headed, and Hairy Woodpeckers, White-breasted and Pygmy Nuthatches, Western Bluebird, Solitary Vireo, Black-throated Gray Warbler, and Purple Finch. The area around the campground at the top of the road is very productive. In summer this is a good area for White-headed Woodpecker, Red-breasted Sapsucker, and Cassin's Finch. The campground has had Flammulated Owl every summer for several years, although they are heard much more often than seen.

Most of the numerous dirt roads that branch off from the highway are not particularly outstanding for birds. The moist canyons are far better. One good canyon trail is up Dark Canyon (1.8), one-quarter mile above Lawler's Lodge. Hike up the stream in summer to find Hermit Thrush, Pine Siskin, Western Wood-Pewee, and other birds. Stone Creek Campground (0.9) and the areas around it are usually worth a look for hummingbirds and the usual mountain birds.

At Pine Cove (1.5), the highest point on this highway (El. 6,300 ft), turn right at the gas station onto Pine Cove Road (1.0). In summer, some hummingbirds may zoom about at feeders. Most are Anna's and Black-chinned, but Calliope, Rufous, and Allen's may occur. Other birds such as White-headed Woodpecker, Black-headed Grosbeak, Western Tanager, and Purple, Cassin's, and House Finches are found. Even in midwinter, there is usually something around.

On the way to **Idyllwild**, you will be treated to fine views of Mount San Jacinto, Tahquitz (TAH-keats) Peak, and Lilley Rock. Check the meadow opposite the Buckhorn Camp (1.4) in summer for Lawrence's Goldfinch and the manzanita thickets in the Idyllwild Picnic Area (0.5) for Rufous-sided Towhee.

There are two campgrounds at Idyllwild (0.7) (El. 5,394 ft); both are good for camping and birding. Mount San Jacinto State Park (fee) is on the right as you enter town. Idyllwild County Park (fee) can be reached by turning right one block past the state park onto Marantha Drive. Immediately, bear left on Lower Pine Crest Avenue, go 3 blocks, and turn right onto County Park Road to the park.

One of the best birding spots is **Humber County Park**, which can be reached by turning left opposite the fire station onto Upper Pine Crest Avenue. Go straight to South Circle Drive (0.6), then left on Fern Valley Road (0.1) to the park (1.8). This is the starting point for the Devil's Slide Trail to the summit of Mount San Jacinto (9.0 miles). Even a short walk up the trail is impressive, but the hike to the top is really rewarding with spectacular views and a chance to bird in the Boreal Life Zone. (A permit may be required.)

Even around the parking lot, you should find White-headed Woodpecker, White-breasted and Pygmy Nuthatches, Mountain Chickadee, and, on summer nights, Flammulated Owl (uncommon). Also look for Mountain Quail. Higher on the trail, there should be Clark's Nutcracker, Townsend's Solitaire, and Red-breasted Nuthatch (rare). Black Swift has been found along the Tahquitz Trail, which branches off the main trail.

Another good birding area is along the road to the **Idyllwild School of Music and the Arts**. To reach that, continue south on Highway 243 and turn right on Tollgate Road (0.8). Anywhere along this road can be good. Lawrence's Goldfinch and Lincoln's Sparrow can often be found in the meadows along the stream near the campus, 1.3 miles along the road.

Beyond Tollgate Road, Highway 243 soon leaves the cool basin and quickly descends the warm south side of the mountain. The brush here is dominated by Ribbonwood, easily identified by its shredding red bark and airy clusters of light-green leaves. Birds are fairly numerous here on the sunny slopes.

Check the dead tops of tall trees in summer for the Olive-sided Flycatcher. Its morning song is a rousing *Quick, three beers!*, but its afternoon call is only a *Hic*.

At Mountain Center (3.7), turn left on the Pines-to-Palms Highway (Highway 74). The **Hurkey Creek Campground** (fee) (El. 4,400 ft) (3.4) is a favorite of birders in all seasons. Look among the pines for Band-tailed Pigeon, White-headed Woodpecker, Clark's Nutcracker (winter), Steller's Jay, Pygmy Nuthatch, Mountain Chickadee, Plain Titmouse, and with luck in fall and winter, Evening Grosbeaks. A flock of Pinyon Jays often wanders noisily around the picnic tables. By hiking up the dirt road beyond the west end of the camp, you can find Mountain Quail, Dusky Flycatcher (summer), Rufous-sided Towhee, and when the manzanita is in bloom in April and early May, Calliope Hummingbird.

Ducks can usually be found on Lake Hemet (0.3) in the winter, but they leave at the start at the fishing season. Common Snipe and other shorebirds like the wet meadows at the upper end of the lake near the highway. A Golden Eagle sometimes makes passes at the American Coots on the lake. Bald Eagles regularly winter here, too. In the dry, open pine forest around the lake you can also find a flock of the noisy Pinyon Jays in any season.

Beyond the lake, the highway enters an area of open pine forest, an excellent area for birds. Birds to watch for here are Band-tailed Pigeon,

Pinyon Jays
Charles H. Gambill

White-headed Woodpecker, Pygmy Nuthatch, Brown Creeper, Brewer's Blackbird, Pine Siskin, and, in summer, Western Wood-Pewee, Violet-green Swallow, Western Bluebird, Western Tanager, Black-headed Grosbeak, and Lawrence's Goldfinch. In winter, Clark's Nutcrackers and Mountain Bluebirds may be found.

If the Pinyon Jays were not at Hurkey Creek, they should be somewhere along the next 5 miles of road. They travel in flocks, and when they go by, you are bound to see or hear them. If you miss them the first time, drive through the pines again.

Past Highway 371 (9.0) the birds seem to fizzle out, so scoot along. If you are adventuresome, try the Santa Rosa Mountain Road (5.3). It is a rough, dirty, 10-mile climb to the summit, but the view is magnificent. On the road up look for Mountain Quail. The area around the summit has produced many interesting summer records (quite-rare Zone-tailed Hawks even nested here from 1978 to 1982). With a lot of luck, you might see Desert Bighorn Sheep on the route. If you decide not to take the climb, you might want to check the area below Highway 74 at the junction of Santa Rosa Mountain Road. This area has produced Wrentit and Gray Vireo.

The campground and housing area at **Pinyon Flats** (3.7) are worth checking. Most of the jays here among the One-leaf Pinyons, California Junipers, and Parry's Nolinas will be Scrub, but you might find a Pinyon.

They often visit the feeding-stations around the cabins. In summer, watch for the very rare Gray Vireo. Also look for Scott's Oriole.

Within the next 13 miles, the road drops 4,000 feet to the low desert and the Lower Sonoran Life Zone. In this scenic section of rocks, cactus, and sand, you will find only an occasional Rock Wren, Black-throated Sparrow, or Ladder-backed Woodpecker. However, it is a rich area for reptiles. Try your luck at the Bighorn Sheep Overlook.

At Highway 111 (15.5) in Palm Desert, turn right for about one mile to Portola Avenue, and then right (south) for a visit to the **Living Desert Reserve** (1.5) (fee). This self-supporting natural history institution has live-animal exhibits and a botanic garden with nature trails. All this gives one an intimate view of the Colorado Desert. The Reserve is open daily 9-5, but is closed during the months of June, July, and August. Common Ground-Doves, Cactus Wrens, and Black-throated Sparrows can all be seen here, and, more importantly, it is a good place to check for migrants.

Return to Highway 111 and continue west through a string of towns that are the winter playground for the rich and famous. As you enter Palm Springs, the highway looks as if it were going to run right into the mountain, but fortunately it suddenly curves right. Midway around the curve, turn left at the signal light onto South Palm Canyon Drive (12.0). This will take you to **Palm Canyon** on the Agua Caliente Indian Reservation (2.8).

A visit to this well-preserved desert reserve (open 9-5, October to June) is well worth the admission fee. Nearly all of the birds, mammals, and reptiles of the desert can be found here among the rocks and lush desert vegetation. Gambel's Quail, Phainopepla, Black-throated Sparrow, and Rock Wren are common. You will also see Antelope and California Ground-Squirrels, Black-tailed Jackrabbit, and lots of lizards.

The main attraction is the large stand of California Fan Palms. These shaggy old trees, nestled in the bottom of the wild, rocky canyons, are but a remnant of a forest that once covered the area. Their skirts of dried fronds shelter the nests of Hooded Orioles, House Finches, and other birds. The clear stream at their feet is a magnet to the many thirsty denizens of this arid land. It is also the home of the Canyon or Desert Treefrog. Be sure to check the hummingbird feeders at the Trading Post.

In late winter, Costa's Hummingbirds zoom in courtship dives over every clump of Chuparosa (*Beloperone*), with its little, red, tubular flowers. In January and February, you should find the hummingbirds easily on the reservation or along the road just before reaching the gate. Later in the spring, they move up the mountain to the yellow-flowered stalks of the Desert Agave or the red-flowered canes of the Ocotillo. When the really hot weather arrives, they will have nested and gone.

Return to Highway 111 and continue north on Palm Canyon Drive into Palm Springs. Notice something different? There are no gaudy billboards. All of the signs are flush against the buildings. Even the street lights are hidden in the palm trees.

When the highway splits into one-way Indian Avenue, continue to Tahquitz-McCallum Way (0.6) and turn left. Go three blocks and turn right on Museum Drive. The **Palm Springs Desert Museum** is on your left. It

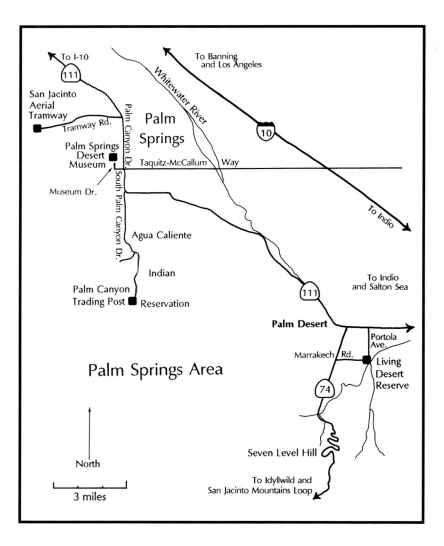

has very good exhibits on the natural history and Indians of the area. The book store always has many tempting books on local subjects.

Follow Highway 111 as it winds through and out of town. On the northern edge, you will see the road leading to the San Jacinto Tramway (2.5), which goes right up the steep side of the mountain. This is an expensive but easy way to reach the Boreal Life Zone. From the top of the tram, you can hike the 5 miles to the summit. Limited amounts of camping equipment are allowed on the tram.

After leaving the city behind, you will cross a barren area of sand-dunes. Even here there is life, for this is the home of the Coachella Fringe-toed Lizard and the Sidewinder. In late winter, the dunes are sometimes blanketed with a colorful carpet of purple Sand Verbena and white Desert Primrose.

The Whitewater Turnoff (6.1) leads across Interstate 10 and up Whitewater Canyon to a trout farm (4.7 miles). The tamarisk and cottonwood trees around the ponds can be loaded with birds during spring migration. It is usually not worth the drive at other seasons, althogh fall and early winter may produce some birds of interest.

Continue on to westbound Interstate 10 (2.7), bear left at Cabazon (5.3), leave the freeway, and cross over to the south side. Then take any road to the left and go about a mile to the wash. This is a good area for LeConte's Thrasher, although you may need a tape to lure it into view. In winter, also watch for Sage Thrasher, Sage Sparrow, and Prairie Falcon.

To return to the starting point, continue on Interstate 10 to Banning (5.6).

You can easily get to the San Bernardino Mountains Loop now—drive west on I-10 for 26.7 miles to I-215. Turn north to San Bernardino (41.6) and follow instructions for starting the route.

There are summer campgrounds throughout the mountains. The one at Pinyon Flats can be used in winter. There are motels at Banning, Idyllwild, and Palm Springs.

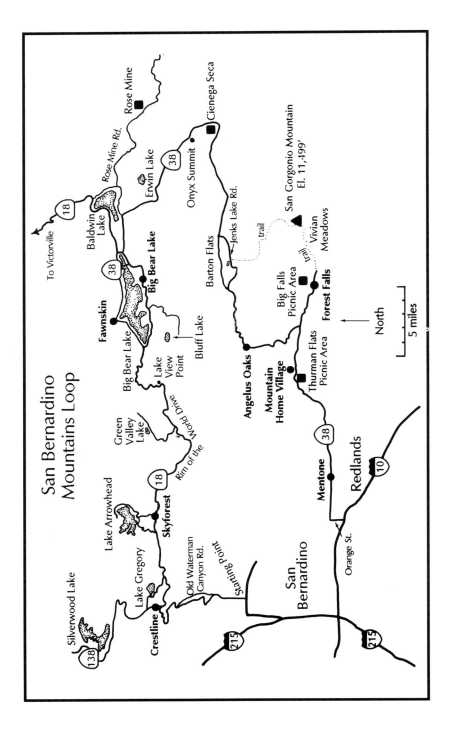

San Bernardino
Mountains Loop

Silverwood Lake

138

Lake Arrowhead

Lake Gregory

Crestline

Old Waterman Canyon Rd.

Skyforest

18

Rim of the World Drive

Starting Point

Green Valley Lake

San Bernardino

215

215

Big Bear Lake

Lake View Point

Bluff Lake

Fawnskin

Big Bear Lake

38

Baldwin Lake

To Victorville

18

Erwin Lake

Rose Mine Rd.

Rose Mine

Cienega Seca

38

Onyx Summit

Barton Flats

Jenks Lake Rd.

San Gorgonio Mountain
El. 11,499'

trail

trail

Vivian Meadows

Big Falls Picnic Area

Forest Falls

Angelus Oaks

Mountain Home Village

Thurman Flats Picnic Area

38

Mentone

Redlands

Orange St.

10

North

5 miles

SAN BERNARDINO MOUNTAINS LOOP

The San Bernardino Mountains are a massive range comprising some 1,000 miles of forests, lakes, rivers, valleys, and lofty peaks. Elevations vary from about 1,000 feet in the sage-covered foothills to 11,502 feet atop the barren summit of San Gorgonio Mountain. Most of the land in the San Bernardino National Forest is public domain, although about a third of it is privately-owned and has been developed into resorts and cabin sites, making this the most densely-populated of Southern California's mountain areas.

The entire area is crossed by a good road grandiosely called Rim of the World Drive; on Sunday afternoons it seems as if the entire population of the world were trying to drive over it. It is wise either to plan your trip for a weekday or to get an early start on the weekend.

The starting point is the intersection of Interstate 215 and Highway 18 in San Bernardino (El. 1,040 ft). Leave Interstate 215 at the Highland Avenue cutoff and follow the signs for the mountain resorts and Highway 18. Turn left onto Highway 18 at the Waterman Avenue freeway exit (2.3), which becomes Rim of the World Drive.

The road quickly begins to climb through the brushy foothills. To check for birds of this habitat, turn right at an unmarked exit onto **Old Waterman Canyon Road** (2.9). The patches of chaparral may yield California Quail, California Thrasher, Wrentit, Bewick's Wren, and California Towhee. Check the Canyon Live Oaks for Band-tailed Pigeon, Acorn and Nuttall's Woodpeckers, Bushtit, Plain Titmouse, and House Wren. Farther up the canyon, in the groves of White Alder, Western Sycamore, and Black Cottonwood, you may find Swainson's and Hermit Thrushes, Downy Woodpecker, and American and Lesser Goldfinches. California Ground-Squirrels are everywhere.

Continue up the canyon to rejoin Highway 18 (3.0), which climbs higher and higher, offering increasingly better views of the valley, if the smog is not too thick. Take the Crestline exit (Highway 138) (4.2) and proceed to the town of Crestline (El. 4,700 ft). Look for Steller's Jays at the

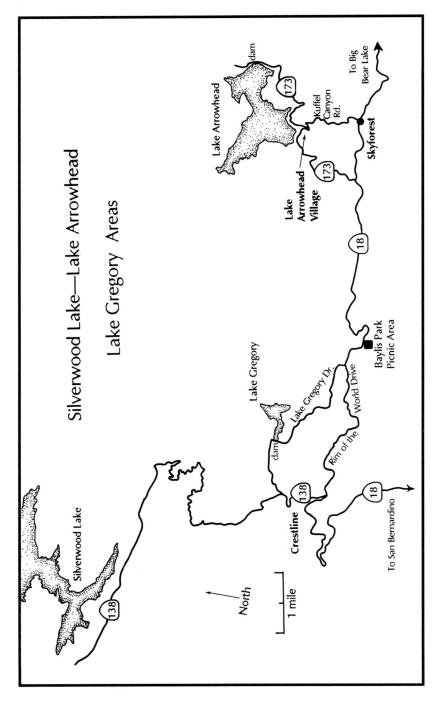

Silverwood Lake—Lake Arrowhead

Lake Gregory Areas

feeding-trays around the cabins. In the center of town you have a choice. If you stay on Highway 138, you can visit **Silverwood Lake State Recreation Area** (9.3). Mountain Quail are often observed along the road in early mornings or evenings. The lake has a few ducks and, in winter, Bald Eagles. During migrations many small birds are found among the trees, especially in the group-camping area.

If you decide not to go to Silverwood Lake, or upon your return from it, continue straight ahead on Lake Drive to Lake Gregory (1.1), which may have a few coots and ducks. Turn right to cross the dam on Lake Gregory Drive. Along this road you will find good stands of Yellow and Sugar Pines, Incense Cedar, and Goldcup and Black Oaks. Stop anywhere to look for Mountain Chickadee, White-breasted and Pygmy Nuthatches, Brown Creeper, Pine Siskin, and other mountain birds.

When you eventually reach Highway 18 (2.3), turn left. Beyond the Baylis Park Picnic Area (0.4), you will see a turnout (0.3) from which the view of the valley is superb. On a clear day, this really does seem to be the rim of the world. The mellow *wook* call of the Mountain Quail can often be heard in the brush below, but the bird is hard to see. At the community of Rimforest (1.3) look for White-headed Woodpecker in the towering, mature Yellow Pines.

Turn left at Highway 173 (2.0) for Lake Arrowhead, which may have a few ducks. To reach the only place on the lake where birders can get an unobstructed view, turn right at the traffic light at the bottom of the hill in Lake Arrowhead Village (1.5). Stay on this road (Highway 173) as it twists its way to the dam at the east end of the lake (2.5).

Retrace your route to Kuffel Canyon Road (2.0) and turn left onto it to rejoin Highway 18 at Skyforest. Turn left and continue on Highway 18 toward Big Bear Lake. For the next ten miles, the highway passes numerous resorts. As you go, you will find many places to pull off to look for birds. One resort worth checking is **Green Valley** (9.8). Watch for Mountain Quail around patches of Buckthorn along the road to the lake (3.3). At the lake and around the campground (1.2) beyond, you may find Common Nighthawk and Williamson's Sapsucker in summer, plus the usual mountain birds. At night, look and listen for Spotted Owl. This is a good place to camp.

Beyond the Green Valley turnoff, the highway climbs even higher until it reaches the summit near Lake View Point (El. 7,207 ft) (4.5) overlooking Big Bear Valley. The habitat here has changed from pine forest to high-mountain brushlands of scrub oak and *Ceanothus*. This is the nesting area for Dusky Flycatcher, Black-throated Gray Warbler, Green-tailed Towhee, and Fox Sparrow. If you do a little squeaking near the

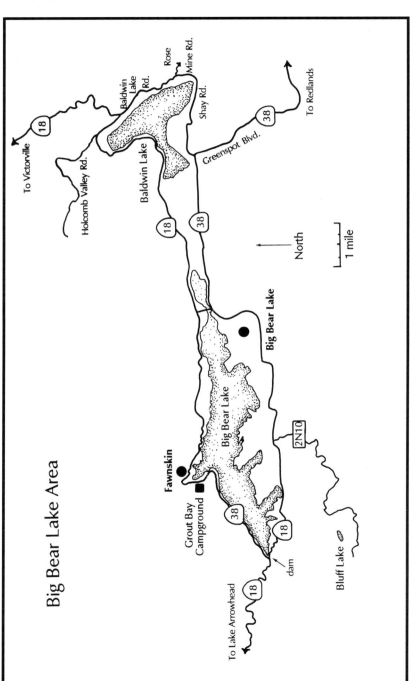

Big Bear Lake Area

brush-patches, they will usually come out into view. In late summer and fall, Clark's Nutcrackers may be common.

If you would like to take a side trip now to a place some birders claim is the finest montane birding in Southern California, you may want to check out **Bluff Lake** (El. 7,900 ft). Even though it is situated only 1.5 miles south-southeast of Lake View Point, the drive to this area is some eight miles. It is most accessible from May through October.

There are a number of locally uncommon species which may be reliably found at Bluff Lake between mid-May and July. Included in this category are Common Nighthawk, Williamson's Sapsucker, Dusky Flycatcher, and Calliope Hummingbird. Other reliable breeding birds include Brown Creeper, Ruby-crowned Kinglet, and Hermit Thrush. The most abundant breeders are Western Wood-Pewee, Violet-green Swallow, Steller's Jay, Mountain Chickadee, Fox Sparrow, Dark-eyed Junco, and Cassin's Finch. A little less common are Townsend's Solitaire and Pine Siskin. Even less common, but present, are MacGillivray's Warbler and Green-tailed Towhee. Other species present in the breeding season, but not necessarily breeding, are Virginia Rail, Sora, Lazuli Bunting, and Red Crossbill. Several species of warblers can also be seen during fall migration, including Hermit and possibly Townsend's. Golden-crowned Kinglets are regular in fall. A big attraction is the Champion Lodgepole Pine.

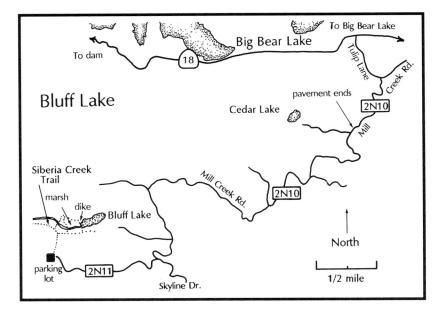

To reach Bluff Lake, continue along Highway 18 to the west end of Big Bear Lake (El. 6,744 ft). Continue on Highway 18 beyond the dam (1.6) until you reach Tulip Lane on the right (1.5) (opposite the stables). Turn right onto Tulip Lane and go to Mill Creek Road (Route 2N10) (0.5), where you turn right. Where the pavement ends (0.8), take the dirt road bearing left. Bear right at the next intersection (0.8), then left (0.5), left again (1.3), continue past a road taking off to the right (0.4), and finally turn right onto Route 2N11 (0.3) to the parking lot (1.0).

The trail to the Champion Lodgepole Pine and Bluff Lake is marked by a plaque at the edge of the parking lot. Birds are found all along this trail. After walking for roughly 300 yards, you will reach a T-intersection. Turn left onto Siberia Creek Trail and follow it for about one-quarter mile through prime coniferous forest and meadow habitat. Retrace your steps to a trail leading left (north) from a Forest Service sign. This trail takes you past the Champion Lodgepole Pine. After you marvel at this 110-foot-tall pine, continue along the trail to a T-intersection at the marsh. Turn left and cross over the foot-bridge.

In 200 feet bear right at the fork; 300 feet farther along bear right again to the dike along Bluff Lake. After crossing the dike, turn right (the area to the left is private property) and walk about 450 feet to the trail (on the left by some cut stumps) leading back to the parking lot. Retrace your way back to the intersection of Tulip Lane and Highway 18 (following the trail of bread crumbs you would have been wise to drop on the outward journey).

Once you are back at the intersection, you may continue east on Highway 18 along the south side of the lake through the town of **Big Bear Lake**. To continue the loop, however, return to to the dam (1.5) and turn right onto Highway 38 to drive along the north shore of the lake. A few waterbirds and Ring-billed Gulls can be found here at any season, and during migration there may be large flocks. Concentrations of over 200,000 American Coots have been recorded. A few linger into winter, which is also the time to look for the Bald Eagle, a regular visitor with up to 25 birds some years.

The **Grout Bay Campground** (2.9) (closed in winter to protect the eagles) is popular with birders. Look among the pine trees for White-headed Wookpecker, Pygmy Nuthatch, Mountain Chickadee, Western Bluebird, and at night Flammulated Owls and Western Screech-Owls. The meadows across the road can be good for Say's Phoebe, Violet-green and Cliff Swallows, and Savannah Sparrow. The wilder areas just north of Fawnskin are good for Spotted and Saw-whet Owls.

East of Fawnskin (0.6) the land becomes more arid. The vegetation changes from Yellow Pine to Western Juniper, One-leaf Pinyon, and sage. More extensive areas of this habitat may be found by following the self-guided Gold Fever Trail (2.2) through Holcomb Valley. The sage flats are the summer home of Common Poorwill, Green-tailed Towhee, and Black-chinned, Brewer's, Lark, and Sage Sparrows. Nocturnal birders find Holcomb Valley of great interest because of its Spotted Owls.

Past the end of Big Bear Lake, Highways 18 and 38 cross. Highway 38 turns south, and you will eventually follow it to complete the loop, but right now you should continue straight ahead on Highway 18 toward Victorville.

When it has water, **Baldwin Lake** (1.0) attracts many birds. It hosts the second-largest breeding population of Eared Grebes in Southern California (Salton Sea has the largest). In late summer and fall, shorebirds and ducks may be common. Cinnamon Teal are present throughout the summer and probably nest. Continue around the lake past the Holcomb Valley Road (2.8) and turn right onto unmarked, dirt Baldwin Lake Road (0.3). If you miss the turn, you will soon top the ridge overlooking the Lucerne Valley far below in the Mojave Desert.

After leaving the highway, you will cross an arid area of sagebrush, where nesting Green-tailed Towhees and sparrows may be common. Up to nine different species of sparrows may be found here or close by. Among those breeding here are Savannah, Vesper, Lark, Sage, Chipping, Brewer's, Lincoln's, and Song. Also, there is the Oregon Dark-eyed Junco, a sparrow.

Midway around the east side of Baldwin Lake is Rose Mine Road (2.1), which goes a rough, dusty 30 miles down the mountain to Yucca Valley. It crosses rather extensive areas of pinyon and juniper where Gray Vireos have nested, although you would be very lucky to find them. Passenger cars will find this road very slow going, but passable in dry weather. Observe desert-travel precautions for there appears to be little traffic on weekdays. Beyond Rose Mine you will enter a valley with Joshua Trees rivaling those in the National Monument.

To continue the loop, however, follow Baldwin Lake Road around the lake, entering an open stand of large old Yellow Pines, where Mountain Bluebirds and Pinyon Jays can usually be found at any season. One of the more unexpected sights is Cliff Swallows building their mud nests on the trunks of large pines under the shelter of the larger limbs. This unusual choice of nesting sites has not been observed elsewhere.

Baldwin Lake Road merges with Shay Road (0.5) and ends at Highway 38 (Greenspot Boulevard) (2.1). If you have time, continue straight ahead to explore the villages along the south shore of the lake.

Continue south on Greenspot Boulevard toward Redlands. You will soon enter forests of Jeffrey Pines. If you don't mind looking stupid, it is easy to tell this pine from a Yellow Pine. Just stick your nose into the deep crevices of the bark and sniff for the odor of pineapple or vanilla.

As the road climbs up from the valley, these pines give way to Western Juniper and One-leaf Pinyon. The brushy area around the Greenspot Picnic Ground (El. 7,500 ft) (3.8) can be good in summer for Black-throated Gray Warbler, Green-tailed and Rufous-sided Towhees, and Dusky Flycatcher. In the vicinity of **Onyx Summit**, you will see a few stunted White Fir. Check here for Clark's Nutcracker, Townsend's Solitaire, and Cassin's Finch.

Onyx Summit (El. 8,443 ft) is the highest point on the highway and the divide between the drainage of the Colorado River to the east and the Santa Ana River to the west. The water from this point seldom gets across the deserts to the Colorado River, but on the other side there is an ample flow in winter and spring into the Santa Ana, the largest river in Southern California.

Just below the summit, there is a grassy area known as Cienega Seca or "dry marsh". Look here in summer for Lincoln's Sparrow and sometimes Lawrence's Goldfinch. As the road drops and drops, it skirts the edges of massive San Gorgonio Mountain and crosses the Barton Flats Recreation Area (8.5). This very popular vacation spot has several public campgrounds and many private organizational camps. It is no place to go birding on a summer weekend, but can be good during the rest of the year. Red-breasted Sapsuckers are fairly common here. Notice the numerous half-inch-diameter holes that they drill in the trunks of the larger pines.

Turn left on Jenks Lake Road (5.0), which leads to a small lake and the road to Poopout Hill, the jumping-off place for the hike up Mount San Gorgonio. A permit is required for the hike, but you may find good birding around the parking lot. The steep, rugged, 8-mile trail to the summit crosses the **San Gorgonio Wilderness** and passes through forests of pine and fir and by delightful lakes and meadows. If you reach the summit at 11,502 feet, you will be in the largest Alpine-Arctic area in Southern California. Here the blue of the sky is matched only by the blue of the numerous Mountain Bluebirds. Jenks Lake Road returns to Highway 38 (1.8).

Many people at Angelus Oaks (5.4) maintain bird feeders, particularly for hummingbirds. In summer, Anna's, Black-chinned, and Calliope Hummingbirds are fairly common. In late summer, they are joined by hordes of Rufous and some Allen's. The Costa's seldom gets this high. It is more common in the sages at lower elevations.

Turn left on Forest Falls Road (5.2) to drive up **Mill Creek Canyon**. The Big Falls Picnic Area (El. 5,560 ft) (4.2) is situated in a grove of large Incense Cedars and Black Oaks at the end of the road. Take the short trail across the river to the falls, where Black Swifts can be found among the more numerous White-throated. American Dippers are found at the falls. By hiking upstream a short way, you can reach **Vivian Meadows**, an excellent spot for Townsend's Solitaire, Cassin's Finch, and Spotted Owl (night). This is also the starting point for the 7.2-mile Big Falls Trail to the top of San Gorgonio Mountain.

Return to Highway 38 and continue down the mountain. Near Mountain Home Village (2.3), turn left on Cienega Road, jog left, turn right on Sycamore Road, and follow it through the little settlement. There are large numbers of birds about the cabins. Fox and Golden-crowned Sparrows are abundant here in winter. You might also try the Thurman Flats Picnic Area (1.3), which is also good for sparrows.

Follow Highway 38 through Mentone to Redlands. Here there are Spotted Doves, European Starlings, House Sparrows, and other city birds if you care to look. You are now close to the San Bernardino County Museum (see *Miscellaneous Areas* section.) Otherwise, turn left at the traffic light on Orange Street (11.0) and join the freeway (I-10) (0.5) going west. This will join Interstate 215 (6.7) and take you north back to San Bernardino.

You are very close to the starting point of the Western Riverside County Loop. To reach it, follow I-215 south to Highway 91 (10.9).

There are 29 public campgrounds in the San Bernardino Mountains and numerous motels and lodges. Some of the campgrounds are on a reservation system in summer. If you are interested, write to the San Bernardino National Forest, 144 North Mountain View Avenue, San Bernardino, CA 92408, and they will tell you the procedure for making reservations.

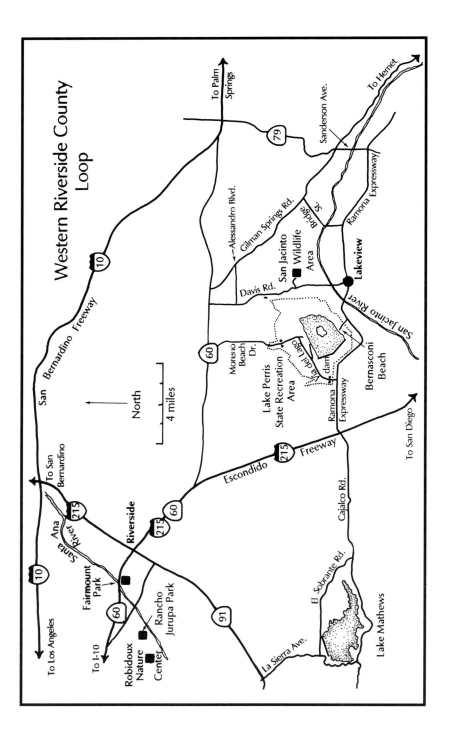

Western Riverside County Loop

To Palm Springs

To Hemet

79

Sanderson Ave.

Ramona Expressway

Alessandro Blvd.

Gilman Springs Rd.

Bridge St.

San Jacinto Wildlife Area

Lakeview

Davis Rd.

San Jacinto River

10

San Bernardino Freeway

60

Moreno Beach Dr.

Lake Perris State Recreation Area

Perris Lake

dam

Ramona Expressway

Bernasconi Beach

North

4 miles

215

Escondido Freeway

To San Bernardino

San Bernardino

Cajalco Rd.

To San Diego

215

Riverside

Santa Ana River

10

60

215

Fairmount Park

Rancho Jurupa Park

Robidoux Nature Center

To Los Angeles

To I-10

91

La Sierra Ave.

El Sobrante Rd.

Lake Mathews

WESTERN RIVERSIDE COUNTY LOOP

by Chet McGaugh

A lthough it is the fastest developing area in California, western Riverside County offers excellent birdwatching opportunities. Some of the most extensive riparian forests remaining in Southern California are found along the Santa Ana River. Lake Mathews and Lake Perris, huge man-made reservoirs supplying water for the exploding population, are wintering areas for large numbers of waterfowl, grebes, gulls, and other waterbirds. The San Jacinto Valley offers some of the best inland-winter birding in the United States, including an exciting variety of birds of prey.

The loop begins at the **Louis Robidoux Nature Center**. From Highway 60, 2.7 miles west of the junction of Interstate 215 and Highway 91 (northwest of Riverside), take Rubidoux Boulevard south to Mission Boulevard (0.6) and turn right. Turn left onto Riverview Drive/Limonite Avenue (0.3), and left again, following Riverview Drive as these two roads diverge (0.6). Follow Riverview Drive to the Louis Robidoux Nature Center (1.2). The Nature Center building, on the left behind a pecan grove, is visible from the road. If the gate is locked (open 10 to 4), park on Riverview Drive and walk in.

Trails from the Nature Center lead to a variety of habitats: riparian, marsh, pond, orchard, scrubby field, and to the Santa Ana River. Although an entire day is easily spent birding here, even an hour or two can be very profitable. Nesting species include Cinnamon Teal, Red-shouldered and Red-tailed Hawks, Great Horned Owl (often nesting in the pecan grove), Anna's and Black-chinned Hummingbirds, Nuttall's and Downy Woodpeckers, Western Kingbird, Ash-throated Flycatcher, California Thrasher, Loggerhead Shrike, Yellow-breasted Chat, Blue and Black-headed Grosbeaks, California Towhee, and Northern Oriole. Listen

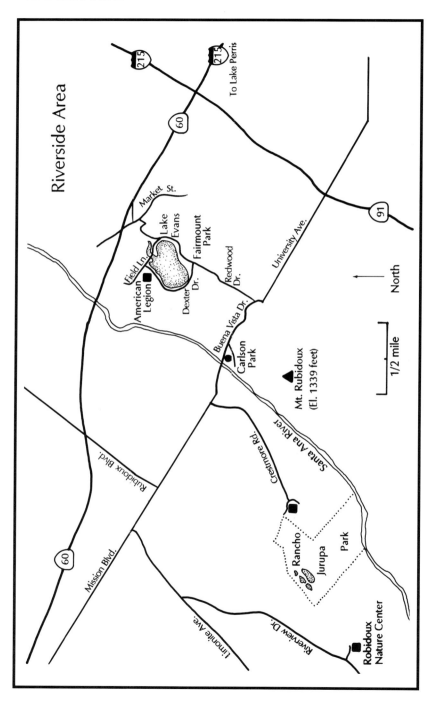

Riverside Area

215
215
To Lake Perris
60
91

Market St.
Lake Evans
Fairmount Park
Field Ln.
American Legion
Redwood Dr.
Dexter Dr.
University Ave.
Buena Vista Dr.
Carlson Park

North

1/2 mile

Mt. Rubidoux
(El. 1339 feet)

Rubidoux Blvd.

Santa Ana River

Crestmore Rd.

Rancho Jurupa Park

60

Mission Blvd.

Limonite Ave.

Riverview Dr.

Robidoux Nature Center

for the quizzical song of Least Bell's Vireo, an endangered subspecies, which was formerly common in willow thickets along the Santa Ana River.

In winter (October-April), the fields and thickets are full of sparrows (White-crowned, Golden-crowned, Lincoln's, Song, Savannah, Fox, and rarely Harris's, Swamp, White-throated, and Green-tailed Towhee), the trees are full of Yellow-rumped Warblers, and the marsh is home to Sora, Virginia Rail, and American Bittern. A flock of a hundred or more Canada Geese can usually be seen loafing on sandbars in the river, as can myriad ducks and shorebirds (Western, Least, and Spotted Sandpipers, Greater Yellowlegs, Long-billed Dowitcher, Common Snipe, and Black-necked Stilt). Sharp-shinned and Cooper's Hawks and Merlin (rare) forage in the riparian thickets and dense scrub. Northern Harriers, Black-shouldered Kites, Ferruginous Hawks, and Prairie Falcons hunt the more open terrain. The air over the river is a bird highway: flocks of ducks, geese, shorebirds, and gulls move up and down the river, visiting favorite feeding and roosting spots. Big Day teams birding the river on foot in January have tallied over 100 species!

During migration, look for Western Wood-Pewee, Olive-sided Flycatcher, Hammond's and Pacific-slope Flycatchers, Solitary and Warbling Vireos, Wilson's, Black-throated Gray, Nashville, Townsend's, and Hermit Warblers, and Western Tanager.

Return to the intersection of Riverview Drive/Limonite Avenue and Mission Boulevard. Turn right (east) and proceed to Crestmore Road (1.0). A right turn here will take you to **Rancho Jurupa Park** (1.2) (fee). You will be paralleling the Santa Ana River (to your left) but will be unable to see it. Check the fields on your right for Prairie Falcon and Ferruginous Hawk (winter). The park, also accessible by trail from the Robidoux Nature Center, has a lake and small ponds that are often full of wintering ducks (Ring-necked, Ruddy, American Wigeon, Redhead, and others). A trail leads to the river and to areas of thick riparian habitat. Watch for Phainopeplas. Gray Flycatcher has wintered in the vicinity of the small ponds in recent years.

Return to Mission Boulevard and turn right. You will cross the river, and, as soon as you do, you'll see a small park on the right (0.4). From Carlson Park you can walk up and down the river or, if you're feeling energetic, you can hike one of the steep trails up Mount Rubidoux and look for White-throated Swift, Cactus Wren (in a cactus patch on the northeast side near the bottom), Rock Wren, and Rufous-crowned Sparrow. It's also a good vantage point for watching the thousands of birds that fly up and down the river on a winter's day.

From the park, proceed east on Buena Vista Avenue (the continuation of Mission Boulevard) and turn left onto Redwood Drive (0.3). Turn left on Dexter Drive (0.5), drive around Lake Evans, and park at the American Legion Hall (0.4), across the street from the army tank. You are now in **Fairmount Park**. This is a popular urban park, so exercise caution. The park is an excellent place to study gulls, since as many as a thousand may be loafing on the lake on a winter afternoon. California, Ring-billed, Herring, and Bonaparte's are the common species; Glaucous, Glaucous-winged, Thayer's, Mew, and Lesser Black-backed have been seen here. Double-crested Cormorant, Great and Snowy Egrets, Great Blue Heron, Belted Kingfisher, and Pied-billed Grebe are usually seen. Many species of waterfowl use the lake; Wood Ducks are fairly common in winter. Birding in the riparian thicket and the open parkland can be very good. Recent winter rarities include Red-throated Loon, Lewis's Woodpecker, Williamson's Sapsucker, Bohemian Waxwing, White-throated Sparrow, and Chestnut-sided Warbler.

From the parking area, make a left turn to reach Field Lane (0.1), where you will turn right. At Redwood Drive (0.2) turn left. Follow Redwood Drive to the park's exit at Market Street (0.2), being careful to make a quick left before entering the area marked "Do Not Enter". A left turn onto Market Street will take you to the eastbound Highway 60 on-ramp (0.1). Get on "The 60" and head east, making sure to avoid the I-215 split (5.9) leading toward San Diego. Exit the freeway at Moreno Beach Boulevard (6.5) and go south until you reach Via del Lago (3.1). Turn left and enter **Lake Perris State Recreation Area** (1.1) (fee).

Lake Perris should be avoided in summer. In winter, however, the crowds are gone and the birds have returned. Horned Grebes occur every winter, joining thousands of Eared, Western, and Clark's Grebes. Greater Scaup, and sometimes Tufted Duck, have been found in the large Lesser Scaup flock that usually rafts near Lot 8. The 1983 Christmas Bird Count team found three species of loons (including Yellow-billed!), Red-necked Grebe, and Black-legged Kittiwake. Pacific Loons, a rarity inland, are found on the lake almost every winter. Other rarities include Oldsquaw, White-winged Scoter, and Western, Heermann's, Mew, and Thayer's Gulls.

Strategies for birding the lake depend on the amount of time you have. A walk out on the dam (3.5 miles round-trip) can be good, as can a walk around the east end of the lake, where the riparian vegetation meets the water. Check the snags for Osprey. Most birders choose to drive and stop at each of the parking lots to scope the little bays, and walk out the "peninsulas" to scope the open water.

The hills of coastal sage scrub around the lake are home to Costa's

Hummingbird, Bewick's, Canyon, and Rock Wrens, California Gnatcatcher (rare), California Thrasher, California Towhee, and Rufous-crowned and Sage Sparrows. Be cautious about identifying gnatcatchers because Blue-gray Gnatcatchers are much more common than the recently-split California Gnatcatcher during most of the year. (Check the undertail; California has dark outertail feathers, while the Blue-gray has white.)

From the guard station at the west end of the park (2.7), drive south to the Ramona Expressway (0.9) and turn left. The expressway takes you past the road to Bernasconi Beach (3.7), another access to Lake Perris and the surrounding hills. After checking Bernasconi Beach, continue on to Davis Road (2.1), turning left. You are now in the San Jacinto Valley and the small town of Lakeview.

The vast, mostly flat San Jacinto Valley is defined, for birding purposes, by Alessandro Boulevard (north), Gilman Springs Road/Sanderson Avenue (east), the Ramona Expressway (south), and Davis Road (west). It is the winter home for an impressive number and variety of birds, allowing the San Jacinto Lake CBC to consistently score among the top inland Christmas Bird Counts in the United States. Ducks and geese (including Greater White-fronted) fly back and forth over the valley, visiting agricultural fields, duck clubs, and the San Jacinto Wildlife Area. Thousands of Horned Larks, and, during most winters, small flocks of longspurs (Chestnut-collared, McCown's, rarely Lapland) forage in the fields. The "longspur field" changes locales based on weather and agricultural practices. Flocks of Mountain Plovers can usually be found. Mountain Bluebirds are common, and Sprague's Pipits have been found in two recent winters.

Drive north on Davis Road (it soon becomes dirt and may be impassable after a rain) to the turnoff for the headquarters of the **San Jacinto Wildlife Area** (2.2) (fee), on your right. Watch the fence along Davis Road for Say's Phoebe and Mountain Bluebird (winter). Turn right at the entrance kiosk to reach headquarters (0.2). To find the rare species it is best to check with the wildlife area's naturalist for current information. The San Bernardino Valley Audubon Society Rare Bird Alert (Phone: 714/793-5599) also has information on recent sightings. Pick up a map and a checklist.

The San Jacinto Wildlife Area is 4,700 acres of wetlands, marsh, grasslands, and rocky hills of coastal sage scrub. It remains a refuge for the endangered Stephen's Kangaroo Rat, the infamous "mouse that roars" at developers in western Riverside County, and is the first of the state wildlife areas to use reclaimed water to re-establish wetlands sacrificed earlier in the century to flood control, agriculture, and development. It is a birder's paradise.

The naturalist can tell you where longspurs and Mountain Plovers have been seen, whether or not there are any Short-eared Owls in the vicinity, where the Long-eared Owls are, and whether or not Bald Eagles are being seen. There's something to see at all times of the year in the wetlands. Nesting species include Eared and Pied-billed Grebes, Mallard, Gadwall, Northern Pintail, Northern Shoveler, Redhead, Ruddy Duck, Virginia Rail, Common Moorhen, American Avocet, Black-necked Stilt, Killdeer, and Yellow-headed, Red-winged, and Tricolored Blackbirds. Grasshopper Sparrows have recently nested. Sage Thrashers may be seen in winter and migration. Recent rarities include Tundra Swan and Little Blue Heron.

In fall the edges of ponds, mudflats, and wet fields are visited by thousands of shorebirds on their way south. Among these are Baird's, Solitary, and Pectoral Sandpipers. Wintering shorebirds are Western, Least, and Spotted Sandpipers, Greater and Lesser Yellowlegs, Dunlin, Black-bellied and Semipalmated Plovers, Long-billed Dowitcher, and Long-billed Curlew, as well as the resident Killdeer, American Avocet, and Black-necked Stilt.

Head north on Davis Road until the pavement begins again (3.4), and continue straight to Alessandro Boulevard (0.1). This is a good place to stop and scan the telephone poles for Ferruginous Hawks, often in the vicinity. Turn right and drive east on Alessandro Boulevard, watching the phone poles and the sky for raptors. Be sure to check the poles (but don't turn) along the side road (1.0) that heads south from Alessandro Boulevard. At Gilman Springs Road (1.0) turn right. Turn right on Bridge Street (5.0).

The fields on both sides of Bridge Street are good for Mountain Plover, Mountain Bluebird, Burrowing Owl, and longspurs. Golden Eagle, Ferruginous Hawk, Northern Harrier, and Black-shouldered Kite are often in the area. When Sprague's Pipits have been found in the valley, they have been found here. Horned Lark, American Pipit, and Savannah Sparrow may be here in abundance, depending on weather and land use. If you want to find longspurs, you must walk the fields. Do not cross "No Trespassing" signs or go through fences; the relationship between birders and property owners in the San Jacinto Valley is fragile. (Many small farm roads leading into agricultural areas can be muddy even two weeks after a rain, or have extremely soft soil. This has caused a few birders to walk miles for a tow.)

By now, if you are doing this trip in winter, you should have an impressive list of raptors, including Bald and Golden Eagles, Turkey Vulture, Osprey, Black-shouldered Kite, Northern Harrier, Cooper's, Sharp-shinned, Red-tailed, Red-shouldered, and Ferruginous Hawks, American Kestrel, and Prairie Falcon. If you're lucky, you may have seen Rough-legged Hawk, Merlin, and/or Peregrine Falcon. Six species of owls are possible: Barn, Great Horned, Western Screech-, Burrowing, Long-eared, and Short-eared. The naturalist at the wildlife area can usually give you information on owl locations. The San Jacinto Valley and the Antelope Valley (see *Miscellaneous Areas* section) are perhaps the best winter raptor areas in Southern California.

After exploring the Bridge Street area, continue to follow this road as it crosses the usually dusty San Jacinto River (1.8) and ends at the Ramona Expressway (0.8). Turn right (west) onto the Ramona Expressway and follow it to I-215 (11.0), then over the freeway. The road you are on is now called Cajalco Road; follow it to Lake Mathews. The lake will appear on your right shortly after you pass El Sobrante Road (6.7). En route, watch for raptors.

Lake Mathews, a metropolitan reservoir, is closed to the public and can be birded only from outside the fence. A scope is a must. Thousands of ducks, geese, grebes (Western, Clark's, Eared, Horned, Pied-billed), and gulls winter here. Common Loons are regularly seen. Golden Eagles are resident in the area; Bald Eagles winter. The drive around the lake is good for Northern Harrier, Black-shouldered Kite, and other raptors. The brushy hills around the south and west end of the lake are California Gnatcatcher habitat.

The strategy for birding the lake is to stop wherever you can get a view of the lake, and approximately two miles beyond El Sobrante Road you will start to get distant views. Bald Eagles are sometimes seen from the shoulder of the road. The road rises and veers close to the lake at a wide shoulder (4.6); stop here to scope the lake and scan the rocky outcrops.

Turn right onto La Sierra Avenue (1.5). You will be driving along the dam and will be as close to the lake as you can get. Bald Eagles often perch on the little islands. Continue to the overlook parking area (1.8) at the northwest corner of the lake for a last scoping.

Continue on La Sierra Avenue to Highway 91 (3.5). Turn right (east) onto the freeway and follow it until you reach Highway 60 (9.4). Get on "The 60" going toward Los Angeles (west) until you return to the Rubidoux Boulevard exit (2.5). Retrace your steps to the Robidoux Nature Center (2.7) to complete the loop. *To start the San Gabriel Mountains loop, take Highway 60 to the Corona Expressway (Highway 71) (19.8), go north on Highway 71 to I-210 (4.4), and stay on I-210 to the La Cañada Flintridge exit (28.7).*

Camping is permitted at Rancho Jurupa Park and at Lake Perris State Recreation Area. Hotels and motels are abundant. There are entrance fees at Rancho Jurupa Park, Lake Perris State Park, and the San Jacinto Wildlife Area.

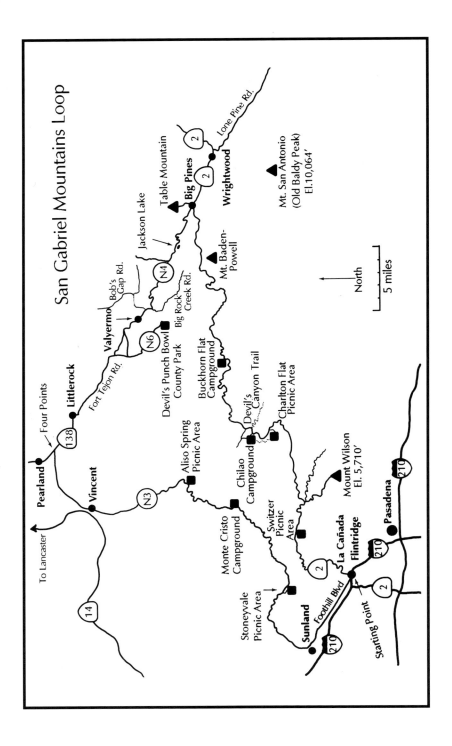

San Gabriel Mountains Loop

SAN GABRIEL MOUNTAINS LOOP

The San Gabriel Mountains stand atop the San Andreas Fault Line with one foot in the desert, one foot on the coastal plain, and their lofty peaks in the clouds 10,000 feet above sea level. Five different life zones and many habitats are represented in this diverse region of snow-covered peaks, forested mountains, steep canyons, and brush-covered foothills. Most of the area is enclosed in the 693,000-acre Angeles National Forest and criss-crossed by roads and trails, all beckoning to be explored.

The best time for mountain birding is during the warmer months, but a visit is worthwhile at any season. The higher roads are often closed after winter storms—or, at least, chains are required. If in doubt, stop at the ranger station for further information and a map of the Angeles National Forest.

The starting point is the intersection of Foothills Freeway (I-210) and the Angeles Crest Highway (Highway 2) in La Cañada Flintridge (El. 1,300 ft). Go north on the Angeles Crest Highway as it rapidly climbs the barren side of the Arroyo Seco.

The sparse vegetation here does not hide many birds, but it is habitat for Rufous-crowned Sparrow and Greater Roadrunner. The drabness is broken in spring by the tall, white-flowered stalks of the Chaparral Yucca. At the Woodwardia Canyon Bridge, you will see a few Bigcone Douglas-firs with their long skinny limbs. The World of Chaparral Nature Trail starts by the pullout at Clear Creek Vista (8.4). It is usually not worth the effort to walk the entire way down into the canyon, but you should try the first few hundred yards. You may find a California Thrasher or a Wrentit.

The **Switzer Picnic Area** (1.4) at the bottom of the canyon is located along a running stream shaded by Coast Live Oaks, Western Sycamores, and Bigcone Douglas Fir. Nearly all of the birds of the chaparral and oak woodlands can be found here, plus a few mountain species. Band-tailed Pigeon, Acorn, Hairy, Downy, and Nuttall's Woodpeckers, Steller's and Scrub Jays, Canyon and Bewick's Wrens, White-breasted Nuthatch, and Western Bluebird can be found here at any season. In summer look for

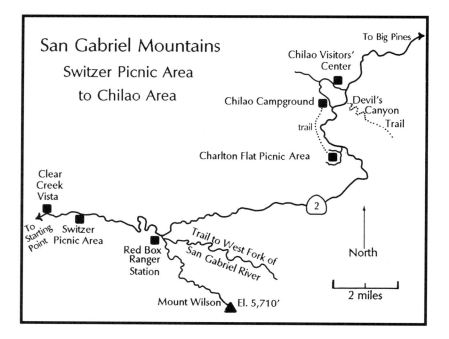

San Gabriel Mountains
Switzer Picnic Area
to Chilao Area

To Big Pines

Chilao Visitors' Center

Chilao Campground

Devil's Canyon

trail

Trail

Charlton Flat Picnic Area

Clear Creek Vista

To Starting Point

Switzer Picnic Area

Red Box Ranger Station

Trail to West Fork of San Gabriel River

2

North

Mount Wilson El. 5,710'

2 miles

Ash-throated Flycatcher, Warbling and Solitary Vireos, Black-headed Grosbeak, and Yellow and Orange-crowned Warblers.

Just before the highway crosses the Arroyo Seco, there is a gated, dirt trail on the right (0.2). Common Poorwills and Great Horned Owls call here at dusk, and, after dark, Western Screech-Owls are often found in the oaks about 100 yards down the dirt trail.

You can turn right at the Red Box Ranger Station (2.3) onto the steep, winding road up Mount Wilson (5.0). From the top (El. 5,710 ft) the view of the Los Angeles Basin can be magnificent on a clear day, and there are occasional clear days in Los Angeles, especially in late fall and winter. In fact, one year there were three. On a smoggy day the trip may not be worthwhile, although in winter, with some snow cover, the birds are often fed by the caretakers of the power station, antennae, and telescope.

At the Red Box Ranger Station's parking lot a dirt road (currently with a locked gate) and a parallel hiking trail lead downhill and eastward into the West Fork of the San Gabriel River. About one mile down the trail you arrive at the bottom of the canyon. Breeding birds in the canyon include Spotted Owl (there is often a pair just after you reach the bottom of the canyon), Nuttall's Woodpecker, Solitary Vireo, and Lazuli Bunting.

A good place to stop at any season is the **Charlton Flat Picnic Area** (El. 5,390 ft) (9.1), which is situated in stands of Yellow Pine and Incense Cedar in the Transition Life Zone. Look here for White-headed Woodpecker, Pygmy Nuthatch, and Purple Finch at any season, and in summer for Western Tanager, Black-headed Grosbeak, Lawrence's Goldfinch, and Violet-green Swallow. If you are lucky, you may find Red Crossbills. During dry weather, many birds can be attracted by turning on a water faucet to a drip for a minute. Or rig a hanging plastic soda-bottle full of water to drip slowly into a pan. The water in the stream along the trail between Charlton Flat and Chilao Campground also lures many birds.

Nearby, there is one of the many burned-over areas (0.5) that have now grown over. This one has been planted to Coulter and Knob-cone Pines. Some of the burned areas are planted with non-native trees, so you may find anything growing there.

You will soon reach the entrance to the **Chilao Recreation Area** (El. 5,200 ft) (1.4). It has about the same birds as Charlton Flat. Check here in summer for Lawrence's Goldfinch, Red-breasted Sapsucker, Great Horned Owl, Northern Pygmy-Owl, and Black-chinned, Fox, and Chipping Sparrows. Although this is the largest camping area in the forest, it is still packed on summer weekends.

As you continue along Angeles Crest Highway, you will come to steep Devil's Canyon Trail (0.8), leading to the primitive Devil's Canyon Wilderness Area. Almost immediately to the left of the trailhead is the Chilao Visitors' Center (0.1). Pick up a bird checklist (open daily 9-5) and look for Mountain Quail. Try looking from the wooden bridge by the entrance at 9 a.m. or 3:30 p.m. The ranger has been feeding the quail at these times for some years now. If you miss the showtime, check the scrub brush behind the Center, where the birds may be awaiting the next feeding. Western Bluebirds are abundant in the picnic areas, and Red Crossbills are possible.

Above 6,000 feet, you will find White Firs, which are indicators of the Canadian Life Zone. Watch for Clark's Nutcracker, Williamson's Sapsucker, and Red-breasted Nuthatch.

The **Buckhorn Flat Campground** (El. 6,500 ft) (7.8) is another fine stopping place. (The entrance is on the left; a very small sign is on the right.) At this higher elevation, the brush-patches will yield Common Poorwill, Dusky Flycatcher, Green-tailed Towhee, and Fox Sparrow. Also look for Olive-sided Flycatcher, Violet-green Swallow, Pine Siskin, and at night Flammulated and Northern Saw-whet Owls. Where the campground exit road rejoins the Angeles Crest Highway, the streamside willows have breeding MacGillivray's and Wilson's Warblers. A few pairs of Hermit

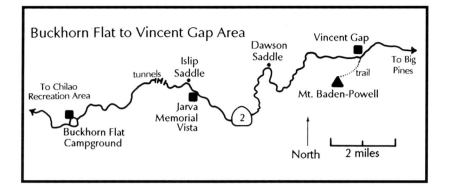

Warblers nest in the pines and firs in this area. A hike downstream from the lower end of the campground may also yield American Dippers. Back on the highway you will soon come to the only tunnels along this highway (4.6). Canyon and Rock Wrens are both resident here, and Bighorn Sheep can often be seen on the ridge above the tunnels. Black-throated Gray Warblers summer in the live oaks in this area. If you need help with the plants, continue on to the Sierra Vista Nature Trail at the Jarva Memorial Vista (0.8).

If the road is open beyond Islip Saddle (occasionally closed November to May), continue on to **Dawson Saddle** (El. 7,901 ft) (5.3), the highest point on the loop. Stop at the pullout on the left for the excellent view of the desert far below. Take time to check the Jeffrey, Sugar, and Lodgepole Pines and White Firs, both above and below the road, for high-mountain species such as Williamson's Sapsucker, Clark's Nutcracker, Red-breasted Nuthatch, Townsend's Solitaire, Cassin's Finch, and Lodgepole Chipmunk. You may also want to stop at Vincent Gap (5.4) and take the 3.5-mile trail that winds through ancient stands of Limber Pines to the summit of Mount Baden-Powell (El. 9,399 ft). This trail is popular with the Boy Scouts, after whose founder the mountain was named.

The highway winds on along the ridge to the **Big Pines Recreation Area** (5.0), a popular spot in both summer and winter. At the intersection, you have a choice of three roads. The one in the center, marked "Table Mountain Road", goes to a campground atop Table Mountain (1.0), a delightful spot. The birds here will be the same observed more easily at previous stops. Still, you can watch White-headed Woodpeckers and Pygmy Nuthatches in the stately pines while enjoying the view of the Mojave Desert far below.

Down the hill to the right on Highway 2 is the little town of Wrightwood (4.0). Check the willows above town for Calliope Hummingbirds and MacGillivray's Warblers. Many of the cabins in town have feeders; in summer there should be a Calliope Hummingbird at one of them. A couple of miles below the town, you will find an area of pinyon and juniper. Gray Vireos have been found here, but you will need all your good-luck charms.

The way to see a Gray Vireo is to step into the growth, listen for a song similar to that of the Solitary Vireo, watch the base of the shrubs or trees, and rapidly follow the bird that you see feeding there. This vireo moves about a great deal, but is not really shy. You just have to follow briskly.

To follow the loop, turn left on the Big Pines Highway (Route N4), which eventually leads to the desert in Antelope Valley. You will soon come to Jackson Lake (2.8), which is too small to attract waterbirds; however, many other birds come to drink. As the road continues to drop down the mountain, the Yellow Pines are replaced by Coulter Pines, and, in turn, by One-leaf Pinyons and Joshua Trees. The Coulter Pine has the heaviest cone of any American pine.

The Fremont Cottonwoods at Big Rock Creek Road (Route 4N11) (4.8) sometimes attract Lewis's Woodpeckers in winter. Check mistletoe clumps in fall and winter for Phainopepla, Townsend's Solitaire, and Western

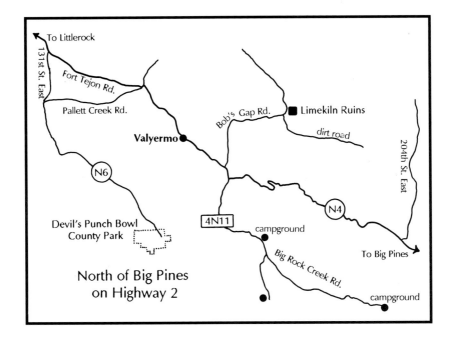

North of Big Pines
on Highway 2

Bluebird. In summer, you can find Cassin's Kingbird, Ash-throated Flycatcher, Warbling Vireo, Yellow-breasted Chat, and other riparian birds in the vicinity of the two forestry campgrounds, which are about 4 miles up Big Rock Creek to the left. Turn right on Bob's Gap Road (0.2) and continue to a dirt road leading right (east) (2.2) just before the historical limekiln ruin site. (They look like huge pillars built into the side of the hill.) There is excellent desert woodland here, with Joshua Trees, California Juniper, and scattered Single-leaf Pinyon. Gray Vireos nest here from April through July (*do not play tapes*—this may be the last remaining Los Angeles County population); also nesting are Scott's Orioles, Ladder-backed Woodpeckers (resident), Black-throated and Black-chinned Sparrows, Mountain Quail, and Verdins—an interesting mix of desert and montane species.

Return to Route N4 and continue west; then turn left at Pallett Creek Road (2.8) toward the Devil's Punch Bowl County Park. The cottonwood and willow-riparian habitat at Pallett Creek Road may be alive with spring migrants and nesting birds. Summer Tanagers occasionally nest here. Go one-half block and turn right on Fort Tejon (Tay-HONE) Road. (If you are interested in a series of unusual rock formations, though, you may want to detour down Pallett Creek Road toward the Devil's Punch Bowl County Park, about 6.5 miles away.) For the next 8 miles, Fort Tejon Road passes stands of Joshua Trees, which harbor Ladder-backed Woodpecker, Verdin, Scott's Oriole (summer) and Cactus Wren. Turn over the dead branches and look for Desert Night Lizards and other reptiles (replace the branches when you're through looking). The delicate little plant with the red stem is a species of buckwheat.

When the pavement ends (8.0), turn right on 82nd Street to Littlerock (El. 2,900 ft) (0.5). The area to the north and east of this little town is famous for its spring wildflowers, and a good spot for finding LeConte's Thrasher. For details on this site and other good birding northward in Antelope Valley, especially in winter, see the *Miscellaneous Areas* section.

Turn left onto the Pearblossom Highway (Highway 138). At Four Points (3.4), turn left toward Los Angeles and the Antelope Valley Freeway (Highway 14) (5.3). Instead of getting on the freeway, keep left under the overpass, and turn left onto the Angeles Forest Highway (Route N3) toward Pasadena.

The first few miles near Vincent are usually drab, but in April the slopes can be vivid with wildflowers. Beyond the electrical installation (1.5) the wash is filled with Great Basin Sage and an occasional California Juniper. This is a good spot for Sage and Brewer's (mostly winter) Sparrows. As you begin to climb the mountain, watch on the left for little Aliso Spring Picnic

Area (7.6) shaded by a few Canyon Live Oaks. The little spring here attracts many birds.

Past the summit (El. 4,900 ft) (0.7) the road drops rapidly into Mill Creek Canyon. Among the White Alders and Western Sycamores below the Monte Cristo Campground (5.2), you can find riparian birds. In winter, look for Hermit Thrush, Ruby-crowned Kinglet, Yellow-rumped Warbler, and Golden-crowned and Fox Sparrows, and in summer for Swainson's Thrush, Black-chinned and Costa's Hummingbirds, Ash-throated Flycatcher, Warbling Vireo, Yellow Warbler, Northern Oriole, Black-headed Grosbeak, and Lazuli Bunting. Check the brushy hillsides for Black-chinned and Rufous-crowned Sparrows.

At the tunnel (2.6) check the rocky cliffs for White-throated Swifts and Canyon Wrens. Turn right down Big Tujunga (Tuh-HUN-gah) Canyon (3.0) toward Sunland. This road is lined with Scotch Broom, which bursts into brilliant yellow blossoms in spring.

Turn left on Vogel Flats Road (5.2) to the **Stoneyvale Picnic Area.** Although crowded with homes, this spot has many birds. Scrub Jay, Western Bluebird, Bewick's Wren, Wrentit, Plain Titmouse, and Rufous-sided and California Towhees are abundant.

Return to the main road and follow it via Oro Vista to Foothill Boulevard (6.3) in Sunland. Turn left to the starting point (7.2).

From here you might wish to stop at the nearby Descanso Gardens or Devil's Gate Reservoir (see Miscellaneous Areas section). Or, if you have conscientiously followed all the birding trips in this book thoroughly and in order, you might like to make your way back to the Santa Monica Mountains to start all over again. It will surely be a different time of the year from when you started, and you should be able to find an excitingly different variety of species in never-static Southern California.

There are numerous campgrounds throughout the mountains. Cabins and motels are available at Wrightwood and at all of the cities on both sides of the mountains.

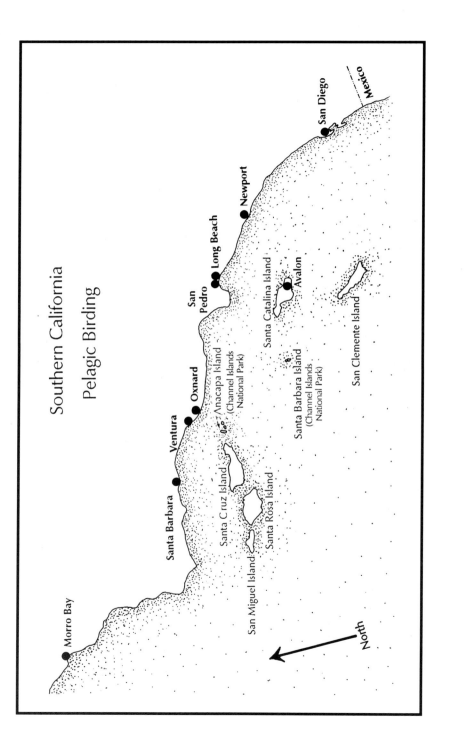

Southern California

Pelagic Birding

Morro Bay

Santa Barbara

Ventura

Oxnard

San Pedro

Long Beach

Newport

San Diego

Mexico

Avalon

San Miguel Island

Santa Rosa Island

Santa Cruz Island

Anacapa Island
(Channel Islands
National Park)

Santa Catalina Island

Santa Barbara Island
(Channel Islands
National Park)

San Clemente Island

North

PELAGIC BIRDING TRIPS

Some 25 or more pelagic species can be found off the coast of Southern California, but there is little hope of seeing them unless you take a boat to their offshore habitat. Even if you don't own a suitable yacht, there are still a number of ways to go out to sea.

The best plan is to sign up for a pelagic birding trip scheduled by local birders. These trips are reasonably-priced and well-conducted by experienced leaders. They are very popular, however, and are often booked solid for weeks in advance, so be sure to make your inquiries and reservations early. A beginning pelagic birder is well-advised to take the first several trips in the company of birders experienced with the territory. Things happen quickly, and often there is simply no time to consult your field guide before another life bird wheels by. Do your homework before getting on board (Stallcup's *Ocean Birds of the Nearshore Pacific*, 1990, was written specifically to help pelagic birders hone their skills), assume that you will get seasick and take the precautions proper for you, and park yourself at the rail within earshot of one of the trip's leaders. Once you've learned to recognize the more common species, keep on trying to identify each bird you are able to get in your binoculars. Eventually you will turn up something new and different.

The **Los Angeles Audubon Society** (7377 Santa Monica Boulevard, Los Angeles, CA 90046; Phone: 213/876-0202) runs several trips a year from San Pedro. While the itinerary may vary from year-to-year, the boats generally head for the waters around Santa Barbara Island and the Osborne Banks, an area of shallower-than-average water well offshore where conditions create a feeding-ground for pelagic species.

The **Morro Coast Audubon Society** (PO Box 160, Morro Bay, CA 93442) usually has at least a fall trip. Contact them in advance for details.

Western Field Ornithologists (4637 Del Mar Avenue, San Diego, CA 92107; Phone: 619/223-7985 or 619/464-7342) schedule very popular trips in May and September departing Mission Bay in San Diego. Tour groups of various sizes often book for these trips well in advance, making early inquiry on your part desirable. These trips may head out as far as possible for a one-day trip or alternately may search the waters around San Clemente Island.

Shearwater Journeys (PO Box 1445, Dept. LSC, Soquel, CA 95073; Phone: 408/688-1990) concentrates its busy pelagic-trip schedule in the waters around Monterey Bay and northward. However, they generally include a September trip departing Mission Bay in San Diego, and have run a number of 3-day trips to the Davidson Seamount, leaving from Santa Barbara. These longer trips search for rarities such as *Pterodroma* petrels and vagrant shearwaters and are quite an adventure for the birder not accustomed to pelagic birding—and even for those who are!

Another option is a luxury trip on the steamer or ferry to **Santa Catalina Island**. This route can be good for pelagic birds, but it varies. On a typical trip in fall and winter you should see Black-vented Shearwater, and if it is a good year for Northern Fulmar (irregular), you should be able to find one or more. Other pelagic species you could see are Parasitic and Pomarine Jaegers, Black-legged Kittiwake (irregular), Common Murre, and Rhinoceros Auklet. You may see Black Storm-Petrel in summer and early fall, and Sooty and Pink-footed Shearwaters in late spring and summer. While you might not see many birds on some of the ferry-crossings, Xantus's Murrelet is always a possibility. Catalina cruises leave daily from San Pedro and Long Beach. The San Pedro terminal is under the Vincent Thomas Bridge; the trips from Long Beach leave from 320 Golden Shore Boulevard. There are at least a few trips a day starting from either location, but the schedule changes seasonally and on weekends. Make reservations at any ticket office, or phone 213/514-3838 or 800/888-5939. (For details on birding onshore on Santa Catalina Island, see *Miscellaneous Areas*.)

An excellent way to find pelagic birds is to go out with the fishermen, but careful inquiries and planning are required to make sure that you get on the best boat for your needs. Birds often follow schools of fish, and fishermen follow the birds to these movable fishing locations. Nearly every pier and marina along the coast has a landing where you can buy tickets for deep-sea fishing boats. The cost runs from $10 to $30, depending on the time and distance traveled. Make sure that the boat is going to the islands or well offshore. Half-day trips to the kelp beds a mile or so off the beach are a waste of money. The best boat-landings for this venture are the Point Loma Landing at Shelter Island in San Diego or one of the landings along Quivira Drive in Mission Bay.

You can take boats from many locations, but most go to the same select fishing areas. Those docking farther away from these areas just take longer to get there. In order to save money and have more time in the good birding waters, arrange to board a boat docking closest to the area you wish to visit. Boats to the **Coronados Islands** and the **Baja California Fishing Banks** should be taken from San Diego; both these locations are in Mexican waters. For **San Miguel** and **Santa Rosa Islands**, take a boat from Santa Barbara Harbor, and for **Santa Cruz** and **Anacapa Islands**, leave from the Ventura Marina, or the Channel Island Harbor at Oxnard.

Fishing trips off Santa Catalina and San Clemente Islands are usually the least productive, but you can take these from Ports O' Call in San Pedro, Pierpoint and Pacific Landings in Long Beach, or Norm's Landing in Newport. Fishing boats out of Morro Bay—at the northern edge of this guide's coverage—often yield good pelagic birds.

The **Channel Islands National Park**, made up of San Miguel, Santa Rosa, Anacapa, and Santa Barbara Islands and the east end of Santa Cruz Island, may also be reached through a private concessionaire, **Island Packers**. Their office is located next to the park headquarters (1867 Spinnaker Drive, Ventura, CA 93001; Phone: 805/642-7688 for recorded schedule and fare information or 805/642-1393 for reservations).

If you can schedule a trip to just Anacapa Island in the late fall or winter months, you should find, with a little luck, such birds as Northern Fulmar (if it is a good fulmar year), Black-vented Shearwater (pretty well guaranteed), Red Phalarope, Pomarine and Parasitic Jaegers, Black-legged Kittiwake (irregular), Common Murre, and Cassin's and Rhinoceros Auklets. From May to September you should find Black and Ashy (rarer) Storm-Petrels and a possible Least Storm-Petrel (late summer to early fall). Another pelagic species which you have an 80 to 100 percent chance of finding (late February to early July) is Xantus's Murrelet (nests on the island). When your boat approaches to within three or four miles of Anacapa Island, start watching for pairs (March to early June is best). Other breeding birds for the island include Brown Pelican, Double-crested, Brandt's, and Pelagic Cormorants, Black Oystercatcher, and Pigeon Guillemot.

The best regularly-run boat trip for birders wishing to go to the National Park is an Island Packers pelagic trip to **Santa Barbara Island**, some 35 miles beyond Anapaca. Plan your trip from late spring through Labor Day; this trip is especially good from May through early June, and mid-August through mid-October. Because of the deeper water beyond Anacapa, you could find such birds as Black-footed Albatross, Flesh-footed Shearwater, and South Polar Skua along with most of the above-mentioned species. Horned Puffins have been seen a few times in late spring, and Red-footed Booby and Brown Booby have each been seen once. Of course, these latter species are casual visitors.

If you are going farther north to Monterey, beyond the scope of this book, plan to take a boat trip there. Monterey is usually the best spot for pelagic birding on the Pacific Coast, and you do not have to go very far off-shore to see the desirable species. Contact Shearwater Journeys for details on their trips.

There are several things to remember when taking boat trips (particularly when going out with fishermen):

1. Take the largest boat available. The higher you are above the water, the more birds you will see.

2. Make sure the boat is going well offshore. Unless you get out over 5 miles (except at Monterey), you are wasting your time.

3. If possible, talk to the captain before buying your ticket and tell him that you are going birdwatching. He will know if his trip is good for that purpose. Sometimes, you can get a reduction in price if you are not fishing. Also ask for permission to get on the upper deck out of the way of the fishermen; you can see more from up there.

4. Take a warm coat at any time of year.

Craveri's Murrelet
Sabine's Gull
Shawneen Finnegan

5. Tripod-mounted spotting scopes are not permitted (and are usually useless) onboard. But you might be able to use a gunstock-mounted scope successfully in calm seas.

6. Do not expect to find all species on one trip. Familiarize yourself with the seasonal status of the pelagic species. To accumulate a large pelagic bird list requires many boat trips.

To find the greatest number of pelagic birds on one trip, you should probably go in the fall (from mid-August to mid-October). This is when most of the shearwaters, jaegers, Arctic Terns, Sabine's Gulls, and petrels are moving by. Even then, you may not see a thing, for pelagic birds are very unpredictable. Winter is the time for Northern Fulmar and most alcids, while the rare Red-billed Tropicbird usually shows up in late summer and early fall. Your best bet is to go to sea every chance you get.

Each January, the American Birding Association's newsletter, *Winging It*, devotes an entire issue to detailing pelagic birding trip opportunities in the U.S. and Canada. Schedules, as well as lists of expected species (often broken down seasonally or for specific trips) are given. Write for a free copy of this issue and information about the ABA's other activities and publications: American Birding Association, PO Box 6599, Colorado Springs, CO 80934.

Winter is also the season for Gray Whales. Some 6,000 or more of these huge creatures, up to 50 feet long, annually migrate from Alaska to the calving bays in Baja California. In Southern California the peak of the southward movement is reached in late December and January, and the northward movement peaks in late March and April. While their spouts may be seen from shore, the best way to see whales is from one of the whale-watching boats, which are operated out of nearly every marina and landing, including Island Packers out of Ventura Marina.

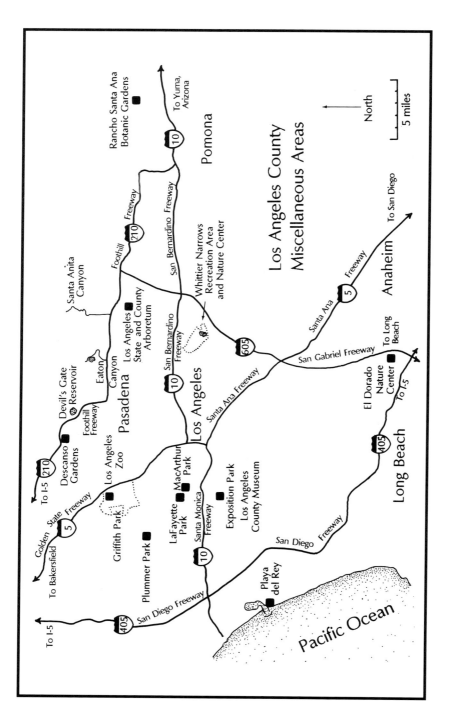

Los Angeles County
Miscellaneous Areas

North
5 miles

To Yuma, Arizona

Rancho Santa Ana Botanic Gardens

Pomona

Foothill Freeway

San Bernardino Freeway

Whittier Narrows Recreation Area and Nature Center

Santa Anita Canyon

Los Angeles State and County Arboretum

Eaton Canyon

Devil's Gate Reservoir

Pasadena

San Bernardino Freeway

Los Angeles

Anaheim

To San Diego

Santa Ana Freeway

San Gabriel Freeway

To Long Beach

El Dorado Nature Center

To I-5

Foothill Freeway

To I-5

Descanso Gardens

Los Angeles Zoo

Golden State Freeway

To Bakersfield

Griffith Park

Plummer Park

LaFayette Park

MacArthur Park

Santa Monica Freeway

Exposition Park
Los Angeles County Museum

Santa Ana Freeway

San Diego Freeway

Long Beach

San Diego Freeway

Playa del Rey

To I-5

San Diego Freeway

Pacific Ocean

MISCELLANEOUS AREAS

The following are miscellaneous birding areas in Southern California that are not dealt with in the main text. (Some are referred to in the chapters, however.) These areas are in the following counties: San Bernardino, Riverside, Imperial, San Diego, Orange, and Los Angeles.

Other fine areas, not dealt with in either the main text or in this section, are just outside the geographical range of this book. They had to be left out—e.g., Death Valley National Monument for migration and winter rarities, and localities up the San Luis Obispo County coast toward the Hearst Castle at San Simeon.

SAN BERNARDINO COUNTY

Cima—Avid birders wishing to build up their California list often go to Cima for thrashers and other desert species. The virtually deserted town is best reached from the Barstow Freeway (I-15) some 25 miles east of Baker. Take the well-marked Cima turnoff and head south.

Watch for Bendire's Thrasher within the first 5 miles. They are fairly common among the Creosote Bushes and Joshua Trees. Also look for LeConte's Thrasher. There can be Gilded Northern Flicker (rare), Ladder-backed Woodpecker, Cactus Wren, Scott's Oriole, and Black-throated Sparrow here. Eventually you will come to a farmhouse (12.7) with a stock pond. The introduced Gambel's Quail and Chukar come here to drink, and so does an assortment of passerines.

At Cima (no facilities) (4.5) turn right, cross the railroad tracks, and drive south toward Kelso on the road following the tracks. Bendire's Thrasher can often be seen on exposed perches along the road. After 4.5 miles turn left (east) on Cedar Canyon Road, a dirt road that crosses the tracks. Again check for Bendire's Thrasher and Gilded Northern Flicker. Follow this road for about 6 miles into the foothills of the Providence Mountains. Look for the rare Gray Vireo on the well-vegetated hillsides among the pinyons and junipers, which are the dominant plants. You may also find Chukar, Pinyon Jay, Cactus Wren, Crissal Thrasher, Black-throated Gray Warbler, Scott's Oriole, Black-throated and Black-chinned Sparrows, Rock Squirrel, and Panamint Chipmunk.

The community of Kelso (no facilities), which was a track-repairmen's town, is dominated by the Kelso Railroad Depot. Until recently the watered lawns and huge shade trees attracted migrants, including some rarities. An effort is presently underway to generate support for restoration of the depot/hotel building. When conditions improve, the area will be at its best in late May and again in early fall.

Mojave Narrows Regional Park and Wildlife Area—Accessible from Interstate 15 about three miles south of Victorville. Exit at the Bear Valley Cut Off. Go east to Ridge Crest Road (3.9) and turn left to the park entrance (2.6) (fee; camping). This 800-acre desert oasis has substantial groves of cottonwoods and willows along the river. Several small lakes and ponds with adjacent open meadows, farmland, and arid desert highlands all combine to make the area a most unusual habitat for a varied assortment of bird life. During migration, numerous warblers and other landbirds are found. In summer look for Black-chinned Hummingbird, Ash-throated Flycatcher, Hutton's and Warbling Vireos, Yellow Warbler, Yellow-breasted Chat, Northern Oriole, Blue Grosbeak, and Lazuli Bunting. Resident birds such as Virginia Rail, Common Moorhen, six species of hawks, six species of owls, four woodpeckers including Ladder-backed, and eleven finches and sparrows are all here. Occasionally, you can find Summer Tanager and Vermilion Flycatcher.

San Bernardino County Museum—2024 Orange Tree Lane (take California Street exit off I-10 in Redlands). Large egg collection, bird exhibits, and bookstore. Sunday 10-5, Tuesday-Saturday 9-5, closed Monday.

RIVERSIDE COUNTY

Desert Center—The Lake Tamarisk Golf Course area is always worth a visit during migrations and winter for landbirds. Rarities—warblers, flycatchers, thrushes—have occurred here. The lake itself is interesting for waterbirds. Some two miles west of Desert Center is the Edmund C. Jaeger Nature Center. Not very birdy and difficult to reach, it can be found by following the road under the power lines along the south side of the freeway, then turning south. It was the discovery site of the hibernating Common Poorwill.

San Timoteo Canyon (Tee-mo-TAY-o)—When you are returning from the desert to Los Angeles on Interstate 10, this old section of the highway allows you to get off the crowded freeway for a few miles. The grassy hillsides along the canyon abound with Black-tailed Jackrabbit, Desert Cottontail, California Ground-Squirrel, and mice that attract Golden Eagle, hawks, Black-shouldered Kite, and Long-tailed Weasel. In winter, also watch for Mountain Bluebird and perhaps a Prairie Falcon. Check the two trout-farm ponds at the RV park for ducks, Tricolored Blackbirds, and Black Phoebes (birders are welcome to free day-use). In summer, look for Bell's Vireo (rare), Blue Grosbeak, Northern Oriole, and Lazuli Bunting in the trees along the stream.

To reach the canyon, go west from Beaumont past the intersection of Highway 60. Go another 1.3 miles and turn south at the well-marked exit for San Timoteo Canyon. When this road ends at Barton Road (16.3), turn left to Waterman Road (3.6), then right to the freeway.

IMPERIAL COUNTY

Cibola National Wildlife Refuge—This 12-mile-long refuge is located on the lower Colorado River, 20 miles south of Blythe. Its southern boundary adjoins Imperial National Wildlife Refuge. The main portion of the refuge is alluvial river-bottom with dense growths of Salt-cedar, mesquite, and Arrowweed. The Colorado River flows through the refuge, in both a dredged channel and through a portion of its original channel. Some 2,000 acres of farmland and 785 acres of desert foothills and ridges are also included within refuge boundaries, for a total of 16,627 acres. Over the years, 232 species of birds have been found here, with 48 species nesting. Nesting species include Great Egret, Great Blue Heron, Black-crowned Night-Heron, Least Bittern, Yuma Clapper Rail, White-winged Dove, Greater Roadrunner, Western Screech-Owl, Great Horned and Burrowing Owls, Lesser Nighthawk, Common Poorwill, Gila and Ladder-backed Woodpeckers, Verdin, Cactus and Rock Wrens, Black-tailed Gnatcatcher, Crissal Thrasher (common), Phainopepla, Blue Grosbeak, and Abert's Towhee (common). Many Canada Geese, ducks, and shorebirds winter here, along with good numbers of Sandhill Cranes.

To reach the area, drive south on Highway 78 from Interstate 10 at the western edge of Blythe. Continue through Palo Verde (16.3) into Imperial County. Palo Verde County Park on Oxbow Lake (1.8) is a good (free) place to camp. At the south end of the lake turn east and jog left and then right to cross the river. (At the jog is another free campground, Palo Verde Oxbow, operated by the BLM). (Also at this point, you can explore a dirt road leading south along the dredged channel for 4.8 miles.)

After crossing the river, immediately turn right (south) to Baseline Road (1.0), where you will turn left to Cibola Road (2.7). (The road that continues straight ahead at the turn follows the left bank of the river for 5 miles.) Turn right (south) on Cibola Road to the headquarters of the Cibola NWR (1.0). Pick up a checklist and a map. The road continues south to Farm Unit #2 (4.3), where you can cross the river to Farm Unit #3. Both units are good in fall and winter for Sandhill Cranes and shorebirds. Back at the junction, Cibola Road continues south to Hart Mine Marsh (good for bitterns, rails, and Common Moorhen) and Cibola Lake (8.3).

SAN DIEGO COUNTY

De Luz Valley—This delightful little valley on the back side of Camp Pendleton can be alive with birds. To reach it, go to Fallbrook. At the north edge of the business district the main highway (S-13), northbound from Highway 76, makes a 90-degree right turn. Turn left at the first block, then bear left at the first junction (1.2). The road follows the Santa Margarita River, then crosses it and continues through chaparral-covered hills for 8.1 miles to the almost-deserted settlement of De Luz. Beyond this, you can follow the road through the hills for 13.2 miles to Rancho California. This is strictly a fair-weather drive because several streams must be forded.

Silverwood—This sanctuary of the San Diego Audubon Society is at 13003 Wildcat Canyon Road north of Lakeside. It is in a fine area of chaparral and oak woodland. Some of the common birds are California Quail, Anna's and Black-chinned Hummingbirds, Northern Flicker, Acorn and Nuttall's Woodpeckers, Ash-throated Flycatcher, Scrub Jay, Plain Titmouse, Bushtit, Wrentit, House and Bewick's Wrens, California Thrasher, Western Bluebird, American and Lesser Goldfinches, Northern Oriole, Black-headed Grosbeak, and, in winter, numerous sparrows. Call the Society (Phone: 619/443-2998) for visitation hours.

ORANGE COUNTY

Santa Ana River—The *Coastal Orange County Loop* covers the lower end of this river, and the *Western Riverside County Loop* covers some river sites in Riverside County. There are other locations in between along the river, in and near Anaheim at the northeast edge of Orange County, that birders regularly cover. Yorba Regional Park, off La Palma Avenue, offers a mix of park birds, ducks, and shorebirds. Given its proximity to the Santa Ana River, it can be good in winter and migration. Shorebirds on the river in winter include Greater Yellowlegs, Western (rare) and Least Sandpipers, Short-billed (rare) and Long-billed Dowitchers, and Common Snipe. Migrations bring many more species. Two other access points along the river—depending on water levels—are Riverdale Park and the dike and bike trail in either direction from the Lincoln Avenue Bridge.

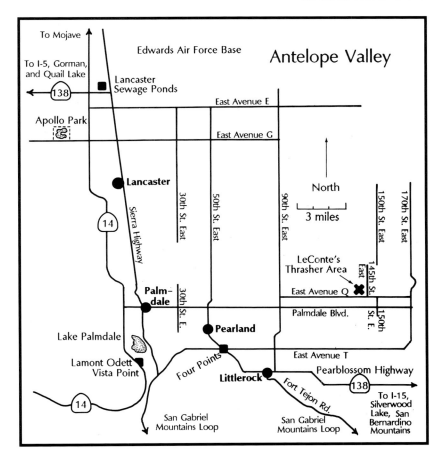

To Mojave

To I-5, Gorman, and Quail Lake

138

Edwards Air Force Base

Antelope Valley

Lancaster Sewage Ponds

East Avenue E

Apollo Park

East Avenue G

Lancaster

14

Sierra Highway

30th St. East

50th St. East

90th St. East

North

3 miles

150th St. East

170th St. East

LeConte's Thrasher Area

145th St. East

Palm-dale

30th St. E.

East Avenue Q

Palmdale Blvd.

150th St. E.

Lake Palmdale

Pearland

Lamont Odett Vista Point

Four Points

East Avenue T

Littlerock

Pearblossom Highway

138

San Gabriel Mountains Loop

Fort Tejon Rd.

San Gabriel Mountains Loop

To I-15, Silverwood Lake, San Bernardino Mountains

14

LOS ANGELES COUNTY

Antelope Valley—The grassy hills along Highway 138 between Gorman and Lancaster are good in winter for Rough-legged and Ferruginous Hawks, Prairie Falcon, and Mountain Bluebird; and, in spring, for wildflowers. Quail Lake, on the north side of Highway 138 about 3 miles east of Interstate 5, should be checked in winter for waterfowl. Tufted Duck has been a regular there.

Antelope Valley is laid out in a regular grid with lettered avenues running from east to west, starting with Avenue A as the northern boundary of Los Angeles County, ascending southward through the alphabet with exactly one mile between each lettered avenue. The numbered streets, which run north to south, are numbered east and west from Division Street. Every tenth street is exactly one mile apart.

Apollo Park, entered from Avenue G and 50th Street West, is good for waterfowl, especially in winter. The **Lancaster Sewage Ponds**, good for waterfowl and shorebirds, are located north of Lancaster at the northeast corner of Avenue D (Highway 138) and Highway 14. (Be sure to check in, and be out by the gate-closing time of 3 p.m.) Drive slowly around the impoundments, which have different, variable water-levels.

If you continue south on Highway 14 to Palmdale (14.0), there is an overlook (Lamont Odett Vista Point) for Lake Palmdale, where one can scope winter ducks and an occasional loon. More importantly, Palmdale is a departure point for finding LeConte's Thrasher. To reach a good spot, go east on Palmdale Boulevard to 150th Street East. Turn left (north) to East Avenue Q, then left to 145th Street East, and park. The birds are regularly found in the area northwest of this intersection. The best time to see them is during the breeding season (February through April), when you may find one singing. They are most active in early mornings and evenings. Walk slowly and scan the bushes far ahead. In the same area you might also find Ladder-backed Woodpecker. (Don't be fooled by the Nuttall's, which are sometimes found here, too.) Look for Verdin and Scott's Oriole.

Agricultural fields or Salt Brush, Creosote, and Joshua Trees once covered the Antelope Valley, but they are quickly being replaced by development to provide a low-cost bedroom community for Los Angeles. Some good agricultural areas still remain in the east end of the valley, roughly bounded by 30th Street East, Avenue E, 170th Street East, and Avenue T. These fields can be checked in fall for the occasional longspur, in winter for Mountain Bluebird and Mountain Plover, in migration for various shorebirds, and at small farm ponds and livestock feed-lots for Tricolored Blackbirds.

Descanso Gardens—(1418 Descanso Drive, La Cañada Flintridge 91011; Phone: 818/790-5571. Beautiful gardens with many common birds. Look for hummingbirds among the flowers and songbirds in the large stand of Coast Live Oaks. Check out the bird-observation station. There are bird walks on the second and fourth Sundays of the month. Open 9-5 (fee).

Devil's Gate Reservoir—This lake, located in Oak Grove Canyon off Interstate 210 at the southeast edge of La Cañada Flintridge, can be good for ducks in winter.

Eaton Canyon—The park and nature center are located in an area of chaparral and oak woodlands, which can be very good for foothill birds. (1750 Altadena Drive, Pasadena 91107; Phone: 818/794-1866)

El Dorado Nature Center—(7550 East Spring Street, Long Beach; Phone: 213/425-8569) This spot has a nature center and riparian woodland and is usually good for casual birding. Stop at the visitors' center for a bird checklist and other information. To reach it from southbound I-605, exit at Spring Street (north of I-405) and watch for the entrance on the left (south). If northbound, exit on Katella Avenue, turn left (north) onto Los Alamitos Boulevard, and left (west) onto Cerritos Avenue, which becomes Spring Street west of I-605. The trails are open from 8 to 4. The Nature Center is closed on Mondays.

This is a pleasant place to bird regardless of the season. In two to three hours, forty to eighty species is an average total. In summer, look for Ruddy Duck, Common Moorhen, Spotted Dove, Allen's, Black-chinned, and Anna's Hummingbirds, Downy Woodpecker, Ash-throated Flycatcher, Western Kingbird, Northern and Hooded Orioles, Orange-crowned Warbler, and most of the "normal" Southern California passerines. This is a reliable place for California Towhee at any season.

There are two lakes, the south one (with a two-mile trail) being better for waterfowl. Between seven and ten species of waterfowl are normal in winter. The area around the front gate and the visitors' center is attractive to warblers, Allen's Hummingbirds, and Ruby-crowned Kinglets (except summer). There is a good assortment of passerines throughout. Rarities show up here fairly often, even though it is not a "hotspot". Time permitting, drive to the northernmost section of the park (Area III) to look for Tricolored, Red-winged, and Yellow-headed Blackbirds (spring and summer), assorted waterfowl, Long-billed Curlew, and American Pipits (winter).

Griffith Park—This is not only the home of the Los Angeles Zoo, but this large park also has numerous trails and a scenic road. The best birding is in the Ferndale area and along the road to the Griffith Observatory. This area can be reached from Los Felix Boulevard, one block east of Western Avenue. The park can be reached by city bus.

Los Angeles County Museum—Located in Exposition Park just off the Harbor Freeway, the museum has extensive exhibits and an excellent collection of birds for those interested in research.

Los Angeles State and County Arboretum—This beautiful old estate at 301 North Baldwin in Arcadia has extensive gardens where birds abound. Many peafowl have nested here for years and now roam all over town. If you are not too particular, you can add them to your life list. The arboretum (fee) can be reached by city bus.

MacArthur and LaFayette Parks—The two parks along Wilshire Boulevard in the downtown district are of interest because of the resident Ringed Turtle-Doves. There is also a lake where many ducks winter.

Playa del Rey (PLY-ah dell Ray)—The rock jetties at the entrance to the harbor attract Brown Pelican, Double-crested and Brandt's Cormorants, gulls, terns, and, in fall and winter, Wandering Tattler, Black Turnstone, and Surfbird. The middle jetty is usually the best. To reach it, go south on Lincoln Boulevard (Highway 1) past Marina del Rey and turn right onto Culver Boulevard, which soon merges with Jefferson Boulevard. At the end of this road, turn right onto Pacific Avenue and go as far as you can. Park (fee) and walk across the old bridge to the middle jetty, or to the Ballona Wetlands for other shorebirds.

Plummer Park—The Los Angeles Audubon Society has its headquarters and bookstore in this park (7377 Santa Monica Boulevard, North Hollywood, 90046; Phone: 213/876-0202). The monthly meetings are also held here.

Rancho Santa Ana Botanic Garden—This very fine collection of native plants is located at 1500 North College in Claremont. It is at its best in April.

Santa Anita Canyon—This pleasant little canyon is great for a few hours of birding. The area near the falls above the picnic grounds is often good for American Dipper, Black Swift, and at night, Spotted Owl. To reach the canyon, go east from Pasadena to Santa Anita Avenue. Turn left (north) to the end of the road.

Santa Catalina Island—Although all species resident on the island can also be found on the mainland, you might want to explore the area around Avalon while waiting for the cruise ship to take you back to San Pedro or Long Beach. (See *Pelagic Birding Trips* chapter for details.) From Crescent Beach Road on Avalon Bay, walk or ride a rental bicycle or golf cart uphill on Catalina Avenue for three blocks. Jog right one block at Tremont Street and turn left onto Falls Canyon Road. Avalon Canyon Road soon splits off to the left; follow it uphill past the golf course and farther (for a total of about 1.7 miles) to the Wrigley Memorial Botanical Garden. Most of Catalina's endemic plants are on display here, as well as a fine collection of succulents from around the world. In summer look for Allen's Hummingbird, Northern Flicker, Black Phoebe, Rufous-sided Towhee, and Chipping Sparrow. Phainopepla and Northern Saw-whet Owl have also been found in or near the gardens. In winter you might see Pacific-slope Flycatcher, Bewick's Wren, Mountain Bluebird (on the ridgetops), Orange-crowned and Yellow-rumped Warblers, Golden-crowned and White-crowned Sparrows, and Dark-eyed Junco. If you have time, hike up Memorial Road (which begins right behind the Wrigley Memorial) to the ridge for a breathtaking view of the town. You'll have a view of the Palisades, a series of cliffs at the east end of Catalina, a favorite perching area for Bald Eagles.

Custom tours to the island's varied habitats—chaparral, coastal sage scrub, oak woodland, and riparian—can be arranged (see *WildBird*, Vol. 1, No. 4 [November/December 1987], pp. 30-37).

Whittier Narrows Nature Center—This sanctuary is located along the west bank of the San Gabriel River about ten miles east of downtown Los Angeles. Its riparian habitat, several lakes, chaparral, and open fields have attracted over 260 species of birds. Wintering waterfowl rest and feed on the lakes while shorebirds utilize the mudflats and sandbars along the river. Hawks and other landbirds are numerous during migrations, and many stay over the summer to nest. The introduced Northern Cardinal is now a rare resident here. The Center, open 9-5 seven days a week, is located on Durfee Avenue and is easily reached from Highway 60's Santa Anita exit, just west of Interstate 605. Go south to Durfee Avenue (0.7) and turn left (east) to the Center (0.5) on your right. Pick up trail maps and a bird checklist.

SPECIALTIES OF SOUTHERN CALIFORNIA

Red-throated (fairly common) and **Common Loons** (common) (both winter visitors) are found in the same areas as Pacific Loons. Rare on larger lakes inland.

Pacific Loon—Uncommon-but-regular winter visitor to coastal waters. Can usually be seen from one of the piers such as at Santa Barbara, Santa Monica, Seal Beach, Newport Beach, Oceanside, or Imperial Beach. The jetties at Playa del Rey and Corona del Mar are also good spots. Large numbers can be seen migrating, in spring, up the coast north of Los Angeles.

Horned Grebe—Uncommon-but-regular winter visitor to coastal waters, bays, and larger lakes. It can usually be found on San Diego or Newport bays, and at the various piers along the coast. Rare at the Salton Sea.

Eared Grebe—Common winter visitor to coastal waters, bays, lakes, and the Colorado River. Common-to-abundant on the Salton Sea. Uncommon summer resident on mountain lakes and occasionally elsewhere, such as at Buena Vista Lagoon and the Ventura sewage ponds.

Western Grebe—Fairly common winter visitor to coastal water and larger, deep-water lakes. Can usually be seen anywhere along the coast. It is most numerous close to shore. Also found on lakes such as Cachuma, Sherwood, Perris, Mathews, and the Salton Sea.

Clark's Grebe—Uncommon winter visitor to coastal waters; slightly more common on inland lakes such as the Salton Sea. Paler than Western Grebe; the white of the face extends around the eye, and the bill is more yellow-orange. Voice a single *creet*.

Black-footed Albatross—Uncommon-but-regular visitor to offshore waters in late spring to early summer. Sometimes seen from boats 30 miles or more at sea. Rarely observed inside Channel Islands.

Laysan Albatross—Casual offshore in late winter and spring. One record for the Salton Sea (1984), and at least two more inland.

Northern Fulmar—Irregular winter visitor, usually rare to uncommon, but may be fairly common. In flight years has been seen from piers and jetties, but most often found on pelagic trips.

Pink-footed Shearwater—Fairly common in summer well offshore, occasionally at other times. Often seen on pelagic trips. Rarely seen from shore.

Flesh-footed Shearwater—Rare spring and fall migrant well offshore. A few records at other seasons farther north.

Buller's Shearwater—Rare-but-regular fall migrant well offshore. Apparently fairly common north of this region, but seldom comes close to shore in Southern California. One record from the Salton Sea (1966).

Sooty Shearwater—Common offshore visitor from mid-April through October. Rare remainder of year. May be abundant in summer and fall. This is the shearwater most likely to be seen from shore (especially May-August north of Santa Barbara), but you will still do better on a pelagic trip. Three records from the Salton Sea.

Short-tailed Shearwater—Rare, or at least seldom-identified, fall and winter migrant (November-March) well offshore. Should be looked for behind boats.

Black-vented Shearwater—Irregular fall and winter visitor to offshore waters. May be common at times. Regularly seen from shore, when present.

Wilson's Storm-Petrel—Very rare fall visitor offshore.

Fork-tailed Storm-Petrel—Casual visitor to offshore waters at all seasons. Nests off Northern California.

Leach's Storm-Petrel—Mainly a spring and fall migrant well offshore only. At times fairly common. Nests on the islets of San Miguel. One record from the Salton Sea.

Ashy Storm-Petrel—Uncommon-to-common fall visitor, less common at other seasons. Nests on northern Channel Islands.

Black Storm-Petrel—Uncommon-to-fairly-common visitor offshore during spring, summer, and fall. Probably more common in summer. Has bred (May-December) on an islet off Santa Barbara Island.

Least Storm-Petrel—Irregular late August, September, and early October visitor from Mexican waters. Seen most regularly off San Diego. One record of several hundred birds from the Salton Sea (1976) following Tropical Storm Kathleen.

Red-billed Tropicbird—Rare-and-irregular summer and fall visitor to offshore waters, especially off the southern Channel Islands. Most birds are immatures without the long tail. Immatures closely resemble Royal Terns, but are larger with a heavier red bill and barred back.

Blue-footed Booby—Rare-and-irregular late summer and fall visitor to the Salton Sea and casual on large lakes elsewhere and at other seasons. In late summer and early fall it may occasionally be found at the north end of the Salton Sea, at Salton City, or at the south end. Most of the boobies stay one or two months before disappearing.

Brown Booby—Very-rare-and-irregular summer and fall visitor to the Salton Sea and the Colorado River, casual at other times. A few records offshore.

Brown Pelican—Fairly-common permanent resident along the coast and on Channel Islands. More common in summer and fall when population is augmented by Mexican birds. The **American White Pelican** is usually found on large inland lakes and at the Salton Sea, not on the ocean.

Brandt's Cormorant—Common permanent resident on Channel Islands. Mainly seen along the coast in the nonbreeding season. Prefers rocky areas and cliffs such as at Point Loma, Point Fermin, and in the Santa Barbara area.

Pelagic Cormorant—Fairly-common permanent resident on rocky cliffs of Channel Islands and north of Pt. Conception. Seen along the mainland in fall, winter, and early spring.

Magnificent Frigatebird—Rare summer visitor along the coast and to the Salton Sea.

White-faced Ibis—Uncommon, permanent resident of Imperial Valley. In larger numbers in migration. Uncommon and local in coastal marshes. Most often found in irrigated fields in Imperial Valley.

Wood Stork—Irregular post-breeding wanderer from Mexico to the Imperial Valley, and casually to the coastal marshes. Most common in late July, August, and September at the south end of the Salton Sea. Numbers have declined recently.

Fulvous Whistling-Duck—Uncommon summer resident of fresh-water lakes and flooded fields in the Imperial Valley, such as Ramer and Finney lakes. Recorded sporadically elsewhere.

Greater White-fronted Goose—Very uncommon winter visitor to Salton Sea and large inland lakes. Easiest to find at the Salton Sea.

Ross's Goose—Fairly common winter visitor to Salton Sea, occasionally elsewhere. Sometimes occurs with tame white ducks in city parks. The majority of these birds winter in the Central Valley of California; only a few drift farther south along the coast.

Brant—Uncommon migrant and winter visitor to the larger coastal bays and estuaries. Some winter at the mouth of the San Diego River, on San

Diego Bay, and at Morro Bay. A bit more widespread in spring; a small number over-summer.

Scoters—All three scoters winter along the coast. The Surf is most common, the Black is very rare, and the White-winged is irregular. Look for them just beyond the breakers on the ocean and on the larger bays. Can usually be seen from the piers and jetties. Small numbers of Surfs over-summer.

California Condor—No longer found in the wild. The last bird in the wild was captured April 19, 1987. There is a captive breeding program of 40 (1990) birds managed by the San Diego and Los Angeles zoos. There are plans to return some of the captive-reared birds to the wild.

Black-shouldered Kite—Uncommon permanent resident of the coastal plain and inland valleys at lower elevations and west of the deserts. More common in winter. Prefers areas of grassy hillsides or meadows which are bordered by densely-topped trees for nesting and perching. Some good areas are along Highway 101 north of Santa Barbara, adjacent to the mouth of the Santa Clara River at Ventura, the Marine Helicopter Base south of Santa Ana, along the Ortega Highway, Camp Pendleton, and Tijuana River Valley.

Harris's Hawk—Formerly an uncommon resident in the Colorado River Valley and the south end of the Salton Sea. It was extirpated by the early 1960s. Recent reports from the Imperial Dam area originate from banded birds reintroduced in the mid-1980s by a cooperative effort of the Bureau of Land Management, the Santa Cruz Research Center, and others. Recent pairing, nest building, and some successful breeding have been documented. There have also been reintroductions in the Salton Sea area.

Prairie Falcon—Uncommon permanent resident of rocky cliffs mainly in the deserts and grasslands. Ranges widely over open country when feeding and in the winter. More common and widespread in winter; a few are found along the coast.

Chukar—Widely introduced in arid regions such as the Mojave Desert. Sometimes locally common. Fairly common in the brushy deserts and hilly country north of Mojave, especially at Galileo Hill Park.

Gambel's Quail—Common permanent resident of brushlands near water in the deserts. Can be seen about oases such as at Twentynine Palms, Palm Canyon, Yaqui Well, Finney and Ramer lakes, and around the Salton Sea.

California Quail—Abundant permanent resident of chaparral and riparian brushlands west of the deserts. If you do much driving in the foothills, you are sure to see a covey scooting across the road.

Mountain Quail—Fairly common permanent resident of brushy terrain in the mountains, mostly above 2,500 feet in elevation. Although widespread, these shy birds can be hard to find. They are perhaps easiest to find in late summer when the young have fledged. Usually chanced upon along some back road. One consistently good place is the road leading to the top of Mount Pinos in summer and along the road between Crestline and Silverwood Lake in the San Bernardino Mountains.

Pacific Golden-Plover (*Pluvialis dominica fulva*)—Uncommon spring and fall transient, and winter visitor, along the coast. Usually not encountered until late August. Some over-winter, especially in the pastureland in the Santa Maria area, but also at Seal Beach National Wildlife Refuge and occasionally the San Diego River mouth area and Playa del Rey. The species may remain into late April. It is a casual transient and winter visitor at the Salton Sea. The **American Golden-Plover** (*Pluvialis dominica dominica*) occurs less regularly in spring and regularly in fall (mostly juveniles). These two subspecies of Lesser Golden-Plover are expected to be raised to the status of separate species.

Snowy Plover—Uncommon, local, and decreasing permanent resident of sandy beaches above the tide line. Occasionally occurs elsewhere, as at the Salton Sea where they are rather numerous. More common in winter. The way to find this bird is to walk the less-disturbed, dry, sandy beaches along the coast in winter.

Mountain Plover—Uncommon winter visitor on barren flats and smoothly-plowed fields of the coastal plains and in the Imperial Valley. The way to find this bird is to scan newly-plowed fields with your binoculars. The bird blends very well with the soil. It prefers fields that do not have large lumps of vegetation. Most easily found in fields in the Imperial Valley and on the Carrizo Plain.

Black Oystercatcher—Uncommon permanent resident on rocky beaches of Channel Islands; occasionally on the mainland on breakwaters at Marina del Rey. More common farther north. Also watch for the very rare **American Oystercatcher**, which sometimes wanders up from Mexico.

Black-necked Stilt—Common permanent resident of marshes, mudflats, and shallow ponds at lower elevations throughout. Abundant at the Salton Sea.

American Avocet—Common permanent resident of marshes, mudflats, and shallow ponds at lower elevations throughout. Not hard to find at Mugu Lagoon, Upper Newport Bay, Imperial Marsh, Salton Sea, and elsewhere.

Wandering Tattler—Uncommon but easy-to-see migrant and winter visitor to rocky shores along the coast. Can be found at Point Loma, La

Jolla, Laguna Beach, Corona del Mar, and Playa del Rey jetties, and elsewhere. Casual at the Salton Sea.

Whimbrel—Uncommon winter visitor on sandy beaches and less commonly on mudflats and fields. Mostly along the coast, but migrates through the Imperial Valley in large numbers, especially in spring.

Long-billed Curlew—Fairly common winter visitor to mudflats and fields along the coast and in the Imperial Valley and along the Colorado River.

Black Turnstone—Fairly common winter visitor on rocky shores along the coast. Casual at the Salton Sea.

Surfbird—Uncommon and local winter visitor and migrant to rocky shores along the coast. Same areas as the Wandering Tattler. Casual at the Salton Sea.

Red Knot—Uncommon migrant and winter visitor on the mudflats along the coast, particularly in coastal Orange County and on the San Diego Bay. Uncommon on the Salton Sea.

Pomarine Jaeger—Common fall migrant in offshore waters. Uncommon in winter and spring.

Parasitic Jaeger—Common fall migrant in offshore waters. Less common in winter and spring migration. Regularly seen chasing terns, and sometimes gulls, along the shore. Rare but regular fall visitor at Salton Sea.

Long-tailed Jaeger—Rare but regular fall migrant. Usually hard to find. Well offshore. Casual inland.

South Polar Skua—Uncommon and irregular spring and fall migrant to offshore waters. Most often seen in late spring.

Heermann's Gull—Common late summer, fall, and winter visitor from Mexico to coastal beaches and Channel Islands. Harder to find in spring. Rare at the Salton Sea.

Mew Gull—Uncommon in winter along the coast; more common farther north. Rare at the Salton Sea.

California Gull—Common winter visitor along the coast, less common in early summer (non-breeder). Fairly common at the Salton Sea, and rarely elsewhere in the interior.

Thayer's Gull—Uncommon winter visitor along the coast. Rare at the Salton Sea. One has to look carefully through the gull flocks to find it. The municipal dump in Santa Maria is one of the best spots; also the Santa Clara River mouth in Ventura. Rare at the Salton Sea.

Yellow-footed Gull—Fairly common summer visitor from Mexico to the Salton Sea. Most numerous July to September. Rare in winter. Casual to the San Diego area.

Western Gull—Abundant permanent resident along the coast and on the Channel Islands.

Glaucous-winged Gull—Fairly common winter visitor along the coastal beaches. Rare at the Salton Sea.

Black-legged Kittiwake—Irregular winter visitor to offshore waters, sometimes quite common. Occasionally seen along the beaches and at piers and jetties.

Sabine's Gull—Regular, uncommon spring and fall migrant to offshore waters. Rarely seen near shore. Casual at the Salton Sea in fall.

Gull-billed Tern—Uncommon summer resident at Salton Sea. Several pairs breed on San Diego Bay.

Elegant Tern—Fairly common post-breeding (July-October) visitor from Mexico along the coast, starting in spring at San Diego. Has nested in San Diego Bay on the dikes at the South Bay Marine Biological Study Area from March through June. Also nests at Bolsa Chica in Orange County.

Arctic Tern—Irregular migrant to offshore waters, sometimes fairly common. Casual at the Salton Sea and on the mainland coast.

Black Skimmer—Fairly common summer resident at Salton Sea. Breeds on San Diego Bay and at Bolsa Chica.

Pigeon Guillemot—Fairly common summer visitor at Morro Bay rock and northern Channel Islands. Very rare elsewhere in Southern California, but fairly common farther north.

Xantus's Murrelet—Uncommon spring and summer visitor to offshore waters. Very rare in fall and winter. Nests on Channel Islands. A good bet is the boat trip to Anacapa Island from Ventura.

Craveri's Murrelet—Uncommon fall migrant from Mexico to offshore waters.

Ancient Murrelet—Rare-to-uncommon winter visitor to offshore waters. A few records from the Salton Sea.

Cassin's Auklet—Uncommon year-round visitor to offshore waters. Nests on northern Channel Islands.

Rhinoceros Auklet—Uncommon fall, winter, and spring visitor to offshore waters. Suspected breeder near Shell Beach in San Luis Obispo County.

Tufted Puffin—Very rare winter visitor to offshore waters; most records are in late spring.

Band-tailed Pigeon—Fairly common permanent resident of oak and pine woodlands in the mountains, foothills, and north coast. Lower elevations in winter.

Ringed Turtle-Dove—Rare permanent resident of parks, mainly in downtown Los Angles, but also other coastal cities. This bird is popular and prolific in zoos and private aviaries. When it becomes too numerous, it is often just turned loose, thus starting another colony. These populations do not meet the criteria as stable and self-generating, and therefore are not "countable".

Spotted Dove—Common permanent resident of residential areas. Introduced into Los Angeles and has spread to Santa Barbara, San Diego, and inland at least as far as Indio. Can usually be seen perched on telephone wires in housing areas with trees.

White-winged Dove—Fairly common summer resident along wooded stream-courses and in brushlands of deserts, such as along the Colorado River and the Salton Sea. A few occur in winter and in other areas, e.g., rare along coast in fall and winter.

Common Ground-Dove—Fairly common permanent resident about farms and wooded water-courses in the Colorado Desert. Particularly common about feed-lots in the Imperial Valley. Occasionally found west of the deserts as at Fullerton, Corona, and in citrus orchards in Ventura County near Oxnard and Ventura.

Ruddy Ground-Dove—Casual fall and winter visitor to low desert areas such as Death Valley (beyond the range of this book) and lower Colorado River Valley.

Parrots—At least five species of parrots, all currently "noncountable", occur in the Los Angeles area. Some small populations are continually "renewed" by escapees (as is the Ringed Turtle-Dove); all are at least suspected of breeding in Los Angeles: **Yellow-headed Parrot** in the suburbs of west Los Angeles and the west San Gabriel Valley; **Lilac-crowned Parrot** and **Red-crowned Parrot** in smaller numbers in the same areas as Yellow-headed; **Canary-winged Parakeet** on the Palos Verdes Peninsula; and small numbers of the **Rose-ringed Parakeet** at various suburban locations, such as Pt. Dume.

Greater Roadrunner—Fairly common (although declining along the coast) permanent resident of open brush in lowland areas from the coastal plain to the deserts.

Flammulated Owl—Very uncommon to rare but hard-to-find summer resident of coniferous forests and high-mountain oaks and pines. Has nested at Palomar Mountain, in San Bernardino Mountains, the San Gabriel Mountains, and on Mt. Pinos. Responds well to taped calls, but stays concealed in dense foliage. Can be lured into view if you walk back and forth across its territory while playing its call.

Northern Pygmy-Owl—Uncommon permanent resident of mixed woodlands in mountains and along canyon bottoms. Responds well to tapes during nesting season, even during the day. Some known sites are

McGill Campground on Mount Pinos, near Dawson Saddle in the San Gabriel Mountains, along the Devil's Slide Trail in the San Jacinto Mountains, and at Figueroa Mountain north of Santa Barbara.

Spotted Owl—Uncommon permanent resident of dense woodlands in steep-sided canyons and shaded ravines, usually near a stream. Some known sites are Santa Anita Canyon, below the Red Box Ranger Station in the San Gabriel Mountains, near Observatory Campground on Palomar Mountain, and in Holcomb Valley in the San Bernardino Mountains.

Lesser Nighthawk—Common summer resident of open areas at lower elevations in the deserts; less common along the coast. Easy to find in the Imperial Valley on a summer evening.

Common Nighthawk—Fairly common local summer resident at Bluff Lake near Big Bear Lake.

Common Poorwill—Fairly common summer resident of open brushlands in the foothills and mountains. Although some hibernate, exact winter status is not known. On a warm winter night they can be heard calling. The way to find this bird is to drive back roads through the brushlands and deserts just after dark and watch for their orange eyeshine on the road.

Black Swift—Rare late-spring and fall migrant west of the deserts, and a rare summer resident near waterfalls. May nest in Santa Anita Canyon, Mills Canyon in the San Bernardino Mountains, and near the Tahquitz Trail and at Lawler Park in the San Jacinto Mountains.

Vaux's Swift—Fairly common spring and fall migrant in most areas. **Chimney Swift** has occurred in Southern California in limited numbers in late spring and summer.

White-throated Swift—Common permanent resident of steep cliffs in all areas. Ranges widely while feeding. Fairly easy to find in mountain canyons and along the freeways in Los Angeles.

Black-chinned Hummingbird—Fairly common summer resident of the woodlands in the foothills and lower mountains. Sometimes abundant about feeders in the canyons, as at Tucker Sanctuary.

Anna's Hummingbird—Common permanent resident wherever it can find flowers for feeding, mostly west of the deserts. Easy to find about gardens in all of the coastal cities.

Costa's Hummingbird—During the late fall and midwinter months, most of these birds are in Baja California, but a few linger in the coastal areas north to Los Angeles and the lower Colorado Desert, where they feed on the flowers of Bladderpod and Tree Tobacco; also in Brawley. As the desert flowers begin to appear in February, the birds begin to increase on the Colorado Desert and become numerous in areas such as Palm Canyon and Yaqui Well. Here they feed and nest in the Chuparosa, cacti, and desert shrubs. When the desert flowers disappear in the spring, the hummers move up into the mountains and over to the coastal chaparral belts, where they feed on White or Black sage. They nest here also, or perhaps this is a second nesting.

Calliope Hummingbird—Uncommon-to-rare spring migrant in the coastal lowlands and mountains. Uncommon summer resident of higher mountains such as Mount Pinos and at Bluff Lake, but may be found around feeders, as at Angelus Oaks in the San Bernardino Mountains and Pine Cove in the San Jacinto Mountains.

Rufous Hummingbird—Common migrant through the lowlands in spring, and the mountains in late summer.

Allen's Hummingbird—Represented by two subspecies. The migratory Allen's Hummingbird is a common migrant through the lowlands in spring, and less commonly in the mountains and foothills in late summer; breeds along the northern coast. The non-migratory Allen's is a common permanent resident on San Clemente and Catalina islands and the adjacent Palos Verdes Peninsula, and, to a lesser degree, on Santa Rosa and Santa Cruz islands. It can always be found in Averill Park, on Point Fermin, and at Point Dume.

Lewis's Woodpecker—Erratic winter visitor to open oak groves and pecan and walnut orchards. Unpredictable and rarely seen. More common farther north.

Acorn Woodpecker—Abundant permanent resident of all oak woodlands. This noisy, colorful bird is hard to miss.

Red-naped Sapsucker—Uncommon winter visitor from coastal lowlands south of Los Angeles to the Colorado River.

Red-breasted Sapsucker—Fairly common breeder in mountains west of the deserts, wintering in the lowlands.

Williamson's Sapsucker—Uncommon permanent resident at higher elevations in the higher mountains. More common farther north in the Sierra Nevada, but still hard to find. In summer, occurs mostly in stands of Lodgepole or Jeffery Pines as at Bluff Lake in the San Bernardinos. Casual in lowlands in winter.

Ladder-backed Woodpecker—Fairly common permanent resident of the lower deserts. Found wherever suitable nesting sites are available, as in city parks, patches of cholla cactus, Joshua Tree woodland, and trees along desert washes.

Nuttall's Woodpecker—Common permanent resident of woodlands in the foothills and lowlands west of the desert. This coastal counterpart of the Ladder-backed is easily found in most oak groves or in patches of riparian woodlands.

White-headed Woodpecker—Fairly common permanent resident of coniferous mountain forests, mainly mature Yellow Pine. Although fairly common, it can be hard to find. Some good spots to look are Mount Pinos, Charlton Flats and Chilao Campgrounds in the San Gabriel Mountains, Green Valley and Grout Bay Campgrounds in the San Bernardino Mountains, and near the fire station at Idyllwild.

Willow Flycatcher—Rare and declining summer resident in dense stands of willow near water and usually adjacent to an open meadow. Fairly common late migrant, especially through the eastern deserts.

Dusky Flycatcher—Fairly common summer resident of patches of dense brush with scattered trees at higher elevations in the mountains. Some known sites are below the parking lot on top of Mount Pinos, near Dawson Saddle in the San Gabriel Mountains, at Lake View Point in the San Bernardino Mountains, and above Hurkey Creek Campgrounds in the San Jacinto Mountains. **Hammond's Flycatcher**, which does not nest in Southern California but migrates through, is most likely to be seen at Point Loma or at the desert oases.

Gray Flycatcher—Uncommon summer resident in arid woodlands of the desert mountain ranges. Uncommon in Joshua Tree National Monument. Rare migrant and winter visitor along the coast.

Pacific-slope Flycatcher—Fairly common summer resident west of the coastal range of mountains, breeding in the cool, shaded canyons of the foothills, migrating from the coast south and east through the lowlands into Arizona. A split of Western Flycatcher. Call note an upward *tseep* as compared to the other split (Cordilleran Flycatcher), which has a two-note call.

Black Phoebe—Common permanent resident near fresh water at lower elevations in all areas. Check under bridges where there is water in the foothills and you may find nesting phoebes.

Say's Phoebe—Common winter visitor in open country in all areas. Uncommon summer resident in the deserts, particularly the Mojave Desert, as in Joshua Tree National Monument. Usually feeds near the ground from a low bush, weed, or fence-line. Nests under the eaves of deserted buildings, bridges, or overhanging rocks.

Ash-throated Flycatcher—Common summer resident of foothill and desert brushlands that have at least some trees with nesting holes. Casual in winter. A shy bird, but not particularly hard to find since it is very active.

Tropical Kingbird—Rare fall and winter visitor along the coast.

Cassin's Kingbird—Fairly common permanent resident of open areas with scattered trees in all areas. Less common in winter. The Western Kingbird is a far more common summer resident but is completely absent in winter.

Violet-green Swallow—Common summer resident of mountain and foothill forests with trees with holes for nesting in the foothills and mountains. Ranges widely while feeding and in migration. A few winter.

Steller's Jay—Common permanent resident of coniferous forests. Noisy and easy to find. Very rare winter visitor to lowlands.

Scrub Jay—Common permanent resident of gardens, chaparral, and oak woodlands west of the deserts. Easy to find. Irregular winter visitor to deserts and the Salton Sea area.

Pinyon Jay—Uncommon permanent resident of pinyon and open pine forests on the arid eastern and northern side of the mountains. Goes about in noisy flocks, often walking on the ground like crows. Some known locations are near Baldwin Lake in the San Bernardino Mountains, along Highway 74 between Hurkey Creek Campground and Pinyon Flats in the San Jacinto Mountains, and in the Providence Mountains southeast of Kelso.

Clark's Nutcracker—Uncommon permanent resident of mountains. In summer found at the very summits of the mountains, where the trees are stunted and separated by rocky slopes and meadows. Moves downslope slightly in winter, but casual at best in lowlands.

Yellow-billed Magpie—Common permanent resident of open valleys with scattered or stream-side trees, from central Santa Barbara County northward. Easily found at Nojoqui Falls County Park south of Solvang in Santa Barbara County.

Chestnut-backed Chickadee—Fairly common local resident in coastal woodlands (especially willows) south to the mouth of Santa Ynez River in extreme western Santa Barbara County.

Plain Titmouse—Common permanent resident of all oak riparian and pine oak woodlands. Usually noisy and conspicuous. Responds well to squeaking.

Verdin—Common permanent resident of brushy areas of low deserts. Can be found in such areas as Yaqui Well, Palm Canyon, and around Ramer and Finney lakes.

Bushtit—Common permanent resident of gardens, chaparral, and woodlands of the plains and foothills west of the deserts. Goes around in twittering flocks, making it easy to find.

Pygmy Nuthatch—Common permanent resident of mature Yellow Pine forests. Usually easy to locate by its twittering calls.

Cactus Wren—Common permanent resident of large patches of cactus throughout much of the region. More common in the deserts, where it may also occur in patches of thorny brush. It is a noisy bird, usually located by its loud, rolling call.

Rock Wren—Fairly common permanent resident of rocky sites in all areas. More common in the deserts. Fairly easy to find in Joshua Tree National Monument and along the rocky foothills near Palm Springs and Borrego Springs.

Canyon Wren—Fairly common permanent resident of steep, rocky canyons with water in the foothills throughout. Fairly noisy, but even after its beautiful descending song or its sharp whistled note is heard, it can be hard to pick out along the canyon walls.

American Dipper—Uncommon and localized permanent resident in Southern California. More common in winter and farther north. Found along clear, fast mountain streams as in Santa Anita Canyon, north fork of San Gabriel River, and along the upper Santa Ana River in the San Bernardino Mountains.

California Gnatcatcher—Fairly common resident. Found in coastal arid sage scrub on lower slopes and in washes. Told from Black-tailed by darker underparts and by call (see *Palos Verdes Peninsula Loop*). Found at Upper Newport Bay, San Elijo Lagoon, in El Toro Cemetery, and at Otay Lakes east of Chula Vista.

Black-tailed Gnatcatcher—Uncommon permanent resident of brushy areas of the lower deserts. Some known sites are along the Colorado River, along Highway 195 at the north end of the Salton Sea, and at Yaqui Well.

Western Bluebird—Fairly common permanent resident of open woodlands of the foothills and lower mountains west of the deserts; at lower elevations in winter. Often sits on telephone wires. Not hard to find.

Mountain Bluebird—Erratic winter visitor to open terrain at lower elevations in all areas. In some winters are fairly common. Often seen hovering over newly-plowed fields. A few spots where they have been seen are Lake Mathews, Tijuana River Valley, in the Imperial Valley, Antelope Valley, and on the Carrizo Plain. Nests from the San Bernardino Mountains and on Mount Pinos northward. Can be found near cabins around Baldwin Lake.

Townsend's Solitaire—Uncommon permanent resident of higher mountain forests. Lower in winter. In summer usually found in areas of mature White Fir or Jeffrey Pine, where it flycatches from the tops of the taller trees. It nests on the ground among the roots of trees, on cliffs, or at the top of road-cuts just under the over-hanging vegetation. If you watch closely when driving dirt roads through the forests, you may see one flying from the nest just under the crest of a bank. In winter it is found in areas with lots of berries, but it is rare in the coastal lowlands.

Varied Thrush—Irregular winter visitor in lowlands and foothills. Rare in deserts, at Salton Sea, and along Colorado River.

Wrentit—Common permanent resident of the chaparral in the foothills. Its marble-dropping call is heard more often than the bird is seen, but if you stop at any patch of chaparral and squeak long enough, you can usually coax one into view.

Sage Thrasher—Uncommon migrant to arid areas with scattered brush at lower elevations. More common in the deserts, as in Joshua Tree National Monument or near Cabazon. Winters in limited numbers near Maricopa, near Red Rock Canyon north of Mojave, on Carrizo Plain near Soda Lake, and around Lake Mathews.

Bendire's Thrasher—Rare and localized early-summer resident of the deserts near the Arizona border. Probably easiest to find near Cima. Will respond to a tape during the nesting season in April and May.

California Thrasher—Fairly common permanent resident of the chaparral of the foothills and lower mountains west of the deserts. Can usually be coaxed into view by squeaking or playing a tape.

Crissal Thrasher—Fairly common but hard-to-find permanent resident of dense brush in lower deserts. Declining overall because of habitat destruction. Some known locations are around Ramer and Finney lakes, along Highway 195 at north end of Salton Sea, and in patches of dense Saltbrush along the Colorado River. Will respond to taped calls.

LeConte's Thrasher—Uncommon, localized, and hard-to-find permanent resident of very arid terrain with scattered bushes. Easiest to find near Maricopa and Palmdale. Responds well to tape in February and March. Can be walked out at other seasons.

Red-throated Pipit—Rare fall migrant. Most records are between October 10-25. Found at estuaries, in wet fields, pastures, and at sod farms along the coast (especially near Oxnard).

Phainopepla—Fairly common to common permanent resident of mistletoe-infested plants at lower elevations in all areas. Uncommon west of the deserts in winter. Usually perches on the top of bushes, making it easy to find. Easy to find at Yaqui Well, Ramer Lake, or any desert oasis.

Bell's Vireo—Rare and very local summer resident in rather dense riparian growth along water courses at lower elevations west of the desert. A fairly nosiy bird that is easily located by its song, but harder than heck to see. Morongo Valley is your best bet. Formerly much more common.

Gray Vireo—Rare and very localized summer resident of dry chaparral and stands of pinyon and juniper. Some known locations are along the dirt road leading south to Oak Spring from Highway 138 just west of Phelan and northeast of Highway 2, the Providence Mountains near Kelso, along the Rose Mine Road below Lake Baldwin, along the base of the Santa Rosa Mountain, and (perhaps the best spots) just north of I-8 east of San Diego (Kitchen Creek Road) and Bob's Gap in the San Gabriel Mountains.

Hutton's Vireo—Fairly common permanent resident of oak woodlands in foothills and lower mountains. Responds well to taped calls, particularly in the spring. Easy to find in Santa Barbara Botanical Garden and at Placerita Canyon State Park.

Virginia's Warbler—Uncommon and local. Nests on Clark Mountain north of Cima, and in the White and New York Mountains. Rare fall migrant along the coast.

Lucy's Warbler—Uncommon and local summer resident at Morongo Valley and along the Colorado River.

Black-throated Gray Warbler—Fairly common summer resident on dry wooded slopes of the higher mountains. Often found in stands of Goldcup Oak. Also nests in the pinyon pines in the Providence Mountains.

Townsend's Warbler—Fairly common migrant and uncommon winter visitor in conifers and live oaks in the mountains, foothills, and coastal lowlands.

Hermit Warbler—Uncommon migrant through the desert and along the coast through the live oaks in the foothills in spring and through the mountain forests in fall. Found in mature pine forests. A few are present in coastal pines in winter.

MacGillivray's Warbler—Hard-to-find migrant in dense cover near the ground in all areas. Rare summer resident in willow thickets in San Gabriel and San Bernardino mountains above 6,500 feet.

Green-tailed Towhee—Fairly common summer resident of high-mountain brushlands. Rare and lower in southern part of the region in migration and winter. Can be found in such areas as Mount Pinos, the sagebrush flats around Baldwin Lake, and along the trail to the top of Mount San Jacinto.

California Towhee—Abundant permanent resident of gardens and brushlands at lower elevations west of the deserts. You will soon be saying, "It's just another California Towhee." Overall much darker than Canyon Towhee, with no spot on breast.

Abert's Towhee—Fairly common but localized permanent resident of thickets near water at lower elevations in the deserts. Because of the clearance of brush for farming, good habitat for this bird is declining. Look for it anywhere along the Colorado River, about Finney and Ramer Lakes, and around the Salton Sea.

Rufous-crowned Sparrow—Uncommon permanent resident of broken chaparral in the foothills west of the desert. Prefers areas where the brush is rather open and not very high. A few sites are below Sweetwater Dam east of Chula Vista, along Old River Road near Bonsall, Irvine Park, the end of Crenshaw Boulevard on Palos Verde Peninsula, near Camarillo State Hospital east of Oxnard, and along Camino Cielo behind Santa Barbara.

Brewer's Sparrow—Fairly common permanent resident. In summer found in sagebrush flats in the mountains, as around Lake Baldwin, and on the deserts in winter. Occasionally elsewhere.

Black-chinned Sparrow—Fairly common but local summer resident of drier chaparral and sagebrush in the foothills and low mountains. In April and May you can hear them singing all over the place and still not see them. They do respond to taped calls and squeaking, but not always very well.

Black-throated Sparrow—Fairly common permanent resident of very arid patches of brush and cactus at lower elevations in the deserts. Easy to find along the base of the San Jacinto Mountains, as at Palm Canyon and Borrego Springs, also in Joshua Tree National Monument and the Providence Mountains.

Sage Sparrow—Fairly common but localized permanent resident of arid chaparral and sagebrush flats west of the deserts. Winter visitor to the deserts. A few sites are lower part of Mount Pinos Road, around Lake Baldwin (summer), and near Otay Lakes east of Chula Vista.

Golden-crowned Sparrow—Common winter visitor in rather dense chaparral and other brushland in the foothills west of the deserts. Try squeaking near patches of dense chaparral.

Tricolored Blackbird—Uncommon but local resident of lowlands west of the deserts. Nests irregularly in large colonies in tule marshes, as at Lake Sherwood, San Jacinto Wildlife Area, and near Temecula. Feeds in open fields with other blackbirds. Somewhat nomadic.

Hooded Oriole—Fairly common summer resident of gardens and woodlands at lower elevations. Very rarely winters, particularly where there are hummingbird feeders and blooming eucalyptus. This oriole shows a preference for palm trees as nesting sites. It is easy to find at the Twentynine Palms Oasis, Palm Canyon, Borrego Springs, and along nearly any city street where there are palms.

Scott's Oriole—Uncommon summer resident of Joshua Trees, Pinyon Pines, and riparian woodlands along the western edge of the deserts and in the Providence Mountains. Some known sites are Butterbredt Springs, Joshua Tree National Monument, Morongo Valley, and Pinyon Flats in San

Jacinto Mountains. Also in Ballinger and Quatal Canyon in Santa Barbara Counties (see Mt. Pinos Loop).

Cassin's Finch—Fairly common permanent resident at higher elevations from San Jacinto Mountains northward. Rarely lower in winter. It shows a preference for the cool arid boreal forests near the tops of the mountains, usually above the range of the Purple Finch. In summer can be found along the trails to the tops of Mount San Jacinto and San Gorgonio and on Mt. Pinos. In fall and winter easy to find around Big Bear and Pine Cove.

Lesser Goldfinch—Common permanent resident of open woodlands, brushy fields, and riparian thickets of foothills, the coastal lowlands, and lower mountains west of the deserts. Easy to find.

Lawrence's Goldfinch—Uncommon and erratic summer resident. In summer most often found in the mountains in oak woodlands and arid pine forests, but also in the foothills. During migration, large flocks are chanced upon in weedy fields in the lowlands. Usually hard to find along the coast in winter, but may be common some years. Shows a strong preference for ornamental plantings of cypress and deodar cedars as nesting sites, often occurring in large numbers, as in Kern County Park near Bakersfield.

BIRDS OF SOUTHERN CALIFORNIA

The bar graphs which follow include all birds which regularly occur in Southern California. A few of the species in the bar graphs, however, are well-known vagrants or accidentals (e.g. Wilson's Storm-Petrel, Blue-footed Booby, Brown Booby, Reddish Egret, Tricolored Heron, Emperor Goose, Zone-tailed Hawk, Brown Thrasher, and Red-throated Pipit). Others that are "seldom seen" or "accidental" (fewer than 10 records) are listed separately on the next two pages.

The bar graphs are designed to show the probability of seeing the bird rather than its abundance. Thus a large bird such as the Red-tailed Hawk may be shown as "hard to miss", while a shy, hard-to-identify, or small bird such as the Black-chinned Sparrow may occur in greater numbers, but be shown as "may see".

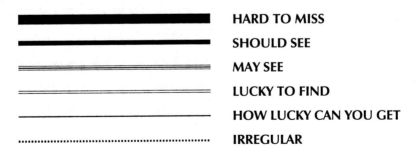

	HARD TO MISS
	SHOULD SEE
	MAY SEE
	LUCKY TO FIND
	HOW LUCKY CAN YOU GET
	IRREGULAR

On your first trip to the area, you may think that some species are harder to find than is indicated. However, if you are in the RIGHT HABITAT and the RIGHT AREA at the PROPER SEASON, you should be able to find the "**hard to miss**" birds on nearly every field trip, the "**should see**" on 3 out of 4 trips, the "**may see**" on 1 out of 4 trips, and the "**lucky to find**" on 1 out of 10 trips—or even less often. The "**how lucky can you get**" species occur at infrequent intervals or take an expert to identify. "**Irregular species**" are those which are sporadic and erratic in *occurrence* and *abundance*.

If you find an unusual bird, take notes and report your find to the regional editor of *American Birds*: Guy McCaskie, San Diego Museum of Natural History, Balboa Park, PO Box 1390, San Diego, CA 92112.

The areas where the birds are found can be broken down as follows:

PELAGIC—open ocean well offshore, and Channel Islands.
COASTAL—inshore ocean, bays, marshes, and mudflats.
LOWLANDS—grasslands, fields, and riparian woodlands.
FOOTHILLS—chaparral, sycamore/oak woodlands, pinyon/juniper.
MOUNTAINS—coniferous forests, high-mountain brushlands
DESERTS—arid lands east of the major mountains.
SALTON SEA—the Sea/Imperial Valley.
COLORADO RIVER—the river and the valley.

BIRDS SELDOM SEEN BUT POSSIBLE

Red-necked Grebe
Laysan Albatross
Cook's Petrel
Yellow-crowned Night-Heron
Roseate Spoonbill
Harlequin Duck
Barrow's Goldeneye
Harris's Hawk
Wild Turkey
Sharp-tailed Sandpiper
Buff-breasted Sandpiper
Horned Puffin
Broad-billed Hummingbird
Broad-tailed Hummingbird
Greater Pewee
Least Flycatcher
Eastern Phoebe
Eastern Kingbird
Scissor-tailed Flycatcher
Gray Catbird
Curve-billed Thrasher
Sprague's Pipit
Northern Shrike

Yellow-throated Vireo
Yellow-green Vireo
Philadelphia Vireo
Northern Parula
Chestnut-sided Warbler
Magnolia Warbler
Cape May Warbler
Black-throated Blue Warbler
Black-throated Green Warbler
Blackburnian Warbler
Prairie Warbler
Bay-breasted Warbler
Prothonotary Warbler
Worm-eating Warbler
Ovenbird
Northern Waterthrush
Hooded Warbler
Canada Warbler
Scarlet Tanager
Painted Bunting
American Tree Sparrow
Bobolink
Common Grackle

ACCIDENTALS

Yellow-billed Loon
Least Grebe
Short-tailed Albatross
Mottled Petrel
Murphy's Petrel
Wedge-tailed Shearwater
Band-rumped Storm-Petrel
Wedge-rumped Storm-Petrel
White-tailed Tropicbird
Red-tailed Tropicbird
Masked Booby
Red-footed Booby
Olivaceous Cormorant
Anhinga
White Ibis
Black-bellied Whistling-Duck
Trumpeter Swan
Baikal Teal
Garganey
Tufted Duck
King Eider
Mississippi Kite
Common Black-Hawk
Yellow Rail
Purple Gallinule
Mongolian Plover
Wilson's Plover
Piping Plover
American Oystercatcher
Spotted Redshank
Gray-tailed Tattler
Upland Sandpiper
Little Curlew
Hudsonian Godwit
Bar-tailed Godwit
Rufous-necked Stint
White-rumped Sandpiper
Curlew Sandpiper
Little Gull
Common Black-headed Gull
Lesser Black-backed Gull
Sandwich Tern

Sooty Tern
Kittlitz's Murrlet
Parakeet Auklet
Ruddy Ground-Dove
Groove-billed Ani
Xantus's Hummingbird
Violet-crowned Hummingbird
Red-headed Woodpecker
Yellow-bellied Flycatcher
Dusky-capped Flycatcher
Great Crested Flycatcher
Sulphur-bellied Flycatcher
Thick-billed Kingbird
Blue Jay
Black-billed Magpie
Veery
Gray-cheeked Thrush
Wood Thrush
Rufous-backed Robin
White Wagtail
Black-backed Wagtail
White-eyed Vireo
Blue-winged Warbler
Golden-winged Warbler
Yellow-throated Warbler
Grace's Warbler
Pine Warbler
Cerulean Warbler
Louisiana Waterthrush
Kentucky Warbler
Connecticut Warbler
Mourning Warbler
Red-faced Warbler
Pyrrhuloxia
Varied Bunting
Cassin's Sparrow
Field Sparrow
Baird's Sparrow
LeConte's Sparrow
Snow Bunting
Streak-backed Oriole
Rosy Finch

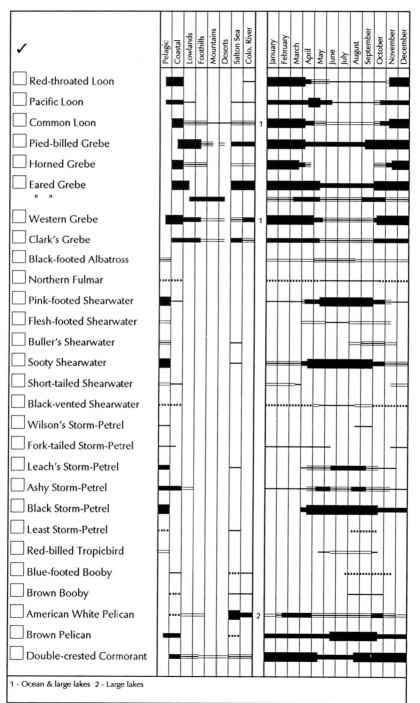

✓

Pelagic | Coastal | Lowlands | Foothills | Mountains | Deserts | Salton Sea | Colo. River

January | February | March | April | May | June | July | August | September | October | November | December

☐ Red-throated Loon
☐ Pacific Loon
☐ Common Loon
☐ Pied-billed Grebe
☐ Horned Grebe
☐ Eared Grebe
   " "
☐ Western Grebe
☐ Clark's Grebe
☐ Black-footed Albatross
☐ Northern Fulmar
☐ Pink-footed Shearwater
☐ Flesh-footed Shearwater
☐ Buller's Shearwater
☐ Sooty Shearwater
☐ Short-tailed Shearwater
☐ Black-vented Shearwater
☐ Wilson's Storm-Petrel
☐ Fork-tailed Storm-Petrel
☐ Leach's Storm-Petrel
☐ Ashy Storm-Petrel
☐ Black Storm-Petrel
☐ Least Storm-Petrel
☐ Red-billed Tropicbird
☐ Blue-footed Booby
☐ Brown Booby
☐ American White Pelican
☐ Brown Pelican
☐ Double-crested Cormorant

1 - Ocean & large lakes   2 - Large lakes

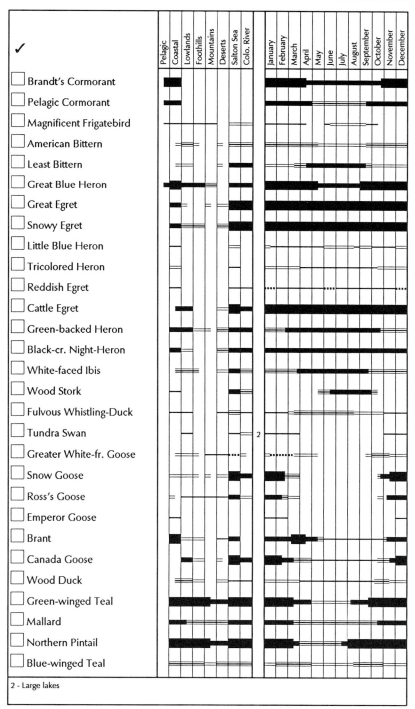

✓	Pelagic	Coastal	Lowlands	Foothills	Mountains	Deserts	Salton Sea	Colo. River		January	February	March	April	May	June	July	August	September	October	November	December
☐ Brandt's Cormorant																					
☐ Pelagic Cormorant																					
☐ Magnificent Frigatebird																					
☐ American Bittern																					
☐ Least Bittern																					
☐ Great Blue Heron																					
☐ Great Egret																					
☐ Snowy Egret																					
☐ Little Blue Heron																					
☐ Tricolored Heron																					
☐ Reddish Egret																					
☐ Cattle Egret																					
☐ Green-backed Heron																					
☐ Black-cr. Night-Heron																					
☐ White-faced Ibis																					
☐ Wood Stork																					
☐ Fulvous Whistling-Duck																					
☐ Tundra Swan								2													
☐ Greater White-fr. Goose																					
☐ Snow Goose																					
☐ Ross's Goose																					
☐ Emperor Goose																					
☐ Brant																					
☐ Canada Goose																					
☐ Wood Duck																					
☐ Green-winged Teal																					
☐ Mallard																					
☐ Northern Pintail																					
☐ Blue-winged Teal																					

2 - Large lakes

✓	Pelagic	Coastal	Lowlands	Foothills	Mountains	Deserts	Salton Sea	Colo. River	January	February	March	April	May	June	July	August	September	October	November	December
☐ Cinnamon Teal																				
☐ Northern Shoveler																				
☐ Gadwall																				
☐ Eurasian Wigeon																				
☐ American Wigeon																				
☐ Canvasback																				
☐ Redhead								3												
☐ Ring-necked Duck																				
☐ Greater Scaup																				
☐ Lesser Scaup																				
☐ Oldsquaw																				
☐ Black Scoter																				
☐ Surf Scoter																				
☐ White-winged Scoter																				
☐ Common Goldeneye																				
☐ Bufflehead																				
☐ Hooded Merganser																				
☐ Common Merganser																				
☐ Red-breasted Merganser																				
☐ Ruddy Duck																				
☐ Turkey Vulture																				
☐ Osprey																				
☐ Black-shouldered Kite																				
☐ Bald Eagle								2												
☐ Northern Harrier																				
☐ Sharp-shinned Hawk																				
" "																				
☐ Cooper's Hawk																				
☐ Northern Goshawk																				

2 - Large lakes 3 - Fairly common nester at Salton Sea

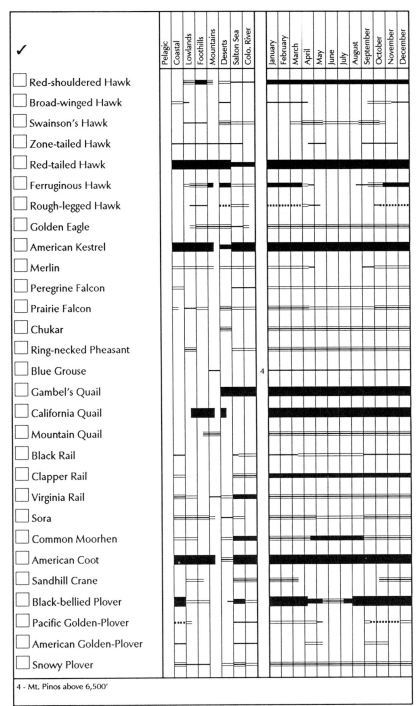

✓	Pelagic	Coastal	Lowlands	Foothills	Mountains	Deserts	Salton Sea	Colo. River	January	February	March	April	May	June	July	August	September	October	November	December
☐ Red-shouldered Hawk																				
☐ Broad-winged Hawk																				
☐ Swainson's Hawk																				
☐ Zone-tailed Hawk																				
☐ Red-tailed Hawk																				
☐ Ferruginous Hawk																				
☐ Rough-legged Hawk																				
☐ Golden Eagle																				
☐ American Kestrel																				
☐ Merlin																				
☐ Peregrine Falcon																				
☐ Prairie Falcon																				
☐ Chukar																				
☐ Ring-necked Pheasant																				
☐ Blue Grouse									4											
☐ Gambel's Quail																				
☐ California Quail																				
☐ Mountain Quail																				
☐ Black Rail																				
☐ Clapper Rail																				
☐ Virginia Rail																				
☐ Sora																				
☐ Common Moorhen																				
☐ American Coot																				
☐ Sandhill Crane																				
☐ Black-bellied Plover																				
☐ Pacific Golden-Plover																				
☐ American Golden-Plover																				
☐ Snowy Plover																				

4 - Mt. Pinos above 6,500'

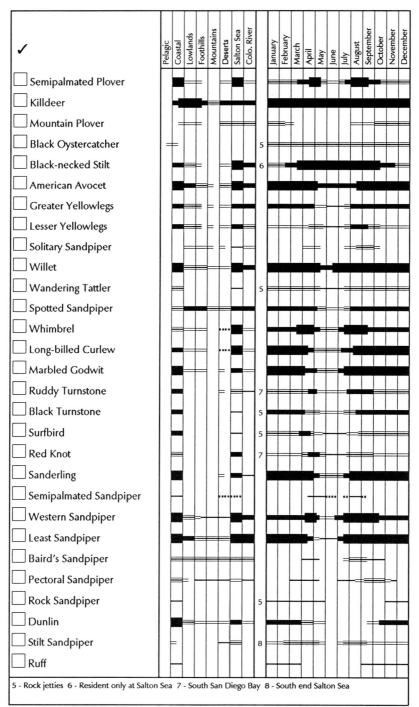

✓	Pelagic	Coastal	Lowlands	Foothills	Mountains	Deserts	Salton Sea	Colo. River		January	February	March	April	May	June	July	August	September	October	November	December
☐ Semipalmated Plover																					
☐ Killdeer																					
☐ Mountain Plover																					
☐ Black Oystercatcher								5													
☐ Black-necked Stilt								6													
☐ American Avocet																					
☐ Greater Yellowlegs																					
☐ Lesser Yellowlegs																					
☐ Solitary Sandpiper																					
☐ Willet																					
☐ Wandering Tattler								5													
☐ Spotted Sandpiper																					
☐ Whimbrel																					
☐ Long-billed Curlew																					
☐ Marbled Godwit																					
☐ Ruddy Turnstone								7													
☐ Black Turnstone								5													
☐ Surfbird								5													
☐ Red Knot								7													
☐ Sanderling																					
☐ Semipalmated Sandpiper																					
☐ Western Sandpiper																					
☐ Least Sandpiper																					
☐ Baird's Sandpiper																					
☐ Pectoral Sandpiper																					
☐ Rock Sandpiper								5													
☐ Dunlin																					
☐ Stilt Sandpiper								8													
☐ Ruff																					

5 - Rock jetties 6 - Resident only at Salton Sea 7 - South San Diego Bay 8 - South end Salton Sea

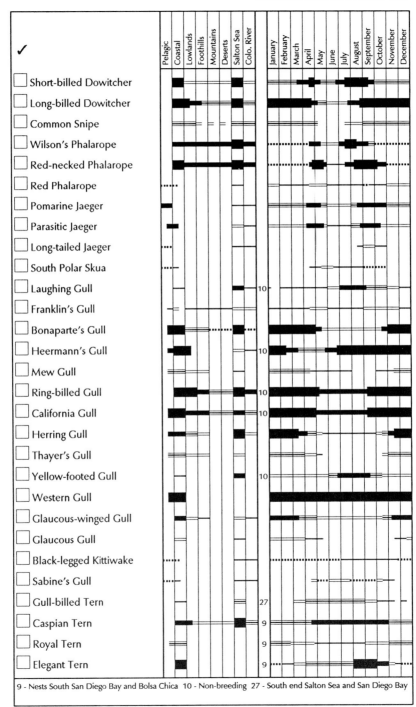

✓	Pelagic	Coastal	Lowlands	Foothills	Mountains	Deserts	Salton Sea	Colo. River	January	February	March	April	May	June	July	August	September	October	November	December
☐ Short-billed Dowitcher																				
☐ Long-billed Dowitcher																				
☐ Common Snipe																				
☐ Wilson's Phalarope																				
☐ Red-necked Phalarope																				
☐ Red Phalarope																				
☐ Pomarine Jaeger																				
☐ Parasitic Jaeger																				
☐ Long-tailed Jaeger																				
☐ South Polar Skua																				
☐ Laughing Gull									10											
☐ Franklin's Gull																				
☐ Bonaparte's Gull																				
☐ Heermann's Gull									10											
☐ Mew Gull																				
☐ Ring-billed Gull									10											
☐ California Gull									10											
☐ Herring Gull																				
☐ Thayer's Gull																				
☐ Yellow-footed Gull									10											
☐ Western Gull																				
☐ Glaucous-winged Gull																				
☐ Glaucous Gull																				
☐ Black-legged Kittiwake																				
☐ Sabine's Gull																				
☐ Gull-billed Tern									27											
☐ Caspian Tern									9											
☐ Royal Tern									9											
☐ Elegant Tern									9											

9 - Nests South San Diego Bay and Bolsa Chica 10 - Non-breeding 27 - South end Salton Sea and San Diego Bay

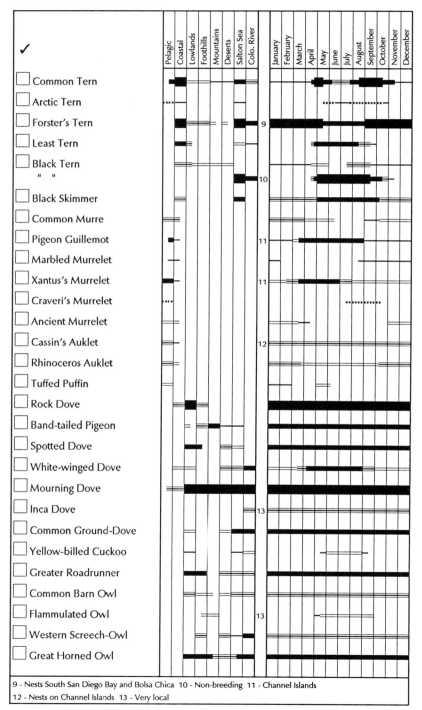

✓	Pelagic	Coastal	Lowlands	Foothills	Mountains	Deserts	Salton Sea	Colo. River		January	February	March	April	May	June	July	August	September	October	November	December
☐ Common Tern																					
☐ Arctic Tern																					
☐ Forster's Tern								9													
☐ Least Tern																					
☐ Black Tern																					
" "								10													
☐ Black Skimmer																					
☐ Common Murre																					
☐ Pigeon Guillemot								11													
☐ Marbled Murrelet																					
☐ Xantus's Murrelet								11													
☐ Craveri's Murrelet																					
☐ Ancient Murrelet																					
☐ Cassin's Auklet								12													
☐ Rhinoceros Auklet																					
☐ Tuffed Puffin																					
☐ Rock Dove																					
☐ Band-tailed Pigeon																					
☐ Spotted Dove																					
☐ White-winged Dove																					
☐ Mourning Dove																					
☐ Inca Dove								13													
☐ Common Ground-Dove																					
☐ Yellow-billed Cuckoo																					
☐ Greater Roadrunner																					
☐ Common Barn Owl																					
☐ Flammulated Owl								13													
☐ Western Screech-Owl																					
☐ Great Horned Owl																					

9 - Nests South San Diego Bay and Bolsa Chica 10 - Non-breeding 11 - Channel Islands
12 - Nests on Channel Islands 13 - Very local

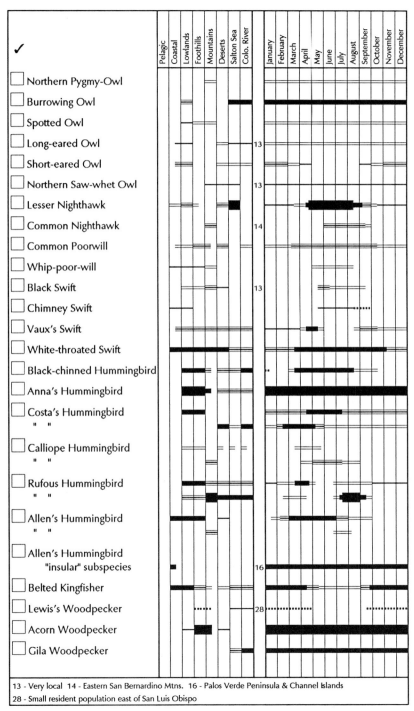

✓	Pelagic	Coastal	Lowlands	Foothills	Mountains	Deserts	Salton Sea	Colo. River		January	February	March	April	May	June	July	August	September	October	November	December
☐ Northern Pygmy-Owl																					
☐ Burrowing Owl																					
☐ Spotted Owl																					
☐ Long-eared Owl										13											
☐ Short-eared Owl																					
☐ Northern Saw-whet Owl										13											
☐ Lesser Nighthawk																					
☐ Common Nighthawk										14											
☐ Common Poorwill																					
☐ Whip-poor-will																					
☐ Black Swift										13											
☐ Chimney Swift																					
☐ Vaux's Swift																					
☐ White-throated Swift																					
☐ Black-chinned Hummingbird																					
☐ Anna's Hummingbird																					
☐ Costa's Hummingbird " "																					
☐ Calliope Hummingbird " "																					
☐ Rufous Hummingbird " "																					
☐ Allen's Hummingbird " "																					
☐ Allen's Hummingbird "insular" subspecies										16											
☐ Belted Kingfisher																					
☐ Lewis's Woodpecker										28											
☐ Acorn Woodpecker																					
☐ Gila Woodpecker																					

13 - Very local 14 - Eastern San Bernardino Mtns. 16 - Palos Verde Peninsula & Channel Islands
28 - Small resident population east of San Luis Obispo

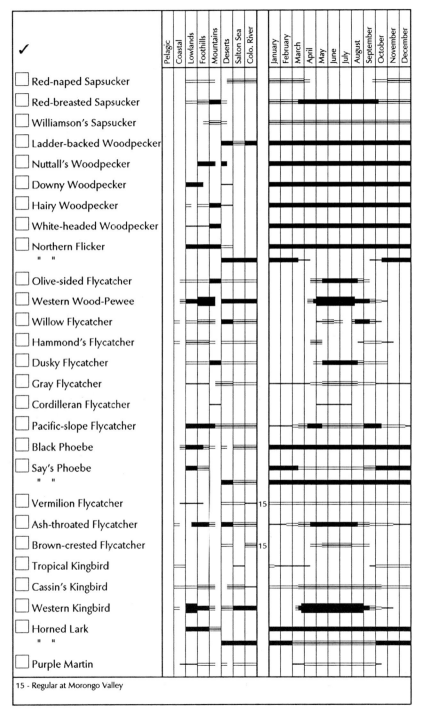

✓	Pelagic	Coastal	Lowlands	Foothills	Mountains	Deserts	Salton Sea	Colo. River	January	February	March	April	May	June	July	August	September	October	November	December
☐ Red-naped Sapsucker																				
☐ Red-breasted Sapsucker																				
☐ Williamson's Sapsucker																				
☐ Ladder-backed Woodpecker																				
☐ Nuttall's Woodpecker																				
☐ Downy Woodpecker																				
☐ Hairy Woodpecker																				
☐ White-headed Woodpecker																				
☐ Northern Flicker																				
" "																				
☐ Olive-sided Flycatcher																				
☐ Western Wood-Pewee																				
☐ Willow Flycatcher																				
☐ Hammond's Flycatcher																				
☐ Dusky Flycatcher																				
☐ Gray Flycatcher																				
☐ Cordilleran Flycatcher																				
☐ Pacific-slope Flycatcher																				
☐ Black Phoebe																				
☐ Say's Phoebe																				
" "																				
☐ Vermilion Flycatcher							15													
☐ Ash-throated Flycatcher																				
☐ Brown-crested Flycatcher							15													
☐ Tropical Kingbird																				
☐ Cassin's Kingbird																				
☐ Western Kingbird																				
☐ Horned Lark																				
" "																				
☐ Purple Martin																				

15 - Regular at Morongo Valley

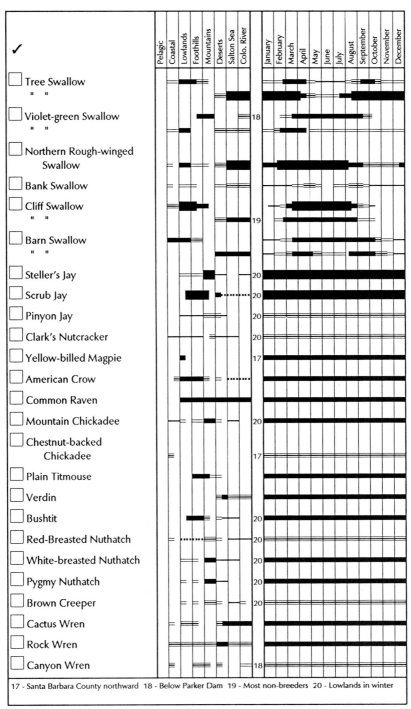

17 - Santa Barbara County northward 18 - Below Parker Dam 19 - Most non-breeders 20 - Lowlands in winter

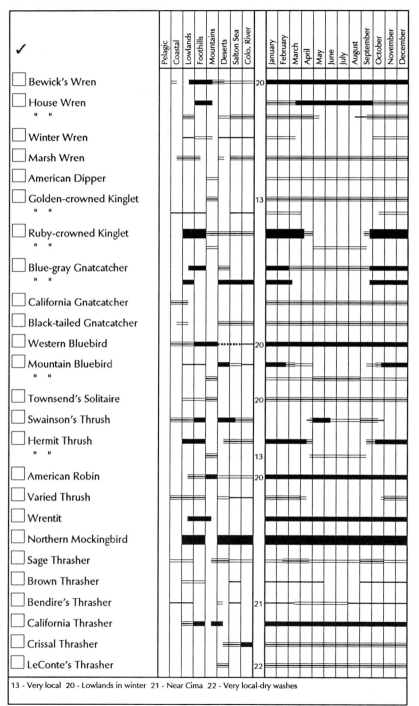

✓	Pelagic	Coastal	Lowlands	Foothills	Mountains	Deserts	Salton Sea	Colo. River		January	February	March	April	May	June	July	August	September	October	November	December
☐ Bewick's Wren								20													
☐ House Wren																					
" "																					
☐ Winter Wren																					
☐ Marsh Wren																					
☐ American Dipper																					
☐ Golden-crowned Kinglet								13													
" "																					
☐ Ruby-crowned Kinglet																					
" "																					
☐ Blue-gray Gnatcatcher																					
" "																					
☐ California Gnatcatcher																					
☐ Black-tailed Gnatcatcher																					
☐ Western Bluebird								20													
☐ Mountain Bluebird																					
" "																					
☐ Townsend's Solitaire								20													
☐ Swainson's Thrush																					
☐ Hermit Thrush																					
" "								13													
☐ American Robin								20													
☐ Varied Thrush																					
☐ Wrentit																					
☐ Northern Mockingbird																					
☐ Sage Thrasher																					
☐ Brown Thrasher																					
☐ Bendire's Thrasher								21													
☐ California Thrasher																					
☐ Crissal Thrasher																					
☐ LeConte's Thrasher								22													

13 - Very local 20 - Lowlands in winter 21 - Near Cima 22 - Very local-dry washes

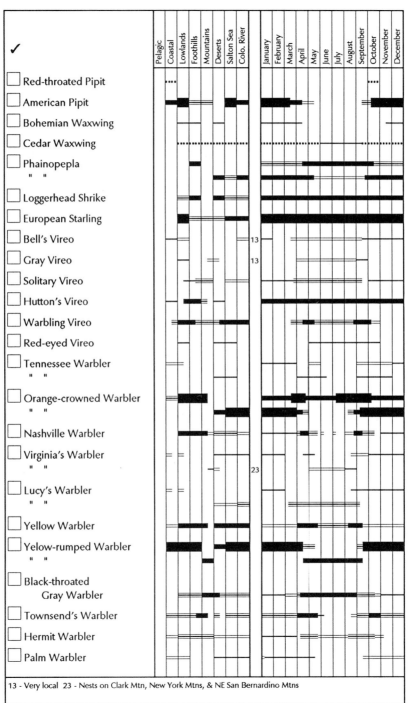

✓	Pelagic	Coastal	Lowlands	Foothills	Mountains	Deserts	Salton Sea	Colo. River	January	February	March	April	May	June	July	August	September	October	November	December
☐ Red-throated Pipit																				
☐ American Pipit																				
☐ Bohemian Waxwing																				
☐ Cedar Waxwing																				
☐ Phainopepla " "																				
☐ Loggerhead Shrike																				
☐ European Starling																				
☐ Bell's Vireo								13												
☐ Gray Vireo								13												
☐ Solitary Vireo																				
☐ Hutton's Vireo																				
☐ Warbling Vireo																				
☐ Red-eyed Vireo																				
☐ Tennessee Warbler " "																				
☐ Orange-crowned Warbler " "																				
☐ Nashville Warbler																				
☐ Virginia's Warbler " "								23												
☐ Lucy's Warbler " "																				
☐ Yellow Warbler																				
☐ Yelow-rumped Warbler " "																				
☐ Black-throated Gray Warbler																				
☐ Townsend's Warbler																				
☐ Hermit Warbler																				
☐ Palm Warbler																				

13 - Very local 23 - Nests on Clark Mtn, New York Mtns, & NE San Bernardino Mtns

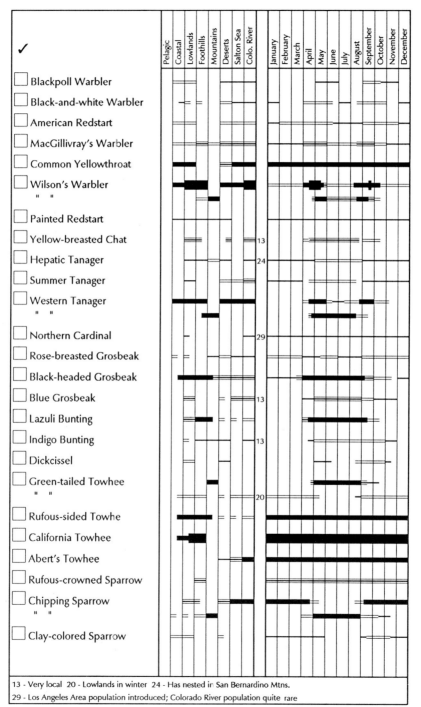

✓	Pelagic	Coastal	Lowlands	Foothills	Mountains	Deserts	Salton Sea	Colo. River		January	February	March	April	May	June	July	August	September	October	November	December
☐ Blackpoll Warbler																					
☐ Black-and-white Warbler																					
☐ American Redstart																					
☐ MacGillivray's Warbler																					
☐ Common Yellowthroat																					
☐ Wilson's Warbler																					
" "																					
☐ Painted Redstart																					
☐ Yellow-breasted Chat								13													
☐ Hepatic Tanager								24													
☐ Summer Tanager																					
☐ Western Tanager																					
" "																					
☐ Northern Cardinal								29													
☐ Rose-breasted Grosbeak																					
☐ Black-headed Grosbeak																					
☐ Blue Grosbeak								13													
☐ Lazuli Bunting																					
☐ Indigo Bunting								13													
☐ Dickcissel																					
☐ Green-tailed Towhee																					
" "								20													
☐ Rufous-sided Towhee																					
☐ California Towhee																					
☐ Abert's Towhee																					
☐ Rufous-crowned Sparrow																					
☐ Chipping Sparrow																					
" "																					
☐ Clay-colored Sparrow																					

13 - Very local 20 - Lowlands in winter 24 - Has nested in San Bernardino Mtns.
29 - Los Angeles Area population introduced; Colorado River population quite rare

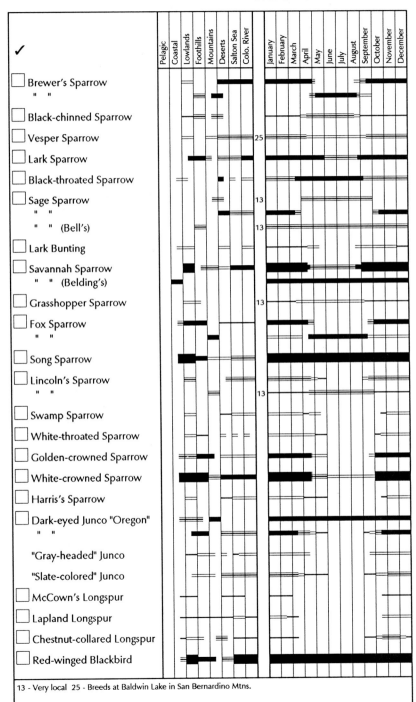

✓	Pelagic	Coastal	Lowlands	Foothills	Mountains	Deserts	Salton Sea	Colo. River	January	February	March	April	May	June	July	August	September	October	November	December

- Brewer's Sparrow
  " "
- Black-chinned Sparrow
- Vesper Sparrow — 25
- Lark Sparrow
- Black-throated Sparrow
- Sage Sparrow — 13
  " "
  " " (Bell's) — 13
- Lark Bunting
- Savannah Sparrow
  " " (Belding's)
- Grasshopper Sparrow — 13
- Fox Sparrow
  " "
- Song Sparrow
- Lincoln's Sparrow
  " " — 13
- Swamp Sparrow
- White-throated Sparrow
- Golden-crowned Sparrow
- White-crowned Sparrow
- Harris's Sparrow
- Dark-eyed Junco "Oregon"
  " "
- "Gray-headed" Junco
- "Slate-colored" Junco
- McCown's Longspur
- Lapland Longspur
- Chestnut-collared Longspur
- Red-winged Blackbird

13 - Very local   25 - Breeds at Baldwin Lake in San Bernardino Mtns.

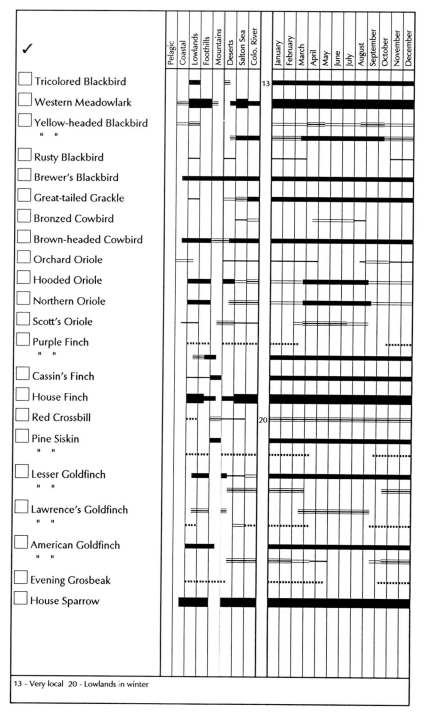

✓	Pelagic	Coastal	Lowlands	Foothills	Mountains	Deserts	Salton Sea	Colo. River		January	February	March	April	May	June	July	August	September	October	November	December
☐ Tricolored Blackbird								13													
☐ Western Meadowlark																					
☐ Yellow-headed Blackbird " "																					
☐ Rusty Blackbird																					
☐ Brewer's Blackbird																					
☐ Great-tailed Grackle																					
☐ Bronzed Cowbird																					
☐ Brown-headed Cowbird																					
☐ Orchard Oriole																					
☐ Hooded Oriole																					
☐ Northern Oriole																					
☐ Scott's Oriole																					
☐ Purple Finch " "																					
☐ Cassin's Finch																					
☐ House Finch																					
☐ Red Crossbill								20													
☐ Pine Siskin " "																					
☐ Lesser Goldfinch " "																					
☐ Lawrence's Goldfinch " "																					
☐ American Goldfinch " "																					
☐ Evening Grosbeak																					
☐ House Sparrow																					

13 - Very local 20 - Lowlands in winter

REFERENCES

Childs, **Where Birders Go in Southern California** (1990) Los Angeles Audubon

Clarke, **An Introduction to Southern California Birds** (1989) Mountain Press Publishing Co., Missoula, MT

Garrett and Dunn, **Birds of Southern California: Status and Distribution** (1981) Los Angeles Audubon

Grinnell and Miller, **Distribution of Birds of California** (1986)

Hoffman, **Birds of the Pacific States** (1927), Houghton Mifflin Co.

Ingles, **Mammals of the Pacific States** (1965) Stanford University Press.

Matelson and Crawford, **The Birds Come Flocking**, *A Field Guide to Santa Barbara County for Birders and Other Travelers* (1978)

Miller and Hyslop, **California: The Geography of Diversity**, Mayfield Publishing Co.

Miller and Stebbins, **Lives of Desert Animals in Joshua Tree National Monument** (1964) University of California Press.

Morro Coast Audubon Society, **Birds of San Luis Obispo County** (1985) checklist

Roberson, **Rare Birds of the West Coast** (1980) Woodcock Publications

Small, **Birds of California** (1974) Winchester Press

Stallcup, **Ocean Birds of the Nearshore Pacific** (1990) Point Reyes Bird Observatory

Unitt, **Birds of San Diego County** (1984) San Diego Museum of Natural History

Webster et al, **Birds of Santa Barbara and Ventura Counties** (1980) Santa Barbara Museum of Natural History

Western Field Ornithologists, **WFO Field List of California Birds** (1987) checklist

The University of California Press (Berkeley) publishes an inexpensive series of natural history guides by various authors. Some of the titles are:

Bailey, **Weather of Southern California**

Booth, **Mammals of Southern California**

Dawson, **Cacti of California**

Hinton, **Seashore Life of Southern California**

Jaeger and Smith, **Natural History of Southern California**

Munz, **California Spring (..Desert..Mountain..Shore..) Wildflowers**

Peterson, **Native Trees of Southern California**

Stebbins, **Amphibians and Reptiles of California**

Mammals, Reptiles, and Amphibians of Southern California

Listed below are the mammals, reptiles, and amphibians that you might see. For more information consult *Mammals of the Pacific States* by Ingles and *A Field Guide to Western Reptiles and Amphibians* by Robert C. Stebbins.

Mammals

Opossum
Ornate Shrew
Gray or Desert Shrew
California Mole
Yuma Myotis Bat
Western Pipistrel Bat
Mexican Free-tailed Bat
Black Bear
Raccoon
Ring-tailed Cat
Long-tailed Weasel
Sea Otter
Badger
Spotted Skunk
Striped Skunk
Coyote
Kit Fox
Gray Fox
Mountain Lion
Bobcat
Northern Sea-Lion
California Sea-Lion
Guadalupe Fur-Seal
Harbor Seal
Elephant Seal
California Ground Squirrel
Rock Squirrel
Mojave Ground Squirrel
Round-tailed Ground Squirrel
Golden-mantled Ground Squirrel
White-tailed Antelope Squirrel
Yuma Antelope Squirrel
San Joaquin Antelope Squirrel
Merriam's Chipmunk
Panamint Chipmunk

Lodgepole Chipmunk
Western Gray Squirrel
Eastern Fox Squirrel
Northern Flying Squirrel
Valley Pocket Gopher
Pocket Mice (9 species)
Kangaroo Rat (6 species)
Beaver
Western Harvest Mouse
Southern Grasshopper Mouse
White-footed or Deer Mice (6 species)
Woodrats or Packrats (3 species)
California Vole or Meadow-Mouse
Long-tailed Vole
Muskrat
Porcupine
Black-tailed Jackrabbit
Desert Cottontail
Brush Rabbit
Mule Deer
Bighorn Sheep
Pacific Bottle-nosed Dolphin
Common Dolphin
Pacific White-sided Dolphin
Long-beaked Dolphin
Right Whale Dolphin
Pacific Pilot Whale
Gray Whale
Fin-backed Whale
Hump-backed Whale
Baird's Beaked Whale
Pacific Beaked Whale
Goose-beaked Whale
Sperm Whale
Pygmy Sperm Whale
Pacific Killer Whale

False Killer Whale
Grampus Whale
Rorqual Whale
Piked Whale
Blue Whale
Pacific Right Whale

REPTILES AND AMPHIBIANS

California Newt
Ensatina
Arboreal Salamander
California Slender Salamander
Pacific Slender Salamander
Western Spadefoot
Colorado River Toad
Woodhouse's Toad
Great Plains Toad
Desert or Red-spotted Toad
Western Toad
Southwestern Toad
Pacific Tree Frog
Canyon Tree Frog
Red-legged Frog
Yellow-legged Frog
Leopard Frog
Bullfrog
Western Pond Turtle
Sonoran Mud Turtle
Spiny Soft-shelled Turtle
Desert Tortoise
Western Banded Gecko
Leaf-toed Gecko
Desert Iguana
Chuckwalla
Zebra-tailed Lizard
Fringed-toed or Sand Lizard
Collared Lizard
Leopard Lizard
Desert Spiny Lizard
Granite Spiny Lizard
Banded Rock Lizard
Side-blotched Lizards
Western Fence Lizard
Sage-brush Lizard
Long-tailed Brush Lizard

Tree Lizard
Small-scaled Lizard
Coast Horned Lizard
Desert Horned Lizard
Flat-tailed Horned Lizard
Desert or Yucca Night Lizard
Granite Night Lizard
Island Night Lizard
Western Skink
Gilbert's Skink
Orange-throated Whiptail
Western Whiptail
Southern Alligator Lizard
California Legless Lizard
Western Blind or Worm Snake
Rosy Boa
Rubber Boa
Western Ring-necked Snake
Spotted Leaf-nosed Snake
Yellow-bellied Racer
Coachwhip
Striped Racer
Western Patch-nosed Snake
Glossy Snake
Gopher Snake
Common Kingsnake
California Mountain Kingsnake
Long-nosed Snake
Western Garter Snake
Common Garter Snake
Checkered Garter Snake
Western Ground Snake
Western Shovel-nosed Snake
Western Black-headed Snake
California Lyre Snake
Arizona Lyre Snake
Night Snake
Western Diamond-backed Rattlesnake
Red Diamond-backed Rattlesnake
Speckled Rattlesnake
Sidewinder
Western Rattlesnake
Mojave Rattlesnake

NOTES

NOTES

NOTES

NOTES

AMERICAN BIRDING ASSOCIATION
Membership Application

All memberships include six issues of **Birding** magazine, monthly issues of **Winging It,** ABA's newsletter, member discounts offered by ABA Sales, and full rights of participation in all ABA activities.

Membership classes and dues:

❑   Individual $24 / yr   ❑   Family $30 / yr

❑   Century Club $100 / yr   ❑   Library $28 / yr

Application Type

❑   New Membership   ❑   Renewal

Member Information

Name _____

Address _____

_____

_____

Phone _____

Payment Information

❑   Check or Money Order enclosed (US funds only)

❑   Charge to VISA / MasterCard (circle one)

     Account Number _____

     Exp Date _____

     Signature _____

         (a $1.00 handling fee will be added for use of credit card)

Sent this completed form with payment to:

ABA Membership
PO Box 6599
Colorado Springs, CO 80934   USA.

Other Birdfinding Guides
in the
Lane Series

A Birder's Guide to Southeastern Arizona (1989)

A Birder's Guide to Colorado (1988)

A Birder's Guide to Florida (1989)

A Birder's Guide to the Texas Coast (1988)

A Birder's Guide to the Rio Grande Valley (1988)

A Birder's Guide to Churchill (Manitoba) (1988)

These and many other publications are available from:

ABA Sales
PO Box 6599
Colorado Springs, Colorado 80934

Toll-free (800) 634-7736

Write or call to order or to request a copy of the most
recent ABA Sales *Annotated Catalog and Pricelist*.

INDEX

226

Parula
  Northern 200
Pasadena 179-180
Peafowl 180
Pelican
  American White 12, 36, 84, 113, 115, 202
  Brown 26, 34, 36, 69, 121, 169, 180, 202
Petrel
  Cook's 200
  Mottled 201
  Murphy's 201
Pewee
  Greater 97, 200
  Western Wood- 29, 47, 70, 73, 82, 90, 104,
    134, 136, 145, 153, 210

Phainopepla 10, 47, 73, 75, 78, 82, 85, 108,
  110, 116, 118, 126-127, 130-131, 137, 153,
  163, 175, 181, 213
Phalarope
  Red 100, 169, 207
  Red-necked 65, 207
  Wilson's 65, 207
Pheasant
  Ring-necked 119, 205
Phil Swing Park 108
Phoebe
  Black 26, 30, 33, 38, 70, 75, 81, 105, 114,
    175, 181, 210
  Eastern 200
  Say's 13, 30, 43, 70, 77, 105, 114, 146, 155,
    210
Picacho State Recreation Area 107
Pigeon
  Band-tailed 10, 22, 29, 48, 78-79, 84, 90,
    104-105, 133, 135, 141, 159, 208
Pine Cove 134
Pine Mountain 48
Pintail
  Northern 69, 87, 156, 203
Pinyon Flats 136
Pipit
  American 12-13, 105, 119, 156, 179, 213
  Red-throated 98, 212
  Sprague's 155-156, 200
Playa del Rey 180
Plover
  American Golden- 205
  Black-bellied 25, 69, 96, 99, 156, 205
  Lesser Golden- 25
  Mongolian 201
  Mountain 25, 43-44, 98, 114, 116, 119,
    155-156, 178, 206
  Pacific Golden- 25, 66, 205
  Piping 201
  Semipalmated 69, 99, 156, 205
  Snowy 15, 17, 20, 26, 97, 120, 205
  Wilson's 201
Plummer Park 180
Point Fermin 61
Point Loma 94
Point Loma Nazarene College 94
Point Mugu State Park 12
Poorwill
  Common 47, 73, 147, 160-161, 174-175, 209
Presidio Park 100
Puffin
  Horned 169, 200
  Tufted 208
Pygmy-Owl
  Northern 48, 90, 133, 161, 208
Pyrrhuloxia 201

White-winged 24-26, 33, 65, 68, 100, 154, 204
Screech-Owl
Western 21, 29, 75-77, 81, 90, 146, 157, 160, 175, 208
Scripps Institute of Onceanography 101
Seal Beach National Wildlife Refuge 65
Senator Wash Reservoir 108
Serra Museum 100
Shearwater
Black-vented 24-26, 33, 58, 68, 96, 100, 168-169, 202
Buller's 202
Flesh-footed 169, 202
Pink-footed 168, 202
Short-tailed 100, 202
Sooty 23, 26, 34, 58, 100, 122, 168, 202
Wedge-tailed 201
Shell Beach 33
Sherwood Lake 12
Shipley Nature Center 64
Shoveler
Northern 69, 87, 156, 204
Shrike
Loggerhead 45, 70, 105, 151, 213
Northern 200
Silverado Canyon 77
Silverwood 176
Silverwood Lake State Recreation Area 142-143
Siskin
Pine 134, 136, 143, 145, 161, 216
Skimmer
Black 65, 69, 71, 100, 114, 118-119, 208
Skua
South Polar 169, 207
Snipe
Common 25, 69, 135, 153, 176, 207
Solana Beach 88

Solitaire
Townsend's 21, 135, 145, 148-149, 162-163, 212
Solvang 21
Sora 10, 57, 64, 69, 99, 110, 126, 145, 153, 205
South Bay Marine Biological Study Area 99
South Coast Botanic Garden 57
South Kern River Preserve 54
Sparrow
American Tree 200
Baird's 201
Belding's Savannah 65, 215
Bell's Sage 215
Black-chinned 21, 47-49, 54, 73, 77-78, 82, 104, 133, 147, 161, 164-165, 173, 215
Black-throated 47, 52, 126, 130, 137, 164, 173, 215
Brewer's 47-49, 52, 54, 114, 120, 125-126, 129, 147, 164, 214-215
Cassin's 201
Chipping 22, 47, 78, 82, 90, 147, 161, 181, 214
Clay-colored 214
Field 201
Fox 21, 48-49, 77-78, 82, 90, 104, 143, 145, 149, 153, 161, 165, 215
Golden-crowned 10, 20-21, 48, 70, 77-78, 82, 98, 104, 149, 153, 165, 181, 215
Grasshopper 73, 85, 101, 156, 215
Harris's 153, 215
House 107, 149, 216
Lark 12, 47-48, 89, 91, 98, 103, 105, 147, 215
LeConte's 201
Lincoln's 48, 70, 82, 135, 147-148, 153, 215
Nuttall's White-crowned 38
Rufous-crowned 13, 21, 35, 59, 73, 76-77, 89, 101, 153, 155, 159, 165, 214
Sage 44-45, 47, 52, 104, 114, 126, 139, 147, 155, 164, 215
Savannah 43, 70, 84, 105, 116, 146-147, 153, 156, 215
Song 75, 78, 82, 87, 147, 153, 215
Swamp 153, 215
Vesper 45, 84, 105, 147, 215
White-crowned 44, 48, 70, 77-78, 81-82, 104, 153, 181, 215
White-throated 153-154, 215
Spoonbill
Roseate 107, 114, 200
Squaw Lake 108
Starling
European 107, 149, 213
Stilt
Black-necked 69, 100, 113, 153, 156, 206
Stint
Rufous-necked 201
Stoneyvale Picnic Area 165
Stork
Wood 114, 116, 119, 203